A Programmer's Guide to Assembler

First Edition

William J. Pervin

*Professor in Electrical Engineering,
Computer Science and Mathematics
The University of Texas at Dallas*

Mc Graw Hill **Custom Publishing**

Boston Burr Ridge, IL Dubuque, IA Madison, WI New York San Francisco St. Louis
Bangkok Bogotá Caracas Lisbon London Madrid
Mexico City Milan New Delhi Seoul Singapore Sydney Taipei Toronto

A Programmer's Guide to Assembler
First Edition

PREFACE

Embedded processors now are included in almost every device and all scientists and engineers now need to be able to program them. While most have C compilers available for somewhat high-level language programming, issues such as speed and code size require the use of assembly language. Thus the study of that subject is still an important part of the educational experience. Learning how an assembler works will better prepare computer users for optimizing their code. In addition, electrical and computer engineers need to study assembler language in order to be introduced to the architecture of a computer.

Our objective does not include making expert assembler language programmers out of our readers. Rather, it is to make high-level language programmers aware of what their compilers must do, what actually happens inside their computers, and how those facts may well affect their programming decisions.

An interesting justification for using a simulator appears in an article by Wolffe, Yurcik, Osborne, and Holliday [SIGCSE Bulletin, Vol. 34, No. 1, March 2002, pp. 176-180] where one can find a partial list of such simulators. The choice of a simulator for the MIPS architecture (particularly as opposed to the Intel architecture) is motivated by the rationale outlined by Dr. C. D. Cantrell in the e-mail quoted on the next page.

The background for the course EE 2310 at The University of Texas at Dallas is as follows. It was developed originally by Dr. C. D. Cantrell under the title "Computer Organization and Design" rather obviously based on the classic text by Patterson and Hennessy. He made available 932 PDF slides for his classes. Dr. Dawn Hollenbeck did further work including laboratory exercises. Finally, Dr. Nathan Dodge added his methods and additional material to the course that was now titled "Introduction to Digital Systems". In the CS Department, Dr. Hermann Harrison has been teaching the equivalent course numbered CS 2310 and has made extremely helpful suggestions for this book, particularly in regard to the material on exception handling. After all this work was done, this author, who benefited by all that previous development, taught some honors sections of the course.

Prerequisite: A basic knowledge of C/C++/Java. (We will use this designation for any pseudo-code based on the common basis of these languages. Readers should have a working knowledge of at least one of these three similar languages before studying assembler language.)

Acknowledgement: This work would have been impossible but for the writing and support of SPIM by Dr. James R. Larus. I also thank him for permission to quote his article as Appendix D.

Dedication: To my children (Edward Charles, James Herbert, Sharon Rachel, and Hannah Esther Pervin), my wife (Susan Phyllis Chizeck), and the memory of my parents (Abraham and Stella Pervin).

MIPS Rationale

The standard -- and, in the view of many, by far the best -- undergraduate textbook on computer organization is "Computer Organization and Design: The Hardware-Software Interface", by John Hennessy and David Patterson.

The authors are the academic parents of RISC architectures, and their textbook reflects this interest by taking the student through the process of designing the datapath and control for a pipelined processor with a much-reduced instruction set. Although the processor that is designed in Chapters 1-7 of the text uses a subset of the MIPS R2000 instruction set, the text discusses the full set of MIPS R2000 instructions in considerable detail. Students taking a Patterson-Hennessy course make use of a MIPS simulator, called SPIM, which runs on all popular platforms, to assemble and run programs. Besides SPIM, which was developed by Jim Larus at the University of Wisconsin, resources developed for the Patterson-Hennessy book by others include the very nice MIPSter Integrated Development Environment (IDE).

The obvious question is, "Why not teach Intel 80x86 assembly language, instead of a language that nobody uses?" There are several answers:

1. Patterson and Hennessy use MIPS assembly language. Given the overwhelming acceptance of their textbook as the standard, this is already a strong argument.
2. RISC architectures actually are dominant. If one looks at a Pentium, one finds that it's actually at least three different processors on one die (a CISC integer unit, a RISC integer unit, and an FPU). Since the "RISC revolution" of 15 years ago, no microprocessor manufacturer has been able to ignore the advantages of RISC architecture from the points of view of overall speed and rapid adaptation to new, lower semiconductor linewidths.
3. From a pedagogical point of view, it's best to teach a subject by going from the simple to the complex. The MIPS R2000 instruction set architecture is probably the simplest in existence for a real processor with a significant market. In contrast, the Intel architecture, which is the result of efforts by many different teams of engineers over a period of more than 20 years, is extremely complex.
4. Optimizing compilers produce embarrassingly good code -- better, in fact, than human-coded assembly language. Precisely because of the current dominance of the 80x86 architecture, optimizing compilers have rendered human-coded Intel assembly language unnecessary.
5. Electrical and software engineers do, in fact, need to write assembly-language programs for embedded processors. Although Intel processors dominate the desktop market, MIPS is one of the dominant architectures in the embedded-processor market. In 1997, MIPS licensees shipped 48 million processors, making MIPS the first RISC architecture in history to exceed Motorola's 32-bit 68000 CISC volume in the embedded market. MIPS intellectual property is in the processors that power the Hewlett-Packard 4000 series of laser printers (which use a customized MIPS R4000), the Sony Playstation (which uses an R3000), the Nintendo 64 (which uses a customized R4000), and the Playstation 2 (which uses a Toshiba processor with a MIPS core). Because of their great speed and processing power, MIPS processors are widely used by OEMs for their embedded systems.

Other system integrators, such as router and telephone-switch manufacturers, make use of embedded processors. For example, some Cisco routers use MIPS processors, and some Nortel switches use Motorola 88000 RISC processors. Other embedded systems use PowerPC or SPARC processors. In all cases, these RISC architectures are extremely similar to the MIPS R2000 architecture that Hennessy and Patterson use throughout their text. A student who has learned the MIPS R2000 instruction set is in a good position to write programs for any embedded RISC processor.

C. D. Cantrell
Professor in Electrical Engineering and Associate Dean
Director, PhoTEC (Photonics Technology and Engineering Center)
The University of Texas at Dallas
Richardson, TX 75083-0688
http://www.utdallas.edu/~cantrell/

REFERENCES

MIPS References

Farquhar, Erin and Bunce, Philip, *The MIPS Programmer's Handbook*, Morgan Kaufmann, 1994 (ISBN 1-55860-297-6)

Kane, Gerry and Heinrich, Joe, *MIPS RISC Architecture*, Prentice-Hall, 1992 (ISBN 0-13-590472-2)

Sweetman, Dominic, *See MIPS Run*, Morgan Kaufmann, 1999 (ISBN 1-55860-410-3)

Computer Architecture Reference

Patterson, David A. & Hennessy, John L., *Computer Organization and Design*, 3rd Ed., Elsevier/Morgan Kaufmann, 2005 (ISBN 1-55860-604-1) [See, particularly, Appendix A (available through http://www.cs.wisc.edu/~larus/SPIM/cod-appa.pdf) which covers the topics of "Assemblers, Linkers, and the SPIM simulator."]

SOFTWARE

SPIM: http://www.cs.wisc.edu/~larus/SPIM/pcspim.zip

MIPSter: http://www.downcastsystems.com/mipster/download.asp

COPYRIGHTS

TABLE OF CONTENTS

CHAPTER ZERO

Bits and Bytes

The first thing we must learn about how our computers store information for us is that it is all kept in the form of simple collections of bits.

0.1 Bits

A **bit** is logically just a single "on" or "off" switch. We usually indicate the state of a bit by using zero to indicate "off" and one to indicate "on." This leads us to make use of the **binary** (base 2) counting system. Since we will not stop using decimal numbers (base 10) in ordinary discussions, we will start to indicate by using subscripts which system is being used.

For BINary numbers we will use the subscript "BIN" (some use "TWO" or "2") and for DECimal numbers, when necessary, we will use the subscript "DEC" (again, some use "TEN" or "10"). We have the following equivalences:

$$0_{DEC} = 0_{BIN};$$
$$1_{DEC} = 1_{BIN};$$
$$2_{DEC} = 10_{BIN};$$
$$3_{DEC} = 11_{BIN};$$
$$4_{DEC} = 100_{BIN};$$
$$5_{DEC} = 101_{BIN};$$
$$6_{DEC} = 110_{BIN};$$
$$\ldots$$

Conversion between these two systems is quite easy. First we should remember that the decimal system uses the position of a decimal digit (zero through nine) to indicate which power of ten is meant. The "powers of ten" are, of course, 1, 10, 100, 1000, … , *etc*. Thus

$$345_{DEC} = 300 + 40 + 5 = 3\times100 + 4\times10 + 5\times1 = 3\times10^2 + 4\times10^1 + 5\times10^0$$

(where we do not always insist on the subscript of "DEC" with the usual decimal digits). In the same way, the binary system uses the position of the binary "digits" (0 and 1) to indicate which power of two is meant. The "powers of two" are, of course, 1, 2, 4, 8, 16, 32, 64, 128, 256, … , *etc*. Thus

$$101011_{BIN} = 1\times2^5 + 0\times2^4 + 1\times2^3 + 0\times2^2 + 1\times2^1 + 1\times2^0 = 32 + 8 + 2 + 1 = 43_{DEC}$$

(where again we avoid the subscript DEC when the meaning is clear).

Given a binary number such as 11010110_{BIN}, one way to obtain its decimal value is to add up the powers of 2 corresponding to the placements of the ones in the number. Thus we would calculate

$$1\times2^7+1\times2^6+0\times2^5+1\times2^4+0\times2^3+1\times2^2+1\times2^1+0\times2^0=128+64+16+4+2=214_{DEC}.$$

Actually, when doing the arithmetic by hand, we would probably work from right to left, doubling 2 mentally and writing down the powers as $2 + 4 + 16 + 64 + 128$ (obtaining the same 214_{DEC}, of course).

A method[1] for doing that calculation working from left to right is as follows. Start with the left-most one giving 1. As long as there is still a digit to the right, double the current value and add that next digit. Finally, add the last digit. In the above case we would have

$$
\begin{array}{rcll}
     & 1 & = & 1 \\
  2 + & 1 & = & 3 \\
  6 + & 0 & = & 6 \\
 12 + & 1 & = & 13 \\
 26 + & 0 & = & 26 \\
 52 + & 1 & = & 53 \\
106 + & 1 & = & 107 \\
214 + & 0 & = & 214 \text{ (again obtaining the same } 214_{DEC}\text{).}
\end{array}
$$

The reverse conversion may be done in a way which builds up the binary number from right to left. Dividing one number by another gives a quotient and a remainder (which is smaller than the divisor). For our purposes we will continually divide by 2 and so always have a remainder that is 0 (for an even number) or 1 (for an odd number), just right for binary numbers. The process is to divide by 2 and use the remainders as the values (from right to left as stated above) and the quotient to continue the process. Thus, starting with 214_{DEC},

$$
\begin{array}{ll}
214 & 0 \\
107 & 1 \\
 53 & 1 \\
 26 & 0 \\
 13 & 1 \\
  6 & 0 \\
  3 & 1 \\
  1 & 1
\end{array}
$$

---

[1] This is a special case of our first example of a technique which applies not only to assembly language programming but also to high-level languages. When evaluating a polynomial use the relation:

$$a_n*x^n + a_{n-1}*x^{n-1} + \ldots + a_1*x + a_0 = (\ldots(a_n*x + a_{n-1})*x + \ldots + a_1)*x + a_0$$

The result of writing from left to right the remainders from bottom to top is 11010110_{BIN}, as expected.

These results for binary integers may be extended to binary fractions. In particular, the positions to the right of a binary point should correspond to negative powers of two just as those to the right of a decimal point correspond to negative powers of ten. Thus,

$$0.101101_{\text{BIN}} = 1/2 + 1/8 + 1/16 + 1/64 = 45/64 = 0.703125_{\text{DEC}}$$

The reverse conversion can be done by a simple doubling process. We repeatedly double the fractional part and use the successive zeros or ones that appear to the left of the binary point as the fractional part of the corresponding binary number. Thus,

	.703125
1	.40625
0	.8125
1	.625
1	.25
0	.5
1	.0

Gives us the 0.101101_{BIN} expected.

0.2 Bytes

A group of eight bits is called a **byte**. In most computers today, addressing in memory is by byte rather than by individual bits. That is, an entire collection of eight bits (at least) will be retrieved even when only a single bit is needed. We will treat arithmetic in more detail later but it is clear that there are exactly 256 possible bit combinations in a byte. They may be listed 00000000_{BIN}, 00000001_{BIN}, 00000010_{BIN}, ... , 11111111_{BIN} but they have no fixed "meaning" until we decide on an interpretation for them.

Of course our first attempt to give a meaning to these bit patterns is to interpret them as representing the decimal numbers to which they would correspond. Thus

$$00000000_{\text{BIN}} = 0_{\text{DEC}},$$
$$00000001_{\text{BIN}} = 1_{\text{DEC}},$$
$$00000010_{\text{BIN}} = 2_{\text{DEC}},$$
$$...,$$
$$11111111_{\text{BIN}} = 255_{\text{DEC}}.$$

This is a natural interpretation and we call them **unsigned integers** and discuss them later.

There are other assignments of meaning to these bit patterns, however. For example, they may be considered representations of characters. The most common system agreed upon is the American Standard Code for Information Interchange (**ASCII**) which gives meaning to the first 128 byte patterns (all with a zero in the left-most place).

Before describing some of the details of ASCII code, we will note that writing eight bits down is rather error prone and boring. We will shortly see that groups of 32 bits are the standard group with which we work in the MIPS computer and it would be almost impossible to write such long strings of zeros and ones down correctly or to read them. For this reason, **hexadecimal** (base 16) numbers are commonly used. For now we will indicate these numbers by the subscript "HEX" (others may use "SIXTEEN" or "16").

Just as binary numbers use two symbols (0 and 1) and decimal numbers use 10 symbols (0 through 9), hexadecimal numbers need 16 symbols available. The standard convention is to use the 10 decimal digits in their usual way and to add the letters A through F to stand for 10 through 15. Thus,

$$A_{HEX} = 10_{DEC},$$
$$B_{HEX} = 11_{DEC},$$
$$C_{HEX} = 12_{DEC},$$
$$D_{HEX} = 13_{DEC},$$
$$E_{HEX} = 14_{DEC},$$
$$F_{HEX} = 15_{DEC}$$

The conversion between binary and hexadecimal notations is trivial. Each hexadecimal symbol corresponds to four binary symbols. Thus, our three notations for the first sixteen numbers are

$$0_{DEC} = 0000_{BIN} = 0_{HEX}$$
$$1_{DEC} = 0001_{BIN} = 1_{HEX}$$
$$2_{DEC} = 0010_{BIN} = 2_{HEX}$$
$$3_{DEC} = 0011_{BIN} = 3_{HEX}$$
$$4_{DEC} = 0100_{BIN} = 4_{HEX}$$
$$5_{DEC} = 0101_{BIN} = 5_{HEX}$$
$$6_{DEC} = 0110_{BIN} = 6_{HEX}$$
$$7_{DEC} = 0111_{BIN} = 7_{HEX}$$
$$8_{DEC} = 1000_{BIN} = 8_{HEX}$$
$$9_{DEC} = 1001_{BIN} = 9_{HEX}$$
$$10_{DEC} = 1010_{BIN} = A_{HEX}$$
$$11_{DEC} = 1011_{BIN} = B_{HEX}$$
$$12_{DEC} = 1100_{BIN} = C_{HEX}$$
$$13_{DEC} = 1101_{BIN} = D_{HEX}$$
$$14_{DEC} = 1110_{BIN} = E_{HEX}$$
$$15_{DEC} = 1111_{BIN} = F_{HEX}$$

For example, $11010110_{BIN} = D6_{HEX}$, which is certainly easier to read. Many high-level languages allow for hexadecimal numbers and invariably allow either upper or lower case letters (A-F, a-f) to be used, even when the language is case-sensitive. In addition, following the convention that variable names must begin with a letter, most languages will require that numbers may not begin with a letter and so hexadecimal numbers are written with 0x or 0X preceding them. Thus our $D6_{HEX}$ would be written 0xD6 (or 0XD6, or 0xd6, or 0Xd6) and would be interpreted as hexadecimal.

Since that is the notation used in almost all computer languages, and will be recognized by our assembler, we will use the "0x" notation rather than the "HEX" subscript almost always. Programmers should get used to that common notation.

The ASCII representations of some of the printable characters include the following:

1) Digits: 0x30 to 0x39 ("0" to "9")
2) Capital (upper case) letters: 0x41 to 0x5A ("A" to "Z")
3) Small (lower case) letters: 0x61 to 0x7A ("a" to "z")
4) Space: 0x20 (" "), Line feed: 0x0A, Tab: 0x09
5) Null: 0x00

A complete list appears in a table printed in Appendix A.

Although the ASCII characters listed above will serve for most applications, the limit of 256 possibilities can be inadequate. For this reason, the inventors of Java decided to use a 16 bit grouping to describe characters. The first 256 agree with the ASCII definitions but there are a total of 2^{16} choices with 16 bits and with that larger number available it is possible to include Chinese, Arabic, Russian, and many other alphabets. This system is called **Unicode** (see http://www.unicode.org for more official information).

0.3 Boolean Algebra

In addition to arithmetic operations such as add and subtract, we recall that computer languages such as C/C++/Java also have logical operations such as AND, OR (inclusive), XOR (eXclusive OR), and NOT built-in. These operations are defined on objects of the type *bool* in Java (that is, either *true* or *false)* and yield a value of type *bool*. The language C, however, was rather untyped and considered the integer 0 to be "false" and any non-zero integer to be "true".

In moving from C to Java then, a programmer must learn to avoid a construct of the form

```
int x; … if (x) …
```

and replace it with such code as

```
int x; … if (x == 0) …
```

or

```
bool x; … if (x) …
```

In assembler, it is very natural to follow the C convention since it was designed with the architecture of the machine in mind. In particular, almost all processors base their branching instructions on comparisons of a value with zero. All that matters is whether an object is less than, equal to, or greater than zero. Indeed, there is almost no typing in assembler and one will frequently find oneself testing whether the representation of a character is the integer zero or not.

Although only zero is considered "false" and anything nonzero is treated as "true" by the hardware, it is conventional to use 1 as the default value when a test is to return "true". Hence, 0 and 1 become the standard representations for "false" and "true" in assembler.

With that convention, the definitions of these operations are as follows. NOT is a unary operation (that is, it takes only one operand) that inverts the bits of its operand; thus, $\text{NOT } 1010_2 = 0101_2$. The other three operators are binary (that is, they take two operands). Their values are given in the following table:

X	Y	X AND Y	X OR Y	X XOR Y
0	0	0	0	0
0	1	0	1	1
1	0	0	1	1
1	1	1	1	0

Exercises

1. Convert the following unsigned 8-bit binary numbers to their decimal equivalents:

    a) 11001100_{BIN}
    b) 00110011_{BIN}
    c) 10101010_{BIN}
    d) 01010101_{BIN}
    e) 11111111_{BIN}
    f) 00000000_{BIN}

2. Convert the following unsigned decimal numbers to their 8-bit binary equivalents:

    a) 0_{DEC}
    b) 255_{DEC}
    c) 85_{DEC}
    d) 170_{DEC}
    e) 51_{DEC}
    f) 204_{DEC}

3. Convert the following unsigned 8-bit binary numbers into hexadecimal equivalents:

    a) 11001100_{BIN}
    b) 00110011_{BIN}
    c) 10101010_{BIN}
    d) 01010101_{BIN}
    e) 11111111_{BIN}
    f) 00000000_{BIN}

4. Convert the following hexadecimal numbers into their 8-bit binary equivalents:

    a) 0x00
    b) 0xFF
    c) 0x55
    d) 0xAA
    e) 0x33
    f) 0xCC

5. Convert 3.14159_{DEC} into binary notation. Convert 10.10111_{BIN} into decimal notation.

6. The following are strings of ASCII characters described in hexadecimal notation. Translate them into readable strings in a left-to-right fashion:

    a) 0x436174
    b) 0x446F67
    c) 0x5465786173
    d) 0x44616C6C6173
    e) 0x60657276696E
    f) 0x4D795053

7. Translate your name into a string of ASCII characters (remembering that a space is 0x20, a period is 0x2E, and a comma is 0x2C; if you need any other special characters – look them up).

8. Evaluate the expressions

    a) 0011_{BIN} AND 0101_{BIN}
    b) 0011_{BIN} OR 0101_{BIN}
    c) 0011_{BIN} XOR (NOT 1010_{BIN})
    d) 0x159B AND 0x34AA
    e) 0xFFFF OR 0x0000
    f) (NOT 0x0000) XOR 0x159B

Note that in English we would carefully distinguish between the inclusive OR ("one or the other, or both") and the exclusive OR ("one or the other, but not both").

CHAPTER ONE

Integers

For scientists and engineers, computers are used to do arithmetic computations. In this chapter we will discuss the basics of how integer numbers are stored and manipulated. Later we will see that real numbers are stored quite differently.

1.1 Unsigned Integers

In Chapter Zero we introduced an interpretation of bit patterns in a byte which included the integers from $0_{DEC} = 0x00$ to $2^8 - 1 = 255_{DEC} = 0xFF$. The MIPS processor that we will study in Chapter Two has registers in which one can store integers that are 32 bits in size so we will usually work with these longer groupings. It is easy to see that these four byte (32 bit) configurations may be taken to represent all the unsigned integers from $0_{DEC} = 0x00000000$ to $2^{32} - 1 = 4,294,967,295_{DEC} = 0xFFFFFFFF$.

Of course we do not want to be limited to non-negative integers so the interesting question is how to represent negative numbers using some of the 2^{32} patterns available. In the next sections we will look at two simple ways that are rarely used and then the actual standard system (2's complement). Still another system will be treated in Chapter 9 since it is part of the standard method used for representing real numbers (IEEE-754).

1.2 Signed-Magnitude Integers

Before considering one of the many ways to represent integers so as to allow for both positive and negative numbers we will agree on a numbering scheme for the bits. It does not matter which decision we make in terminology but it may be convenient to use zero for the least significant bit. Thus in a 32-bit register we will call the right most or least significant "bit 0" and count towards the left up to "bit 31" for the most significant. One advantage is that for the unsigned integers described above the nth bit is associated with the power 2^n.

|31|302928272625242322212019181716151413121110090807060504030201 00|

In order to allow for signed numbers we may choose to use bit 31 to indicate the sign of the number and the other 31 bits to give its magnitude. This system is called the **signed-magnitude** association. It is convenient to use bit 31 equaling zero to indicate positive numbers and one to indicate negative numbers. Thus,

$$0x00000000 = +0_{DEC},$$
$$0x00000001 = +1_{DEC},$$
$$...,$$
$$0x7FFFFFFF = 2,147,483,647_{DEC} = +(2^{31} - 1)$$

while

$$0x80000000 = -0_{DEC},$$
$$0x80000001 = -1_{DEC},$$
$$...,$$
$$0xFFFFFFFF = -2,147,483,647_{DEC} = -(2^{31} - 1)$$

Although this interpretation is simple for humans to use, the existence of both a +0 and a -0 makes it somewhat difficult for computer use. Testing whether a number is equal to zero is probably one of the most frequent operations and it might require two tests using the signed-magnitude system.

1.3 One's Complement

Another reasonable system is to invert every bit in a number to represent its negative. This is called the **1's complement** of a number. Since bit 31 would change from 0 to 1 we could keep our convention that 0 means positive and 1 means negative. For example,

$$11111111111111111111111111110101_{BIN} = 0xFFFFFFF5$$

would be the 1's complement of

$$00000000000000000000000000001010_{BIN} = 0x0000000A = 10_{DEC}$$

and so would represent -10_{DEC}. Taking the 1's complement a second time would return the original number and so satisfies a natural requirement for consistency. However, there would still be the problem of having both a positive zero (0x00000000) and a negative zero (0xFFFFFFFF).

1.4 Two's Complement

Finally, we reach a somewhat more complicated (for humans) system which turns out to be easy to implement in hardware and is used in almost all computers. Again bit 31 is used to indicate the sign of the number and positive numbers are associated with their magnitude. Negative numbers are obtained by taking the 1's complement and then adding one to the result (ignoring any carry into the non-existent 33rd bit position). This defines the **2's complement** of a number.

The non-negative integers are then associated as before:

$$0x00000000 = +0_{\text{DEC}},$$
$$0x00000001 = +1_{\text{DEC}},$$
$$\ldots,$$
$$0x7FFFFFFF = +2,147,483,647_{\text{DEC}} = +(2^{31} - 1)$$

Now consider 0xFFFFFFFF. Its 1's complement is 0x00000000 and so its 2's complement is 0x00000001. Hence we associate 0xFFFFFFFF with -1_{DEC}. Next, 0xFFFFFFFE has 1's complement of 0x00000001 and so adding one yields 0x00000002 thus associating it with -2_{DEC}. We may continue in this way down to 0x80000001 with 1's complement of 0x7FFFFFFE, 2's complement of 0x7FFFFFFF which is 2^{31} - 1, and so the value is $-(2^{31} - 1)$. There is still the pattern 0x80000000 to deal with. Its 1's complement is 0x7FFFFFFF and so its 2's complement is itself! Since it is in the form of a negative number (bit 31 is one), we will associate it with -2^{31}, the next number in order. In summary,

$$0x80000000 = -2,147,483,648_{\text{DEC}} = -2^{31}$$
$$0x80000001 = -2,147,483,647_{\text{DEC}} = -(2^{31} - 1)$$
$$\ldots$$
$$0xFFFFFFFE = -2_{\text{DEC}}$$
$$0xFFFFFFFF = -1_{\text{DEC}}$$

In this system there is now only one zero: 0x00000000. On the other hand, there is one negative number with no corresponding positive number. This explains why we are told in C/C++/Java that an *int* variable can take on all values between -2^{31} and $+(2^{31} - 1)$ and so the range is not symmetric about zero. We should note, however, that the 2's complement of the 2's complement does return the original number as required.

1.5 Arithmetic and Overflow

In addition to the law of double negation (- - x == x), we may check that the sum of a positive and a negative integer in 2's complement form does yield the correct result (again ignoring any carry into the 32nd bit position). For example, the sum

$$0xFFFFFAD3 = 11111111111111111111101011010011_{\text{BIN}} = -1325_{\text{DEC}}$$
$$+\ 0x00001666\ \ \ = 00000000000000000001011001100110_{\text{BIN}} = +5734_{\text{DEC}}$$
$$0x00001139\ \ \ \ = 00000000000000000001000100111001_{\text{BIN}} = +4409_{\text{DEC}}$$

is correct. Although addition is always correct in this case, it is important to note that adding two positive or two negative numbers may give an incorrect result.

Let us consider a simple example of the problem. Adding

$$0\text{x}7\text{FFFFFFF} = 01111111111111111111111111111111_{\text{BIN}} = +(2^{31}-1)$$
$$+\ 0\text{x}7\text{FFFFFFF} = 01111111111111111111111111111111_{\text{BIN}} = +(2^{31}-1)$$
$$0\text{xFFFFFFFE} = 11111111111111111111111111111110_{\text{BIN}} = -2_{\text{DEC}}$$

We see that in general adding two large positive numbers together may give a negative number (we may check that adding small numbers is correct). The same type problem can occur when adding two negative numbers together; it might produce a positive number. The cause in each case is **overflow**; that is, bits are carried into the sign bit incorrectly when a result should be larger than can be represented in 31 bits.

The overflow problem can occur with most high-level languages. In any problem in which large numbers can appear one should check for this condition. Depending on the language, compiler, operating system, and supporting hardware, different results may be obtained. In some cases the problem is ignored and it is completely up to the programmer to watch for errors. We will demonstrate this later. At the other extreme, in some cases the system will terminate our program, giving us no opportunity to take corrective action after it happens. An intermediate case is when an **exception** is signaled and our program can decide on what action to take (see *try-catch* statements in Java).

Another law of arithmetic we want satisfied by the 2's complement representation is that $x - y = x + (-y)$ should always be true, where $-y$ is the negative of y. In other words, we would expect to do subtraction by doing an addition. It is easy to see that the 1's complement representation would lead to a simple hardware solution since all that would be needed would be to invert each of the bits in the subtrahend. It turns out that the 2's complement representation is equally easy to implement.

In a study of arithmetic circuits we see that an integer adder could be made from 32 adders of individual bits. Each of these would give as output both the one bit sum of the two inputs and the "carry" bit sent to the next adder. This reminds us that each bit adder actually has three inputs: the two input bits to be added together and the carry bit from the lower order adder. The 0-bit, however, has no lower order adder attached so when subtracting rather than adding one can use that input wire to complete the final step of adding one to the 1's complement.

1.6 Bitwise Operations

In addition to arithmetic operations, almost all computers include some operations which act on the individual bits in bytes. The logical functions AND, OR, XOR and NOT used in C/C++/Java and introduced in the previous chapter are one type of example. We will use the AND operation with a predetermined set of bits on (equal to one) to pick out the values of those certain bits from a byte or group of bytes. Thus, 0x000000FF, when used as one of the two 32-bit operands to AND, will give a result equal to exactly what is in the lowest order eight bits of the other operand. We call a pattern such as 0x000000FF a **mask** when used in this way.

In a similar way, we may use the OR operation to turn on certain bits. For example, the mask 0x80000000 would turn on the highest order bit of the other 32-bit operand of OR giving us a negative number no matter what the sign was originally. (Note that in 2's complement notation it would not be the negative of the original number.)

Another group of bitwise operations consists of the shift operations. Again, almost all computers have such operations. There are two types of shifts: to the right and to the left. Let us consider the right shifts first (as applied to 32-bit operands). The *srl* (**Shift Right Logical**) operation usually takes as one of its operands the count of how far each bit is shifted to the right while zeros are inserted on the left end. Bits that are shifted off the end to the right are lost (fall into the "bit bucket" is sometimes said). For example, a series of one bit right shifts of 0x01010101 would give 0x00808080, then 0x00404040, then 0x00202020, then 0x00101010, then 0x00080808, etc. It is an exercise to contrast these right shifts with division by two.

A problem arises if we consider the result of starting with 0x80808080. Then the very first right shift would give us 0x40404040. That's fine if we are only considering the bits but not if we look at the values as two's complement integers! The first is negative while the second is positive! This shift is no longer the same as division by two as mentioned above. Because of this, there is another right shift operation *sra* (**Shift Right Arithmetic**). There is no difference if the high-order bit is zero (a positive number) but when the high-order bit is one (a negative number), ones are inserted on the left instead of zeros. For example, the 0x80808080 would give 0xC0404040, then 0xE0202020, then 0xF0101010, then 0xF8080808, etc. It is an exercise to contrast these arithmetic right shifts with division by two.

For left shifts, there is no choice but to bring in zeros from the right and so there is no difference between *sll* (**Shift Left Logical**) and *sla* (**Shift Left Arithmetic**) and there may or may not be two different mnemonics for this operation. It is an exercise to contrast this left shift with multiplication by two. Note, however, that there may be overflow just as with actual multiplication by two! Thus 0x40404040 would shift into 0x80808080 and change from positive to negative. In some machines such a change is noted in some way and can be checked for in software; in others, it is ignored.

Exercises

1. With our natural representation of unsigned integers, what is the largest such number (in base 10) that can be expressed using 32 bits?

2. If we used the signed-magnitude representation for integers, in base 10 what are the largest positive integer and the most negative integer that can be expressed using 32 bits?

3. Calculate the signed decimal values of the following 2's complement 32 bit numbers:

   a) 0x10101010
   b) 0xF0F0F0F0
   c) 0x89ABCDEF
   d) 0x01234567
   e) 0xABADDEED

4. Prove that the two's complement of the two's complement is the original number (Law of Double Negation).

5. Explain why the sum of any positive 2's complement integer and any negative 2's complement integer gives the correct value (no overflow).

6. Show that if there is no overflow, addition of 2's complement numbers is correct.

7. Exactly what decimal value would the addition 0x70000000 + 0x70000000 yield using our 2's complement representations?

8. Justify all the comments regarding shift operations. In particular, compare them to multiplying or dividing by two.

9. There are also "rotate" operations which shift left or right but, instead of losing the bits which go off one side, have the bits appear on the other side. They are *ror* (**RO**tate **R**ight) and *rol* (**RO**tate Left). Justify a use for such instructions.

CHAPTER TWO

MIPS Architecture

The specific processor we will use in this book is the MIPS computer. There have been many generations of processors designed by MIPS Technologies Inc. but we will consider only the very basic one, the R2000. It will serve as one of the cleanest and easiest of examples of the **RISC** (**R**educed **I**nstruction **S**et **C**omputer) architecture. Additional justification for using an architecture of that type, and MIPS in particular, is given in the Preface. After we have introduced the features of this architecture we will return to the basic question of the philosophy that led to the many decisions involved in designing such a computer.

2.1 Registers

Our MIPS processor has 32 "general purpose" registers, each containing 32 bits. Almost every operation will use operands contained in these registers and will leave its result in one of the registers. (The choice of 32 bits is not the only one possible. Older computers used 8 and then 16 bits; the newest now often use 64 bits. The ideas remain the same, however.) These registers are named **R0** through **R31** and, in MIPS assembly language they may be referred to by the notation *$0* through *$31*.

These registers are usually called "general purpose" because they may be used in almost any way the programmer wishes. However, the programmer is really are not quite free to assign meaning to registers arbitrarily. For example, R0 has the number zero hard-wired into it so if one writes *$0* as the place to put a result, the result is lost. In addition, R31 is where the hardware places a return address when calling on a subroutine using the normal *jal* (**J**ump **A**nd **L**ink) command or the *jalr* [**J**ump **A**nd **L**ink **R**egister] command (by default although one can choose a different register) explained in Chapter Five.

In addition to these hardware restrictions, there are some software restrictions on the use of registers. R1 may be used by our assembler at any time and so is not really available to the programmer. Finally, R26 and R27 are reserved for the operating system and should not be used. That leaves just 27 registers free.

Many of the other registers have meanings assigned by convention. While an individual programmer may ignore most of those conventions, professional programmers usually work in groups and have standards required of them. The conventional uses are as follows: R4 through R7 are to contain arguments being passed to functions; R2 and R3 would then contain the results of a function call; R28, R29, and R30 are used to contain pointers to important data structures such as a global area, the stack, and the frame (to be explained later – if at all).

After taking these hardware, software, and conventional restrictions into account we are left with just 18 completely general purpose registers. According to studies on register usage in similar machines this is rather at the low end of the number necessary to give good performance. It will certainly be more than sufficient for the small programs written during a beginning class but might be a tight squeeze for major projects. The point is that we want to have all the variables we use held in registers since, as we will discuss in later sections, bringing data to and from memory is very slow and hurts our performance greatly. On the other hand, the choice of 32 registers means that exactly 5 bits are necessary to address them. If we increase the number at all, 6 bits would become necessary (making 64 register names available). That is quite a bit more than experiments show is necessary for good performance. This is just one example of the trade-offs done by designers.

The 18 general purpose registers we have left are usually divided up according to a final convention. Eight of them are to be preserved by a function (the call**ee**) when it is called while the other ten may be changed during the running of the function's code (and must be saved by the call**er** if necessary). This leads to the following mnemonic names for the registers:

```
R0  = $0  = $zero    contains the constant value zero
R1  = $1  = $at      reserved for use by the assembler
R2  = $2  = $v0      value of a function call
R3  = $3  = $v1      value of a function call
R4  = $4  = $a0      first argument to a function
R5  = $5  = $a1      second argument to a function
R6  = $6  = $a2      third argument to a function
R7  = $7  = $a3      fourth argument to a function
R8  = $8  = $t0      temporary register: not preserved
...                  ...
R15 = $15 = $t7      temporary register: not preserved
R16 = $16 = $s0      saved register: preserved by function
...                  ...
R23 = $23 = $s7      saved register: preserved by function
R24 = $24 = $t8      temporary register: not preserved
R25 = $25 = $t9      temporary register: not preserved
R26 = $26 = $k0      reserved by operating system kernel
R27 = $27 = $k1      reserved by operating system kernel
R28 = $28 = $gp      global pointer
R29 = $29 = $sp      stack pointer
R30 = $30 = $fp      frame pointer
R31 = $31 = $ra      return address register
```

In this text we will almost always save both the saved registers *($s0-$s7)* and the temporary ones *($t0-$t9)*. This choice is dictated by the fact that in many systems, particularly those with fewer registers, it is a common convention (see Chapter Five) to save all the registers (whether changed or not) before calling a function. On other systems, it is completely the function's responsibility to preserve all the registers other than those which are specifically to be changed. The fact that MIPS generally takes this intermediate stance is quite useful but may confuse those who are used to one or the other of the extreme conventions. In the interest of safety (paranoia), it would seem prudent to have a function always return with all registers unchanged unless change is specifically required.

There are also a few special purpose registers in the MIPS processor. One is the **Program Counter (PC)** that contains the address in memory of the next instruction to be performed. It also contains 32 bits and that is a limitation on the amount of memory containing both our program and our data that can be addressed. It is updated early in the process of performing instructions and may be changed completely by jump (*goto*) instructions.

While some early computers did not have hardware multiplication built into them, our MIPS processor does include a multiplier unit. However, multiplying together two 32 bit integers may give a 64 bit result and that cannot fit in a 32 bit register. For this reason there are two additional registers, **HI** and **LO**, each containing 32 bits into which the result of an integer multiply always goes. Rather obviously the high order bits 32 bits go into HI and the lower order 32 bits go into LO. If the numbers are all small enough, the answer may have HI equal to zero and the entire result could be moved into one of our general purpose registers from the LO register. There is no test made for this when it happens, however, so the programmer should test the value of HI before assuming it is zero. (This requires moving HI into one of the other registers since almost all operations, including testing, take place in the general purpose registers.)

The HI and LO registers are also used by the divide instruction. When we divide two integers (in registers), the quotient is put into LO and the remainder is put into HI. This is very convenient since both are often needed. There is also a complete set of registers associated with floating-point operations that we will treat later in Chapter 10.

2.2 Register Operations

Almost all the operations of the processor take place in the general purpose registers. The arithmetic operations of addition and subtraction, the logical operations of AND, OR, XOR (exclusive or), the shift and rotate operations, and many others all take place totally in the registers. That is, the two operands and the result are all values found in registers. (There are systems in which operands can be in memory but MIPS is not one of them.)

The operations themselves are indicated by specific bit patterns within the instruction. Luckily, we almost never have to remember the detailed pattern of any machine instruction. The advantage of assembler language over the actual machine language is that mnemonics are used rather than arbitrary numbers. Thus *add* is, as one would expect, the mnemonic for **ADD**ition. (Different systems have different mnemonics. *add* might be simplified to *A* in another computer.)

A basic fact about the MIPS processor is that it is a **3-address** machine. That is, many of the instructions contain three addresses in them: two addresses for the two operands and one more address for where to put the result.[1] This is another reason why the choice of 32 registers, while minimal for good performance, was a good one. Using an additional bit in each address would require three more bits in each instruction for addressing and might leave too few for other purposes.

The actual use of an add instruction in assembly language would be in the form

> *add $s3, $s1, $s2*

This is equivalent to *add $19, $17, $18* but we usually do not have to remember more than our mnemonic names for the registers. Our simulators always display the registers giving both names. In addition, the major improvement of assembler language over actual machine language is that we do not have to remember or figure out that the machine language for that instruction is *0x02329820*. Again, the assembler listing will show us that hexadecimal number if we need it.

That assembler statement would correspond to the C/C++/Java code of

> *S3 = S1 + S2;*

using obvious variable names in our high-level language. Notice that the order of the operands and result is the same as for our high-level language. (However, remember that some 3-address machines may not follow this order. In particular, the sum of the first two might be placed in the third.) Note that the registers do not have to be different. In particular, the C/C++/Java code of

> *S0 = S0 + S0;*

would be translated into the assembly language code

> *add $s0, $s0, $s0*

We will consider other instructions in assembly language later.

---

[1] In systems that are 2-address machines, one of the two-operand addresses is where the result is to be placed. If that value is needed, the programmer must save it in advance. An example of a 1-address machine would be a pocket calculator in which one of the operands and the place for the answer is always the display. Finally, Burroughs Corporation, starting with its B5000 series of stack-oriented computers, built wonderful 0-address machines. In their case both of the operands were always found on the top of the stack and the result was always put on the top of the stack.

2.3 Memory

Another important design decision made by the MIPS inventors was to have it be a **load and store** machine. That means that the only operations that are concerned with memory are the load and the store instructions. They bring register data from (load) and to (store) memory. As we will see in Chapter Twelve, this allows those instructions that do not access memory to proceed faster. The problem is that accessing memory is much slower than the speed at which the processor is capable of running and we therefore try to have any operands already in quickly accessible registers.

Computer memory itself consists of as many bytes as we can afford to buy. Each byte is given an address and these addresses must fit in a 32-bit register and so are limited to 2^{32} locations. As before, this is certainly sufficient for simple exercise programs but might be inadequate for very large systems. Some computers have hardware and software to allow a larger address space than actually exists. This **virtual memory** is treated in detail in Operating Systems courses.

In hexadecimal notation, the addresses of bytes in memory range from 0x00000000 to 0xFFFFFFFF. Since registers contain four bytes, which we will call a **word**[2], there are two ways by which the word may be constructed. The first word would certainly start at address 0x00000000 and the second at 0x00000004, etc. The question is when we put those four bytes starting at 0x00000000 into a register, where will each byte go? These four bytes at locations 0, 1, 2, and 3 could be placed so that byte 0 goes at the least significant (bits 0 through 7) end or the most significant (bits 24 through 31) end.

When we look at our PCSPIM simulator in the next section we will see that when areas in memory are printed out, four consecutive words (with addresses increasing from left to right) have bytes numbered

    3 2 1 0   7 6 5 4   B A 9 8   F E D C

in short hexadecimal form. This tells us that PCSPIM stores bytes into words in a **little endian** fashion; that is, the smallest address goes into the least significant position[3]. On some other systems (such as the SUN using XSPIM) the storage is in **big endian** order; that is, the smallest address goes into the most significant position. (These names come from the political argument in Swift's satire "Gulliver's Travels".)

The four words above would have bytes numbered

    0 1 2 3   4 5 6 7   8 9 A B   C D E F

---

[2] On 16-bit machines a "word" usually refers to just 2 bytes (16 bits). Thus, the meaning of "word" is machine dependent in the industry while a "byte" is universally 8 bits.

[3] Actually, PCSPIM is not completely consistent in this regard. When we store integers from registers into memory we will find them readable in normal big endian fashion.

in big endian fashion. Regardless of the endian choice, we would address the words by 0, 4, 8, and 0xC (that is, the smallest value for the address of a byte). It is interesting to note that the actual MIPS processor can process data in either endian order. Our simulators, however, will usually only use the order imposed by the particular hardware.

The next decision regarding memory usage is how these bytes are to be referenced by the hardware. The underlying hardware allows for only one addressing scheme although the assembler allows some other modes from which it can construct actual addresses in that one fixed form. The address of a byte (or the first byte of a word) is found by adding together the value found in one of the registers (called the **base register**) given in the instruction and a **displacement** (or **offset**) which is a signed (2's complement) 16-bit integer also given in the instruction. In assembler language this is written generically as *D($R)* where *D* is the displacement and *R* the register. We call this **base-displacement addressing**.

[Other computers may have many other addressing schemes. For example, some allow an address to be calculated from a form such as *D($B,$I)* where *D* is the displacement and *B* a base register as before and *I* is an index register. The address is found by adding together the contents of the two registers and the displacement. The index register is useful for accessing values out of an array.]

Fortunately, again the assembler comes to our rescue in determining the addresses of memory locations in most cases. In assembler we will be allowed to designate the address of a location by a name in a way similar to how one does that in high-level languages. That is, a variable name is really associated with a location in memory. We will associate a label with a location and let the assembler figure out how to turn an address expression (which may include an offset from a labeled location) into a *D($R)* form.

2.4 Instruction Formats

A very important basic decision to allow improved pipelining (see Chapter 11) was that all instructions take exactly one word (32 bits) for their code. As opposed to those architectures in which there are variable length instructions, the MIPS processor can know immediately where the next instruction in order is located (assuming no jump) without the need to first decode the instruction being performed.

There are actually only three instruction formats; which again was a design decision. The 3-address *add* instruction described above is just one of the **R-type** (Register type) instructions. Others are all the logical and shift instructions. They all have the bit pattern form that looks like the following:

```
|313029282726|2524232221|2019181716|1514131211|1009080706|050403020100|
|     OP      |    RS     |    RT    |    RD    |    SA    |     FN      |
```

As in all instructions, the first field (bits 31 down to 26) of six bits contains the actual operation code. By placing the operation code (OP) always in the same position, the part of the circuitry concerned with decoding the instruction can start on the next instruction immediately. Even though the designers chose to make the processor a RISC-type machine, 64 instructions (6 bits) turns out to be rather restrictive and so some instructions are given the same operation code and are distinguished by the Function Number (FN) part of the instruction. The Shift Amount (SA) field is used by shift instructions and is zero if not needed.

The remaining 15 bits are used to designate the three registers involved; 5 bits for each as expected. The RS and RT registers are the two source registers holding the operands and the RD register is the destination register for the result. Further details will be given in the next chapter after we have a simulator with which to observe these instructions.

A second type of instruction format is the **I-type** (Immediate type) in which one of the two operands is a 16-bit signed number appearing in the instruction itself. Many of the R-type arithmetic and logical instructions have corresponding I-type formats which allow one to avoid the use of another register to contain a small number. They all have the bit pattern form that looks like the following:

```
|313029282726|2524232221|2019181716|15141312111009080706050403020100|
|     OP      |    RS    |    RT    |            IMMEDIATE            |
```

The immediate field is in 2's complement form and is **sign extended** to 32 bits before being used. That is, if positive (0 in bit 15), 16 more zeros are appended before the number; if negative (1 in bit 15), 16 more ones are appended so the final number is of the correct sign and magnitude. For arithmetic and logical operations, RS is the source register and RT the destination register.

For example, the ***ADD Immediate*** instruction

    addi   *$s3, $s1 , -0x25*

takes the value in register $s1$ (=\$17) and adds the 32 bit representation of -25_{HEX} to it and places the result in register $s3$ (=\$19). Note that $0x25 = 37_{DEC} = 00100101_{BIN}$ so, taking the 2's complement, $-0x25 = 11011011_{BIN}$ or $11111111111011011_{BIN} = 0xFFDB$, and those are the 16 bits which appear in the immediate field of the instruction. When extended to 32-bits, we obtain $0xFFFFFFDB$ and that is what is used in the addition.

This corresponds to the C/C++/Java code of

    S3 = S1 + (-0x25);   // or S3 = S1 – 37;

In addition to arithmetic and logical operations, the conditional branch instructions (*e.g.*, branch if two registers contain equal values) use the I-type instruction with the 16 bit immediate field giving the offset (*i.e.*, how far to jump if the condition is true). Since 16 bits does not allow for a large jump and every bit is significant in the architecture, a clever trick is used to extend the range of the jump. Since all instructions are 32 bits = 4 bytes long (an earlier design decision), the address of every instruction has two zeros in the lowest order bits. Since they must be zero, it is unnecessary to show them and so the hardware will shift the 16-bit field left two places automatically. Thus there are virtually 18 bits available for the jump amount. In case that is still insufficient, there is a *jr* (**Jump Register**) command that allows a jump to any 32-bit address placed in a register.

For load and store operations, the RS register and immediate field are treated as the base register and displacement in the standard *D($R)* form to access memory. In these cases the RT register may serve as either the source (for store) or destination (for load) register.

The final form of an instruction is the **J-type** (Jump type). It is used for jump instructions which reset the Program Counter (PC) to the indicated address so computation proceeds from that place. They all have the bit pattern form that looks like the following:

31 30 29 28 27 26	25 24 23 22 21 20 19 18 17 16 15 14 13 12 11 10 09 08 07 06 05 04 03 02 01 00
OP	TARGET

The same trick is applied to the 26-bit target field in order to allow for a virtual 28-bit distance for the jump. The 26 bits are shifted left two bits and the four highest order bits are taken from the Program Counter (PC) to form the 32 bit address of the next instruction to be performed.

Exercises

1. Suppose register $8 = *$t0* contains the number 0x00010001. What is the result if the computer multiplies *$t0* by itself?

2. Suppose register $9 = *$t1* contains 0x21 and $10 = *$t2* contains 7. What is the result if the computer divides *$t1* by *$t2*?

3. What is the result of the instruction *add $0, $1, $2*?

4. Suppose *$s1* contains 1, *$s2* contains 2 and *$s3* contains 3. What will be in those registers after the instruction *add $s3, $s1, $s2* is executed?

5. Using obvious variable names, what would be the assembly language equivalent of the C/C++/Java statement *T5 = T7 + S5;* ?

6. If each word holds four characters, what would your name look like in memory if stored in little endian fashion? How about big endian order?

7. Suppose register $8 = *$t0* contains the number 0x00010001. Exactly where in memory is the location described by *25($t0)*? Give your answer in hex format.

8. With the same *$t0* as in #7, describe location 0x00010101 in *D($R)* form.

9. What will be the contents of the 15 bits from 25 down to 11 corresponding to the R-type instruction *add $s3, $s1, $s2*?

10. If an add instruction contains 111011111010001 as the 15 bits from 25 down to 11, what would be the corresponding assembler language statement?

11. The operation code for *addi* is 001000. What is the machine language corresponding to the assembly language statement *addi $t8, $s5, 30*?

12. Suppose the immediate field of a conditional branch instruction contains 0x1000. How far will the computer go for the next instruction if the condition is true? What if the immediate field contains 0x9000?

13. The jump instruction has operation code 2. If the instruction 0x08000010 is at location 0x10101010, where is the next instruction to be found?

14. If the contents of register *$t0* are 0x00010001 and you use the two address command *mult $t0,$t0*. Exactly which registers are changed and to what?

CHAPTER THREE

SPIM and MIPSter

We are now ready to actually do some assembly language programming. Fortunately, there are software packages available which will help us accomplish our goal. The first of these was the MIPS simulator SPIM by James R. Larus. With the aid of PCSpim in particular we will be able to watch the registers and memory as our code is executed. As mentioned in the Preface, we are even better off with the simulator than with the real thing since it will be easy to "single-step" through the code we have written and see exactly what each individual command accomplishes. Of course we will probably lose the opportunity to find out some things about the real processor (such as detailed timing facts and some advanced concepts including pipelining) but we will find out more than enough to give us a good feel for how assembler languages and their associated machines work. A second very helpful package is the MIPSter IDE (**I**ntegrated **D**evelopment **E**nvironment) by Dave Haynes. Programmers who have used such IDE's as Visual C/C++/Java are used to having their text editor just a part of an environment in which their code can be immediately compiled and run. MIPSter will do the same thing for us.

3.1 Assemblers

Almost all assembly languages are based on the same idea. A computer's processor is designed to take its instructions in "machine language" as described before. Assembly language is, at its core, just machine language using mnemonics. For example, two instructions that access memory in our load and store MIPS processor are **L**oad **W**ord (operation code 100011_{BIN} in bits 31-26) and **S**tore **W**ord (operation code 101011_{BIN} in bits 31-26). Programmers almost never have to try to remember all the operation codes since assembler language allows one to use mnemonics for them. In particular, *lw* and *sw* are the mnemonics for these two operations in our MIPS assembly language. Obviously, these are much easier to remember.

A second basic fact about assemblers is that they are invariably line oriented. That is, each line of code is a separate "statement" as opposed to the usual free-form source code for languages such as C/C++/Java. Just as the ";" indicates the end of a statement in C/C++/Java, so does a new line indicate the end of an assembler statement. The general form of an assembly language statement is a line that looks as follows:

```
label:        operation   operands    # comments
```

The four fields are all optional and blank lines are allowed if desired. Assembler languages are notoriously difficult to read and so it is conventional to use many more comments than with "self-documenting" high-level languages. In addition, it is expected that assembler programmers will indent their code very carefully in order to help the reader. The old IBM360 assemblers expected programmers to use columns 1, 10, 16, and 40 for these four fields. It's no longer required to be that careful in that most assemblers are free form within each line. Nevertheless, it is strongly recommended that indentations be consistently used. Let us consider the form of each of these four fields.

The first field is an optional label. It serves the same purpose as a variable name in high-level languages: it gives a name to a location in memory. The programmer can then refer to that location by name and leave it up to the assembler (or compiler) to figure out the actual address of the location. Labels in SPIM are constructed in a similar manner to variable names in C/C++/Java in that they consist of a string of alphanumeric characters starting with a letter. They are terminated by a colon (":") and are case sensitive. We do not consider the colon to be part of the label.

We must mention that almost all the detailed information given here about our assembler may well differ from that for another assembler, even for the same MIPS processor. Assemblers are just software programs (as are compilers) and the authors may well have included different features in their code. Indeed, one of the main selling points used by our friendly salesperson is what fancy extra features that particular software includes (and this may well include bugs that they have been unable to fix). As an example of this problem we will point out that different assemblers (for MIPS and for other architectures) usually allow a small set of non-alphanumeric characters in labels. Characters such as underscore ("_"), period ("."), dollar ("$"), percent ("%"), and others may be allowed (sometimes counted as a letter with which a label may begin and sometimes not). A very good practice is to avoid all such special characters since a programmer often has to write assembler (or even C/C++/Java type language) code for different machines and different assemblers (or compilers) and that's just one more unnecessary thing to try to remember.

The second field is the operation desired. Mnemonics for all the machines instructions are available (and a convenient list appears in a frame in the Toolbox of the MIPSter IDE). See Appendix D for a list of instructions used by SPIM. We have mentioned *add*, *lw*, and *sw* already and we will learn more as we go. Trying to memorize all of them at one time is probably impossible. The best way to learn them is to use them.

The original concept of an assembler was that each mnemonic stood for a specific machine instruction; the translation was one-to-one. In fact it soon became normal to allow in the operation field what are called assembler **directives**. These do not correspond to machine instructions to be performed when the final program is run but are orders directed to the assembler itself. We will have directives that give the assembler some of the information it needs to turn our source code into machine language that then may be executed. When we start MIPSter we will see a template for a SPIM program and it will include the two directives *.data* and *.text* to remind us that most programs need these. The *.data* directive tells the assembler that we want it to put specific data elements starting at that position. The *.text* directive tells it that what follows is actually assembler code to be executed. All the assembler directives begin with a period and are listed in Appendix D and in the MIPSter toolbox.

Another difference between the original concept and our SPIM assembler is that the RISC (**R**educed **I**nstruction **S**et **C**omputer) architecture has reduced the number of instructions wired into the processor to the extent that some very natural instructions need to be performed by a different instruction or by two or more actual machine instructions. For example, it would be natural to load a small number into a register with an *li* (Load Immediate) command. Its form would be *li $R,immediate* where *$R* is the desired register and *immediate* is the 16 bit signed number to be loaded. We will use this command regularly but it turns out that there is no such instruction wired into the MIPS processor. The reason is that the same result can be obtained by the command *ori $R,$0,immediate* for which there is a machine instruction. Our assembler is helpful enough to allow us to use the *li* **pseudo-operation** but translates it into the legal *ori* (**OR I**mmediate) instruction for us. In some other cases the assembler will allow us to use a natural mnemonic for an action that will take two or more machine instructions to perform.

The third field is a list of operands for the operator. This list can be somewhat free form in that spaces may be used to improve readability. We will use the comma (",") to delimit the elements of the list but they are really not necessary. Whatever a programmer chooses to do, however, it is recommended that it be done consistently.

Finally, comments are placed on almost every line. Everything following a pound sign ("#") is ignored by the assembler and so serves as a comment[1]. As mentioned above, more comments are to be expected in assembler but an often stated requirement that every line have a comment may be going a bit too far. Just as *n=n+1;* (or *n+=1;* or *n++;*) are so obvious that it should not be necessary to put the comment *"// increment n by 1"*, so also some statements in assembler will become so obvious that nothing is necessary. However, it can rarely hurt to be explicit. Any trick – or even thinking – that is necessary should be carefully documented since even the author of the code will forget the details quickly.

3.2 MIPSter

Almost all assemblers expect their input to be ASCII source code. Many text editors are available to produce this source code. The simple programs *Notepad*, *WordPad*, and even *EDIT* under MSDOS will work fine. In UNIX systems both *emacs* and *vi* are useable. One should probably avoid the complicated word processing systems such as MS Word since they usually save their files in special formats other than straight ASCII code and are unnecessary. In the case of MIPS programming, we have an excellent IDE (Integrated Development Environment) in MIPSter and it is recommended that code be written using that editor. Source files for SPIM and MIPSter should be saved with the suffix ".*s*" which is a default for both. (Other systems may use ".*asm*" or ".*txt*" as the preferred suffix.)

When we first bring up MIPSter we see the following screen:

---

[1] Actually the "#" character may appear in a quoted string and have its normal meaning. Older version of MIPSter, however, may not color code it correctly (see the next section).

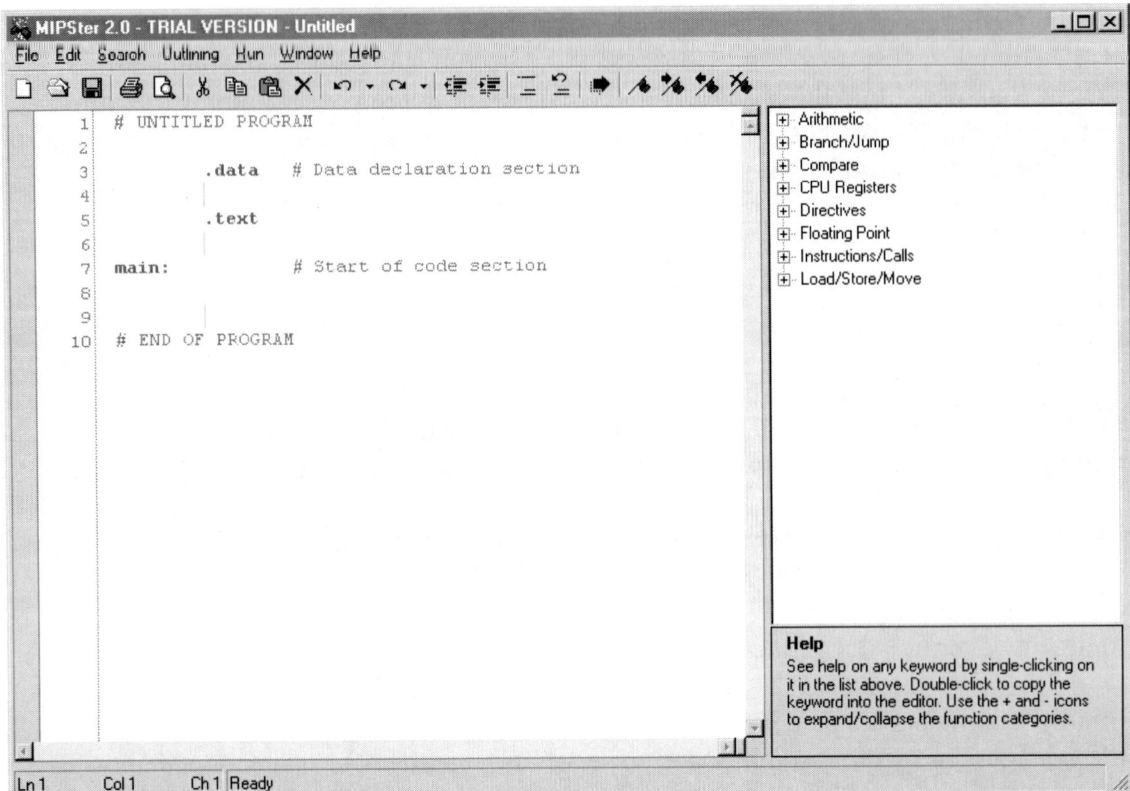

The top banner shows that this is a new file with no name associated with it yet. (In fact, if we save it now it will have the name "untitled.s".) The pull-down "File" and "Edit" headings have subcommands all with the usual meanings. A new heading is "Run" under which is found "Start with SPIM" and "SPIM Properties". By clicking on "Start with Spim" (or pressing **F5**) we can try out our code and stay within this environment.

Notice that the expandable lists in the right column give us the mnemonics for almost all the instructions we may use. When an instruction is selected, a short description appears in the comment line below.

Let's bring up the usual "Hello World!" program and consider the details. By typing at the appropriate places in MIPSter we can have the following code

```
# UNTITLED PROGRAM

        .data        # Data declaration section
banner:
        .asciiz      "Hello, World!"
        .text
main:                # Start of code section
        li    $v0,4
        la    $a0,banner
        syscall
        li    $v0,10
        syscall
```

```
    # END OF PROGRAM
```

If we press **F5** a command window appears that looks like:

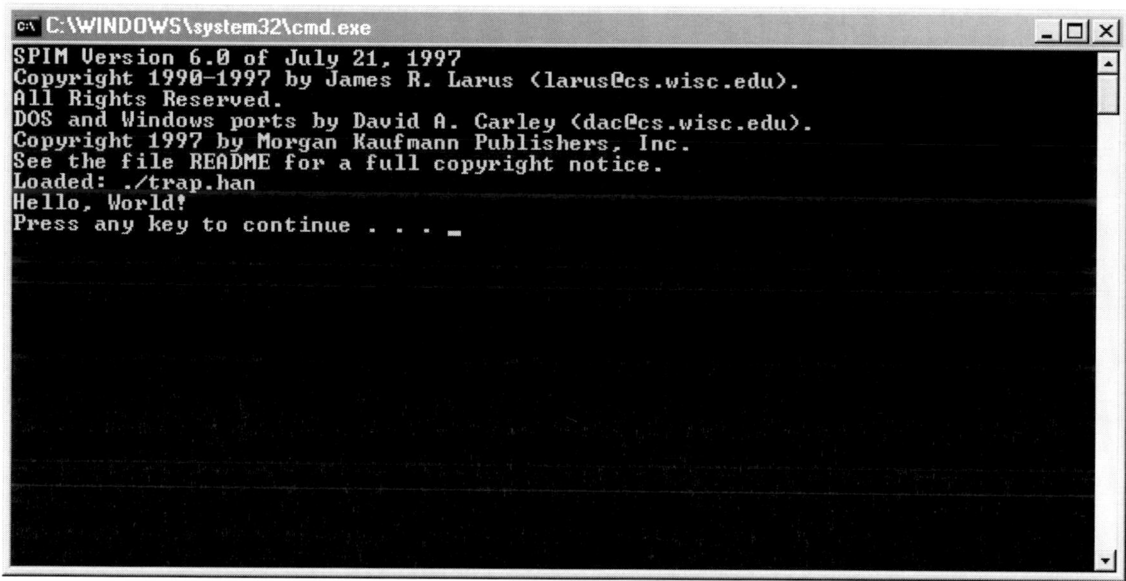

Within the command window we see copyright information, some system notices and then the actual output of the program that is to print "Hello, World!" on the screen. The system then prompts us to press any key to continue (which allows the window to remain visible as long as we wish). [We will note later that this uses an older version of SPIM.]

Now we can analyze this code. Although the grey-scale printing of the pictures does not show us colors, we can see on our computer screen that MIPSter color-codes our source. This is extremely helpful. Labels appear in red and if they do not have the correct color it is clear that the assembler does not understand what we meant (only what we actually typed); for example, we might have forgotten the colon following the label. Comments appear in green while instructions, directives, and pseudo-operations all appear in blue. Registers appear in maroon and other operands appear in black. The colors usually indicate how the assembler will interpret our source code and that encourages us to make immediate corrections. (The "#" character embedded in a quoted string and some unusual instructions may not be recognized correctly.)

The data declaration section (indicated by the *.data* directive) here contains only one labeled location (*banner*). Thus "banner" may be used to indicate the address at which the assembler places the data described. The directive *.asciiz* tells the assembler to store the operand (which is the string "Hello, World!") as a string of ASCII characters terminated (as in C/C++/Java) with a "Null" or zero (0x00) byte.

Within the code section (indicated by the *.text* directive), we find it starting with the label *main* which has the same meaning as in C/C++/Java: it indicates where the operating system is to start in our code when running the program. (Some MIPS systems may require some slightly different labels such as __*start,* but we will stick to PCSpim's convention. In addition, the directive *.globl main* is usually used before the *main* label but it is not necessary in most of our small programs using PCSPIM.) All our complete programs will contain a *main* label but we will often give just the functional part of a problem assuming that the reader can write all the input and output code and call on the critical function easily.

Finally, we get to the actual code for our example. The first line uses the pseudo-operation mentioned before: *li*. We have no real reason to remember that there is no such instruction wired into the processor. We should use it in a natural way to describe exactly what we want to happen. In particular, we want to Load into register *$v0* the small **I**mmediate operand 4. Later, when we look at this same code through SPIM we will see that the assembler actually turns this into *ori $2,$0,4* which does exactly that.

The second line also uses another pseudo-instruction: *la* (**L**oad **A**ddress). In some cases *la* may be translated into two instructions but, in this case, it becomes just one. Again we don't have to think about how the assembler does it, just assume it is correct. When we look at SPIM we will see that it actually loads into the upper half of the register *$a0* = $4 the immediate value 0x1001 because it knows that the system will place our data starting at the address 0x10010000. Thus the actual code will be an *lui* (**L**oad **U**pper **I**mmediate) instruction with operands $4 and 4097 (decimal notation is the default in SPIM) and machine language 0x3c041001 (which we really do not need to know). The point is that it loads the address of *banner* into *$a0*.

All that's left to explain in this short program is the meaning of the operation *syscall*, short for "**SYS**tem **CALL**", which we will do in the next section.

3.3 System Functions

If we go to the listings on the right, we can expand the "Instructions/Calls" listing. Ten of the items are simple calls to the operating system to perform eight possible I/O operations, a memory allocation operation, and, obviously, a normal exit from our program. In each case, register *$v0* is to be loaded with the number (1 through 10) of the desired operation.

These ten are the main calls available through MIPSter at this time. PCSPIM has a number of other possible calls that we will consider in Chapters Six, Eight, and Ten. We will treat float and double numbers later but will give the details of integer and string operations now. Here is a partial table of the meanings of the calls we need immediately:

Code	Name	Argument and Result Registers
1	print_int	$a0=integer
4	print_string	$a0→string
5	read_int	;$v0=integer
8	read_string	$a0→buffer, $a1=length
10	exit	

To print the value of an integer in decimal notation on our terminal, we load that integer into register *$a0*, put the code number 1 in register *$v0*, and issue a **syscall** instruction. The system will then print the integer on our screen. It will be placed wherever the curser is at the time and will not issue a carriage return, line feed, or even a space after it is done. If we want a space between numbers or after a prompt, we have to put it there ourselves. This is another basic fact about assembler language: you have to do almost everything yourself.

Practice: After the label *main* and before the *li $v0,4* line, add the following lines to the source code of *HelloWorld.s*:

```
li      $v0,1
li      $a0,1234
syscall
li      $a0,0x1234
syscall
```

Now run the program by pressing **F5**. (If told that the file has changed and asked if you want to save the latest version, you must answer "yes" in order for the program to run.) You should see the output line now read:

```
12344660Hello, World!
```

This tells you that the default for integers is decimal, that hexadecimal numbers are acceptable in our standard format ($4660_{DEC} = 0x1234$), and that no spaces or other characters are inserted unless we specifically ask for them. Also notice that the *syscall* did not change the value of *$v0* when we performed function code number one.

Another type of object we can print is a Null-terminated string. As stated above, the directive *.asciiz* tells the assembler to store the operand as a "Null" or zero (0x00) terminated string of ASCII characters. System function four is designed to print such strings. While we again place the function code number, 4 this time, in *$v0*, we do not put the string we wish to print in *$a0*. In fact, since *$a0* consists of only 32 bits (4 bytes) there is not room for more than 4 ASCII characters in that register and one would have to be the terminating "Null". What is actually put in *$a0* is a **pointer** to the string we wish to print. By a pointer to an object we mean the address of the object. The assembler will calculate the address for us. We indicate a pointer by using the character "→" in our table of calls.

The line *la $a0,banner* then is the result of compiling code similar to *A0 = &banner;* in C/C++. While Java is said to not have pointers, every object identifier is really a pointer – you just are not allowed to do any pointer arithmetic. Assembler language uses pointers and pointer arithmetic frequently and so the *la* (**L**oad **A**ddress) pseudo-instruction is very important.

Here is one way to get the three outputs of the above practice exercise on separate lines. In the *.data* section insert a line such as

```
NL     .asciiz   "\n"        # NewLine character (Null terminated)
```

We see that SPIM uses the backslash in the same way that C/C++/Java does, it allows for special characters (and "\t" stands for TAB as expected). Now if we place the three lines

```
li    $v0, 4
la    $a0, NL
syscall
```

between our output statements, we will get the new lines desired. Notice, however, that we can no longer count on $v0 to contain 1 (particularly since we specifically change it to 4). Thus we must put in the code to return $v0 to 1 each time it is needed.

Remember, we do not put the actual NewLine character and Null terminator in $a0; we must put there a pointer to the string consisting of just those two characters. If we forget and try it with the characters themselves in $a0, SPIM will assume that we have an address in that register and will start printing at that location no matter where it is. It will continue printing until it finds a Null byte; again, no matter how far away it is. Lots of garbage output can appear for no obvious reason in assembler!

The other system function call we have already used is number 10. We should end all our programs with

```
li    $v0, 10
syscall
```

that tells the operating system to terminate our program normally by closing any open files and cleaning up memory.

Input of integers is very simple. If one loads the number 5 into $v0 and issues a *syscall*, the system will bring up a console window and wait for the *<Enter>* that terminates the input of the integer. There is, however, no error checking in our simulator. If a letter appears in the input string of digits, it also terminates the integer as far as the system is concerned. The integer itself appears in register $v0 thus writing over the previous value of 5. (As usual, different systems may differ in regard to error checking of input. If one is critically concerned about it, one could always read in the input as a string of characters and convert proper input into an integer value oneself!)

Finally, we may also input (Null-terminated) strings of characters using *syscall* number 8. Just as in our discussion of printing a NewLine, there is not room in one register for a Null-terminated string of more than three characters. We must, therefore, make room for the string somewhere in our data segment. The assembler directive *.space* is used as follows:

```
buffer:   .space 100 # a place for our string of 98 characters + 2
```

and means that we want the assembler to leave 100 bytes of memory at a location which we may refer to by the label "buffer".

Now we can issue a *syscall* such as

```
li    $v0, 8
la    $a0, buffer
li    $a1, 20 # read 18 characters, NL, and add a Null-terminator
syscall
```

The system will wait for an *<Enter>* before proceeding. Notice that we must designate a length for the string in register *$a1* and the system will then try to read two less than that length so as to leave room for the NewLine character (0x0a) and Null terminator (0x00). The *<Enter>* indicates the end of our input and that input may be smaller than the length specified. If our input is longer than the length given in *$a0*, the remaining characters will be ignored and even the NewLine character will be discarded.

Practice: It is now possible to modify our HelloWorld program to include input and output of integers and strings. This is an opportunity to add a **prompt** to our input. That is, we should print out a string such as "Please input an integer: " or "I'm waiting for a string followed by a carriage return! " so that the user knows why there is no activity from the system and for what it is waiting. In addition, it is often good programming practice (unless the specifications do not allow it) to **echo** the input so that the user can see exactly what the system has taken to be its input. Labeling the echo with some string such as "I think you entered: " or "Thank you for entering: " is helpful for the user (albeit irritating if too cute).

3.4 SPIM

Even if it assembles, our program may not work perfectly (a very likely situation). The MIPSter system does very little to help. In order to "debug" an assembly language program we usually have to get down to the level of watching what happens in the registers and in memory as we step through the code generated by the assembler. The SPIM program (under the title PCSpim for Windows) is useful for debugging and helps us understand exactly how a computer's architecture works. If we bring up PCSpim we get a screen like this:

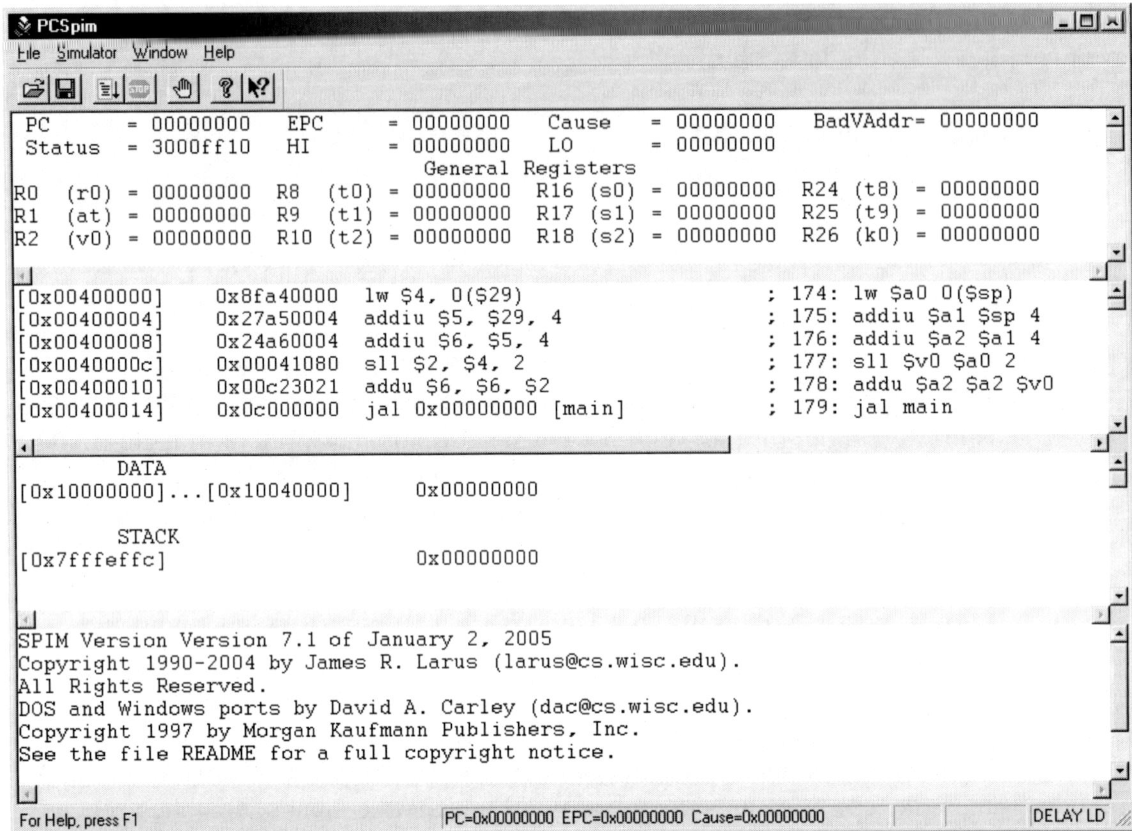

This is the usual appearance of the PCSpim user interface. The main screen consists of four subwindows. The top window shows the contents of the registers. Listed first are the special registers, some of which we have mentioned previously: PC (Program Counter) and HI and LO which are used for multiplications and divisions. In addition it appears that there are some other special registers that we will use later (see Chapter 12). All but the Status register have been initialized to zero since we have not yet loaded any program into the system.

Under the title "General Registers" we find the 32 general-purpose registers with their mnemonic names. Scrolling down we can see that *$gp* and *$sp* have been initialized to some values by the system but the others are all zero. Beneath these registers is a list of all the floating-point registers that we will use later (but note that their values seem to be in decimal format). From the appearance of *$sp* it is clear that the general purpose registers are displayed in hexadecimal format. (Note that under the pull-down list titled "Simulator" there is a subheading called "Settings" in which one can change the default format of these registers!)

The second window in PCSpim contains the *.text* segment of our program; that is, the actual code to be executed. At the far left is a list of the locations of the instructions. They will always start at 0x00400000 by convention agreed to by PCSpim and the operating system. Since all instructions take exactly 4 bytes, the (hex) addresses of succeeding instructions always end in 0,4,8,c,0,4,8,c,0,.... . The second column contains the actual machine instructions that will be performed displayed in hex format. The assembly language programmer almost never needs to investigate this field since it is usually assumed that the assembler can do simple operations correctly. That is, it can always easily look up the actual machine instructions associated with our assembler language mnemonics such as *li, la, add*, etc. and do other straightforward bookkeeping chores.

The third field (terminated by a ";") is a modified version of our assembler language source. All the mnemonics for registers have been replaced by (decimal) numbers and the pseudo-instructions have been translated to equivalent assembler statements that are in one-to-one correspondence with machine instructions. Some of our labels will appear here for convenience (but are not significant in our machine code). Since we have not loaded any program into PCSpim yet, we see the instruction `jal 0x00000000 [main]` there now as a place holder. It is a call on *main*, which is where we want the program to start, but there is no program yet so the assembler does not know what address to place there and just leaves it at zero.

The final field on the right will contain our assembler source code, with our comments, together with the assembler code inserted by the system to smoothly start and stop our program. The comments of "#argc" and "#argv" remind us of the calling convention in C for command line parameters to a program. We don't have to be concerned with that code at this time. Here is where we can see the transformation of some of our pseudo-instructions into actual machine instructions.

Let us now load a new version of our *HelloWorld.s* program into PCSpim. Under the "File" heading, there is an "Open…" subheading from which we can find our source code.

```
# HelloWorld.s

        .data           # Data declaration section
banner:
        .asciiz         "Hello World!"
        .text
main:                    # Start of code section
        li      $v0, 4
        la      $a0, banner
        syscall

        li      $v0, 10
        syscall

# End of HelloWorld.s
```

Once PCSpim has loaded this program, if it is successful in assembling it there will be message to that effect in the fourth window. If it is not successful, we must go back to our editor (MIPSter seems best) and correct any errors. Our screen now looks like this:

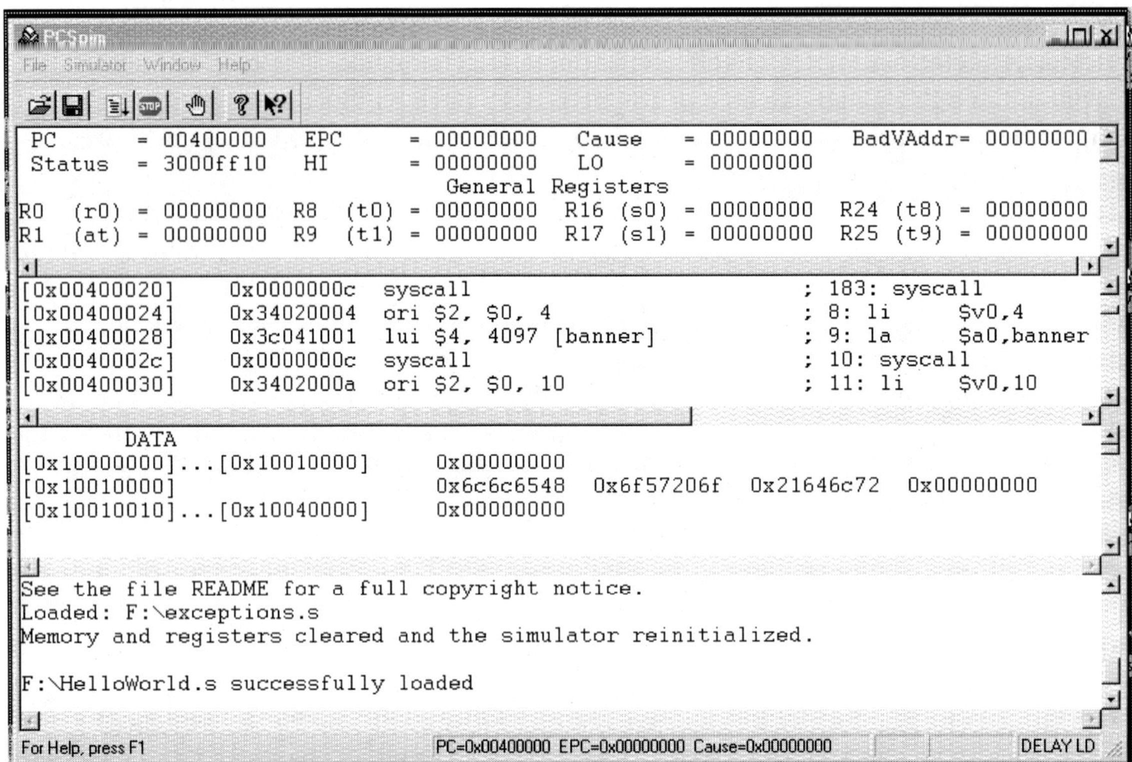

The last line tells us that we have been successful in loading *HelloWorld.s* into PCSpim and it has been assembled with no syntactic errors (but there might well be logical errors). Now let us consider the changes made to the registers and in memory before running the program. Looking at the Program Counter (PC) we see that 0x00400000 now appears (on some older versions the programmer must set this register to that value using the "Simulator" pull-down menu, choosing "Set Value…" and then filling in "PC" as the register to change to 0x00400000). That is the location at which this assembler and operating system have agreed to put the setup code for all its programs. It is not the address at which our program's *main* label is placed. We recall that the system puts some preliminary code at the beginning that includes a call on our *main* that may be much later. The other registers are unchanged.

In the second window we may scroll down and find our code starting at the instruction located at 0x00400024. In the right column we see that it is actually the 10th line of the source code.[2] As promised, the *li $v0,4* pseudo-operation is translated into the actual assembler code of *ori $2,$0,4* which becomes the uninformative 0x34020004 machine instruction (although we can see the 16 bit immediate operand of 4).

Notice that the *la a0,banner* pseudo-operation is translated into *lui $4, 4097 [banner]* . (We could use some other label for *banner* since it does not matter as long as we are consistent.) The result is to place in the upper half of $4 = *$a0* the number 0x1001 =

---

[2] This assumes that we are using the standard "exceptions.s" supplied with PCSPIM by Larus. In Chapter 12 we will consider writing our own versions that might change the number of commands to be executed before our code starts.

4097_{DEC}. Now we may look in the *.data* segment in PCSpim (the third window) and find 0x1001000 on the third line of our display; where we expect to find "Hello World!" … :

```
[0x10010000]        0x6c6c6548   0x6f57206f   0x21646c72   0x00000000
```

If we look up the ASCII codes in the table in Appendix A, it reads from left to right:

```
   lleH      oW o     !dlr     ⊘⊘⊘⊘
```

where the character ⊘ stands for actual Null (zero) byte. The small endian behavior of our processor is obvious here. We can read printable characters in the data segment but it's a little difficult to read strings because of the endian problem. Nevertheless, the string we want is there. (On a big endian machine we would have "Hell o Wo rld! ⊘⊘⊘⊘" instead.)

3.5 Single Stepping

Once we have loaded a version of *HelloWorld.s* which has no syntactical errors into PCSpim, we may run it by pressing **F5 (Go)**. A window will pop-up asking for "Run Parameters" and requesting the "Starting Address" in particular. Modern versions of PCSpim have already placed the correct value: 0x00400000 in the window and the "OK" button starts the system. (If the Starting Address is still zero, one must manually change it to 0x00400000.) When it runs, a Console window will appear with our output ("Hello, World!") in it. If we do not like the output, we have to go back to a text editor such as MIPSter to change our source code and try again. We can run the same code again by going to the "Simulator" pull-down menu and "Reload" the source file.

The "Simulator" menu lists some more advanced choices, most of which we will wait to discuss until we have more experience. The "Single Step" option, however, is helpful from the beginning and we see that **F10** is a shortcut for it. Let us again load the file *HelloWorld.s* into PCSpim and this time watch the behavior of the registers and memory as we execute the code one instruction at a time.

When we are ready to start the **P**rogram **C**ounter (PC) should be at 0x00400000 and the corresponding instruction is highlighted in the second window. Scrolling down the register window we see that all the registers are zero except R28 (*$gp*) and R29 (*$sp*). The actual value in *$sp*, the **S**tack **P**ointer, agrees with the address in the *.data* window that shows us that the stack does start where the register points and has nothing in it yet. The portion of the *.data* segment starting at 0x10010000 has our string in it as described above. There is some "Kernel" data starting at 0x90000000 but we do not have to be concerned with that; it's the operating system's problem until Chapter 12.

Now let's concentrate on the second window in which the actual instructions appear. As we saw above, even before we loaded our own program into PCSpim, the system places some startup code at the beginning address of 0x00400000. If we push **F10 (Single Step)**

PCSpim will execute just one instruction at a time and we can watch the effect of each instruction.

The first time you press **F10** there doesn't seem to be much happen; in fact a zero value at the location in memory pointed to by the stack pointer *$sp* (that's memory location 0x7fffeffc) has been moved into register *$a0* which was already zero! That's not very visible!! The PC has changed to 0x00400004 and so we are ready to perform the next instruction. The second push on **F10** does something visible, however. The instruction highlighted was *addiu $a1,$sp,4* and the mnemonic stands for **ADD** **I**mmediate **U**nsigned (no overflow). That is, add the immediate value of 4 to the contents of *$sp* and place the answer in *$a1*. A simple calculation shows that 0x7fffeffc + 4 = 0x7ffff000 and that's what we find in R5 = *$a1*. It did it!

The third **F10** will have PCSpim execute the third instruction *addiu $a2,$a1,4* and we see that the immediate value 4 is added to the number in *$a1* and the result is placed in *$a2*. Again the PC is increased to point to the next instruction at 0040000c. The fourth F10 performs a *sll* (**S**hift **L**eft **L**ogical) instruction with operands *$v0,$a0,2* (which means move the bits in *$a0* two places to the left while bringing zeros in from the right but ignore any bits lost on the left – including, in particular, changes in the sign bit due to overflow) placing the result in *$v0*. Since *$a0* is zero in this case (the first instruction did that), nothing is visible.

The fifth **F10** will add *$v0* to *$a2* but, again, that is invisible. Finally, the instruction at 0x00400014 (that is *jal 0x00400024 [main]*) is performed. This is a complicated instruction with more than the usual amount of affects *jal* stands for **J**ump **A**nd **L**ink so this is an instruction which causes a jump (*goto*) to a different location in our code than the normal "next in order" instruction. Although the PC would usually the incremented to 0x00400018, the *jal* instruction here places the address of *main* in the PC instead. PCSpim has calculated where that location actually is and we do not have to count bytes ourselves to figure it out. It turns out to be at 0x00400024 and that's where our program really starts. Note that *jal* places 0x0040001c in *$ra* (**R**eturn **A**ddress). That's the "And Link" part of the instruction and we will see what that does for us later.

When single stepping through a program we will always have the first six[3] instructions given to us by the system and we have to go through them to get to our own code. Now let's take a moment to watch our HelloWorld.s actually run.

The first instruction at 0x00400024 is the *li $v0,4* on line 10 which was translated into *ori $2,$0,4*. If we press F10 we get the value 4 in *$v0* = $2 as expected. The next instruction is our *la $a0,banner* which we see is translated into *lui $4,4097 [banner]*. The "banner" is there just to help us read the code and is ignored in the final analysis. The 4097 is a decimal number corresponding to the 0x1001 the system needs in the upper half of the register *$a0* because there has been an agreement to place our data starting at 0x10010000 (where we see the string labeled *banner*). The *la* pseudo-instruction will

---

[3] See previous footnote

often generate two instructions, one to set the correct upper half and another to adjust the lower half of the register.

When we get to the *syscall* instruction, a console window will pop-up with the output of the program. Clicking on the "x" in the upper right, as usual, will close that window. The final exit *syscall* just returns us to the kernel and so does not act as we would expect. Nevertheless, by the time we get to that instruction we hope to have found any problems with our code.

We will next treat more complicated coding problems and see how to use the stack and other features of MIPS assembler language.

Exercises

1. Write and test a SPIM program that will print your name, address, and telephone number on separate lines.

2. Although the line orientation of assemblers is basic, it is possible to put more than one statement on a line in our assembler. Just as in C/C++/Java, a ";" indicates the end of a statement and may be followed by another assembler statement. This is not a recommended procedure since it leads to unreadable code such as

    ```
    .data;s: .asciiz "\nHello, World!\n"
    .text;main: li $v0,4; la $a0,s;
    syscall; li $v0,10; syscall
    ```

    Rewrite this code in standard indented form.

3. In addition to the *.asciiz* directive, we find in the "Directives" listings in MIPSter the directive *.ascii* (without the *z*). This directive tells the assembler to place the operand as a string of ASCII characters next in memory but not to terminate it with a Null character (0x00). Since labels just name locations, there is no difference between

    ```
    banner: .asciiz "Hello World!"
    ```

    and

    ```
    banner:   .ascii  "Hello "
              .asciiz " World!"
    ```

    Demonstrate this fact using the SPIM simulator.

4. Use SPIM to check that the instruction *la $a0,banner* is translated into a *lui* instruction as mentioned in 3.2.

5. Use SPIM to single-step through code that inputs integers using system call number 5. See what happens with erroneous input.

6. Use SPIM to single-step through code that inputs strings using system call number 8. See what happens with strings longer than the length given in *$a1*. See what happens to shorter strings.

CHAPTER FOUR

Arrays and Pointers

A computer is only useful for handling large quantities of data. If all we wanted to do was add two integers in registers *$a0* and *$a1* and put the result in register *$a2*, the single assembler statement *add $a2,$a0,$a1* would suffice (as would a pocket calculator). When we want to sort many integers, particularly an indefinite number, we need to be able to store all the integers in memory and access them quickly in a loop. Our first job, then, will be to determine how we can input a large number of integers or long strings as data for our code. With high level languages it is most appropriate to construct a large file containing test data and then run the program we are debugging repeatedly with that data set. Using a command such as

c:\> program.exe < data.dat

when in a command window will ask the operating system to run the compiled code called *program.exe* on the c: drive (presumably the "execute" program put out by our compiler) using as input the file *data.dat* which we have constructed earlier.

The MIPS simulator SPIM has a group of system calls that allow us to use files for input and output (they are not available in MIPSter). They are very complicated operations and we will delay studying them until Chapter 6. Here we will require that the user must be prompted for the program's input and must enter it every time the program is tested. This limits the amount of data with which one can reasonable expect to test a program. An alternative is to have the program itself generate its own test data as a separate part of the code unrelated to the actual purpose of the program. We will demonstrate both methods here.

We will use the pseudo-operation *.space* to tell the assembler the place to put a large amount of data. For example,

```
array:      .space      100
```

is the assembler directive to leave 100 bytes (25 words) of memory locations in the *.data* section and allow us to refer to it by the label "*array*" rather than have to calculate ourselves exactly where it is within the *.data* section. The label "*array*" is sometimes called a **relocatable** symbol since the actual address at which it is stored may change due to decisions made by either the assembler or the operating system.

Note that there is no typing information in that statement so 100 bytes of characters or 25 integer words would equally fit in that space. Although the assembler can help in some cases, it is usually the programmer who must be careful to avoid errors in typing.

In C/C++/Java we would define an array by a statement such as *int[] array;* and access the elements by pointers in C and by references in Java. As usual, assembler is even more basic and we are required to do pointer arithmetic frequently when accessing array elements.

4.1 Arrays

We recall that the only method of addressing memory in the MIPS processor is by using the base-displacement form *D($R)* where *R* is a register and *D* is a 16-bit 2's complement displacement. Fortunately, the assembler and the operating system have an agreement as to where the *.data* segment will be placed and can assist the programmer. For example, suppose we have the following code:

```
           .data
array:     .space   100
           .text
           ...                        # some code
           la        $t0,array
```

The SPIM assembler will give us a line of code such as

```
   0x3c081001   lui  $8, 4097 [array]          ; 7: la $t0,array
```

The "*[array]*" note is just to help the programmer and is not part of the code. The instruction itself (*lui $8,4097*) places 0x1001 = 4097_{DEC} in the upper half (*lui* = Load Upper Immediate) of register 8 (*$t0*). The agreement is that our portion of the *.data* segment is to start at location 0x10010000 and that is what is put in *$t0*.

Now suppose we started our .data segment differently:

```
           .data
begin:     .asciiz  "Begin:  "
array      .space   100
end:       .asciiz  "End"
           .text
           ...                        # some code
           la        $t0,array
```

The assembler will give us two lines of code such as

```
   0x3c011001   lui $1, 4097 [array]             ; 8: la $t0,array
   0x34280008   ori $8, $1, 8 [array]
```

This time the space we left for "*array*" has been displaced by the eight bytes of the string "Begin: " (seven characters – there is a space after the colon - and the terminating Null byte) and so the assembler this time placed 0x1001 in the upper half of $1 = *$at* but then used an **OR I**mmediate (*ori*) command to put 8 in the lower half as it stored the result in *$t0*. The desired result of 0x10010008 will appear in *$t0* but the assembler has used register $1 without any warning to us and this justifies our earlier statement that we should never use that register ourselves.

If we look in the *.data* segment listing of PCSPIM, we see the prompt followed by 100 zero bytes all starting at 0x10010000.

```
[0x10010000]        0x69676542  0x00203a6e  0x00000000  0x00000000
[0x10010010]...[0x10010068]     0x00000000
[0x10010068]        0x00000000  0x00646e45
[0x10010070]...[0x10040000]     0x00000000
```

After those zero bytes we find the other Null terminated string "End". Notice that if we issue the instruction *la $t1,end* then the assembler will give us

```
0x3c011001  lui $1, 4097 [end]                    ; 10: la $t1,end
0x3429006c  ori $9, $1, 108 [end]
```

Thus it has calculated for us exactly where the string "End" begins ($108_{DEC} = 0x6C$ bytes past the beginning of our data) within the *.data* segment. Of course it is possible for us to count up carefully exactly how long and where each piece of data is but it's much easier and more likely to be correct if we allow the assembler to do it for us. That's what computers can do best.

Before considering how to address the individual bytes within an array, let us look at one additional feature. Suppose the length of the first string is changed as follows:

```
        .data
begin:  .asciiz    "Begin:"       #NOTE: no space
array   .space     100
end:    .asciiz     "End"
        .text
        ...                       # some code
        la         $t0,array
```

All that happens is that the entire data from the beginning of "*array*" to the end is moved up one byte. [Try it!] Now let us contrast that with the following:

```
        .data
begin:  .asciiz    "Begin:"       #NOTE: no space
worda:  .word      0xffffffff
array   .space     100
wordb:  .word      0xeeeeeeee
end:    .asciiz    "End"
        .text
        ...                       # some code
        la         $t0,array
```

Now we get

```
[0x10010000]        0x69676542  0x00003a6e  0xffffffff  0x00000000
[0x10010010]...[0x1001006c]     0x00000000
[0x1001006c]           0x00000000
[0x10010070]        0xeeeeeeee  0x00646e45  0x00000000  0x00000000
[0x10010080]...[0x10040000]     0x00000000
```

Notice that the *.word* directive not only leaves space for a four-byte integer and initializes it, it also assures that it lies on a word boundary! That is, an address that is divisible by 4. That is almost the only form of typing with which the assembler will help us. It will put words on word boundaries (most instructions expecting a word as an operand will not work otherwise).

Now let us address the bytes in "*array*". If we have placed the address of the beginning of the 100 bytes in register *$t0* as above, then they are in locations *0($t0)* through *99($t0)*. Since the assembler may not take care of typing for us, if we wish to store integers (words) in that space we must be aware that there is room for only 25 of them (1 word = 4 bytes). One way to loop through these values would be to place the instruction *addi $t0,$t0,4* at the end of the loop and leave the displacement zero in our *D($R)* form to simulate what would be the following for-loop in C/C++/Java.

```
for( i == 0 ; i < 25 ; i++) {array[i] = i;}
```

The assembler code for this statement could be:

```
# assume: $t0 contains the address of the 100 bytes
# (maybe after an la $t0,array instruction)
# assume: $t1 contains the integer 25
# (the number of words desired)
# assume: $s0 contains the counter i; first initialize it to zero
        li    $s0,0   # or move $s0,$0 or some other initialization
loop:   beq   $s0,$t1,done  # when i == 25 we are finished, branch
        sw    $s0,0($t0) # array[i] = i;
        add   $t0,$t0,4  # each integer is 4 bytes long
        add   $s0,$s0,1  # increment the count by 1
        j     loop       # go back and do the loop test again
done:                    # ready for the next instruction; however,
# $t0 no longer contains the address of the 100 bytes = 25 words!
```

The *beq $R₁,$R₂,Label* has the effect of testing whether the two registers $R₁ and $R₂ are equal, and, if they are, taking the next instruction from the location indicated by the label. There are many such branch instructions that are found in the Branch/Jump Toolbox in MIPSter. Their mnemonics are usually self-explanatory; e.g., *beq* = **B**ranch if the registers are **EQ**ual. The *j* instruction is an unconditional **J**ump to the label indicated. [Note that branch instructions are I-type and so have only 16 bits to indicate how many words from the present location to go. J-type instructions have 26 bits available and so can go much further. The *jr* (**J**ump **R**egister) and *jalr* (**J**ump **A**nd **L**ink **R**egister) refer to the contents of a 32 bit register and so can go anywhere!]

Note that counters may go by one while the addresses go by four!

Of course there are many other ways to accomplish this task. Another way to write it in C/C++/Java would be:

```
i=0; while(i < 100){array[i] = i; i++;}
```

and this would lead to about the same assembler code. It would also be reasonable to do a "count down" of the counter *i* starting at 25.

After the above code is run, the values placed in the *.data* segment can be found on the following snapshot of the PCSPIM interpreter:

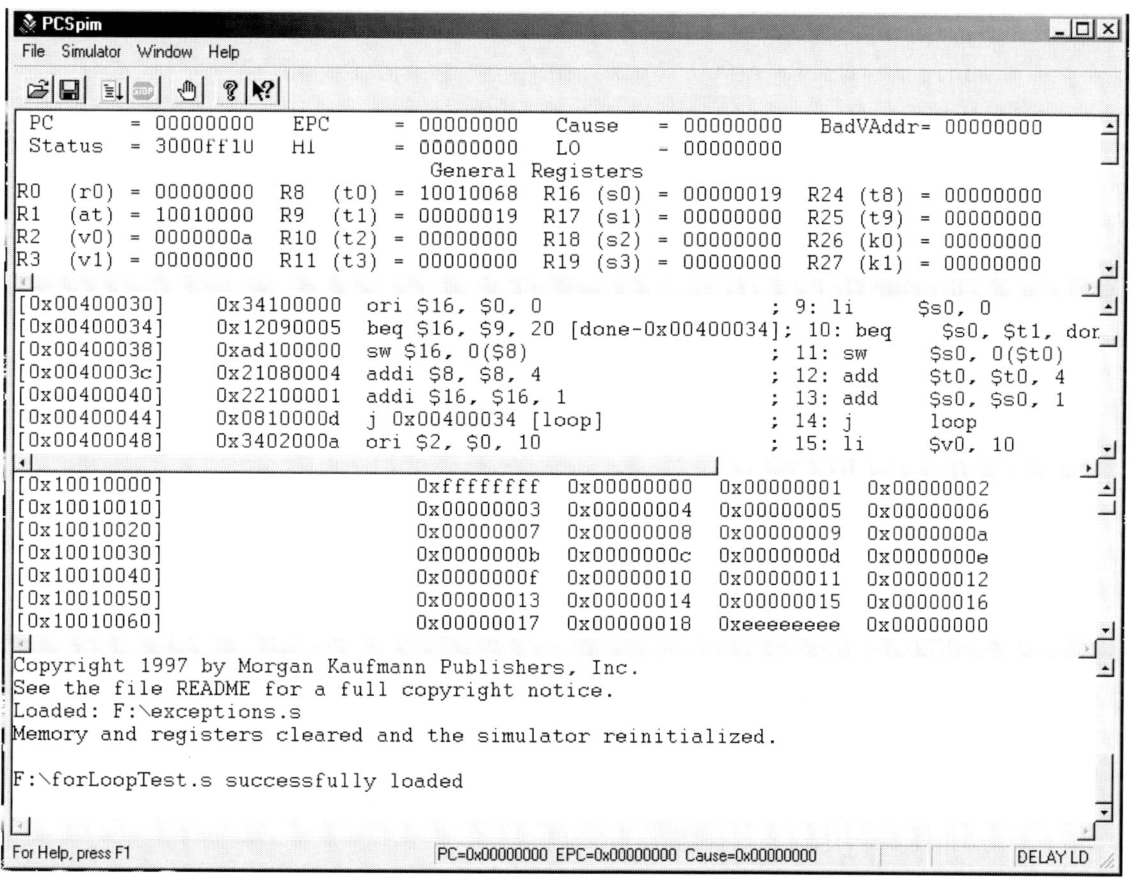

After the integer 0xffffffff there are the 25 integers from 0 through 24 (0x18). After that is the integer 0xeeeeeeee. All as expected from the code from a driver program called "forLoopTest.s".

In the Load/Store/Move Toolbox of MIPSter we can find the instruction we used to **S**tore a **W**ord: *sw Rsrc,addressWord*. The *Rsrc* stands for the source register and *addressWord* is clearly the address of the word into which the value is to be stored. Looking at the other instructions we can see that one can also **S**tore a single **B**yte (*sb*) and some other pieces of data with the MIPS processor.

4.2 Addressing

While we have noted that the MIPS processor actually uses only the Base-Displacement form of addressing: $D(\$R)$, most assemblers will allow a more general form to be used by the programmer as long as it is able to figure out which location is desired. We will use the general notation $L{\pm}D(\$R)$ to describe this form of addressing. The new symbol L stands for a label within the *.data* segment of the program. When L is the label of an array of locations in memory, the register R is often called an **index register** since it can be used to contain the index of each element in the array.

Let us generate an array of "random" numbers that might be used as test data for some other program. For more information about "random" numbers, see Knuth[1] and Chapter 10. Here is some code:

```
# random.s gives us an array of pseudo-random numbers in the
# range 0 <= n < 100 based on Knuth's advice.
# X[n+1] <- (aX[n] + c) mod m
# using m = 2^16 = 65536 which works on a 16-bit machine well
# using a = 32445 so that a mod 8 = 5 and 99m/100 > a > m/100
# using c = 1
# using X0 = 31416 in $s0 as seed
        .text
main:
        li      $s0, 31416          # X0 - initialized (could be input)
        li      $t0, 32445          # a - initialized
        li      $t1, 0x0000FFFF     # mask to do modulo - initialized
        li      $t2, 396            # counter - initialized 4*100-4
        li      $t3, 100            # limit so values 0-99
Loop:   bltz    $t2, Exit           # Stop when counter passes zero
        mul     $s0, $s0, $t0       # X = aX
        addi    $s0, 1              # now X = aX+c
        and     $s0, $s0, $t1       # now X = (aX+c) mod m
        move    $a0, $s0            # save X in $s0
        srl     $a0, $a0, 8         # divide by 256 (use upper 8 bits)
        bge     $a0, $t3, Loop      # only want those < 100
        li      $v0, 1              # op code for print_int
        syscall                     # print value 0 <= X < 100
        sw      $a0, list+0($t2)    # store them in reverse order
        la      $a0, NL             # print a new line
        li      $v0, 4              # op code for print_str
        syscall
        add     $t2, $t2, -4        # decrease counter (4 bytes)
        j       Loop
Exit:   li      $v0, 10             # standard return to OS
        syscall
#
        .data
NL:     .asciiz "\n"
        .word   0xeeeeeeee          # also aligns to word boundary
list:   .space  400                 # room for 100 integers
        .word   0xffffffff          # also easy to find
```

---

[1] *The Art of Computer Programming: Vol. 2 / Seminumerical Algorithms*, 2nd Ed., Addison-Wesley, 1981

When we run this code we find 100 integers between the 0xeeeeeeee and 0xffffffff words in the reverse order to which they were printed. While they may look somewhat "random", they obviously cannot be truly random numbers since we will get exactly the same results every time we run this code! Again it is suggested that a careful reading of Knuth's material would be helpful and will justify a recommendation that any random number generator a programmer uses (including those in expensive packages) should be tested as much as possible.

Using PCSPIM we can find out what code is actually generated by the assembler to correspond to the *sw $a0, list+0($t2)* instruction. This time it takes three machine instructions to accomplish the desired result. In the code segment we find

```
0x3c011001  lui $1,4097[list]; 28: sw $a0,list+0($t2)# store them
0x002a0821  addu $1, $1, $10
0xac240008  sw $4, 8($1) [list]
```

First the address of the *.data* segment is stored in $1. Next, the contents of the index register *$t2* = $10 are added to what is in $1. Finally, a **S**tore **W**ord (*sw*) instruction is done using the basic *D($R)* form where the displacement 8 is where the assembler has calculated that *list* starts relative to the beginning of the *.data* segment. (The offset of zero is actually added to that displacement.)

4.3 Pointers

The use of pointers seems to be one of the most difficult concepts in C programming. Misuse of pointers led the inventor of Java to try to get rid of them completely. In assembler, however, we are required to use pointers and do pointer arithmetic regularly. Here is an example of code using pointers. The comments explain the purpose of the program.

```
# reverse.s
# Input: Any string
# Output: The reverse of that string
###################################
            .data
prompt:    .asciiz    "Input any string: "
echo:      .asciiz    "\nThe reverse of \n\t"
is:        .asciiz    "is \n\t"
buffer:    .space     78
           .word      0              #Null for reversed string
#
           .text
# Input string with prompt and echo
main:      li         $v0,4          #string print function
           la         $a0,prompt     #prompt string
           syscall
           li         $v0,8          #string read function
           la         $a0,buffer     #where to put it
           li         $a1,78         #how many characters max
           syscall
           li         $v0,4          #string print function
```

```
        la          $a0,echo         #echo string
        syscall
        li          $v0,4            #string print function
        la          $a0,buffer       #buffer (including LF)
        syscall
        li          $v0,4            #string print function
        la          $a0,is           #"is"
        syscall
#start actual processing
        la          $s1,buffer       #get address of start of buffer
        addi        $s1,77           #point to end of buffer
#find end of actual string
look:   lb          $t1,0($s1)       #loading a byte
        bnez        $t1,found        #finally not Null
        sub         $s1,1            #back up 1 byte
        j           look             #keep looking
#reverse the string in place
found:  sub         $s1,1            #ignore LF (0x0a)
        la          $s2,buffer       #point to beginning of string
#here is the loop for reversing (s1 → end; s2 → beginning)
rev:    bgt         $s2,$s1,done #middle found
        lb          $t1,0($s1)       #\
        lb          $t2,0($s2)       #  interchange
        sb          $t1,0($s2)       #  the bytes
        sb          $t2,0($s1)       #/
        add         $s2,1            #update the pointer
        sub         $s1,1            #update the pointer
        j           rev              #do it again
#now print result
done:   li          $v0,4            #string print function
        la          $a0,buffer       #reversed string with LF and Null
        syscall
        li          $v0,10           #standard exit
        syscall                      #return to OS
```

The comments in this code should be somewhat self-explanatory. We have used the **Load Byte** (*lb*) and **Store Byte** (*sb*) commands to do the reversal of the two characters. Unlike integers, we can input an entire string using *syscall* 8 giving it an address at which to begin placing the string and a maximum number of characters.

4.4 Binary Search

We will study various data structures later along with associated algorithms. One of the most important processes, however, will justify a look at a sorting algorithm in the next section. The process is searching for a value within a list of values. It is easy to see that searching for a key which is in a list of n randomly ordered elements by starting at the beginning and continuing to look at each one until found, will take, on the average, $n/2$ accesses. Should the key not actually appear in the list, we would have to look at all n elements to find that fact out.

Having the list sorted allows us to use the Binary Search method to find the key. At each stage we cut in half the number of places at which the key could appear. Since that can only happen about $log_2 n$ times, even in the case where the key does not appear, this method is far superior (particularly for large values of n). Should the list contain $2^{20} =$ 1,048,576 elements, at worst 21 accesses would be necessary rather than an average of 524,288 when it appears in the list and 1,048,576 when it does not appear in the list.

Our code follows directly from some C/C++/Java code such as

```
int binary_search(int[] array, int size, int key)
{
    int low = 0, high = size - 1;
    while( low <= high)
    {   int mid = (low + high) /2;
        if( array[ mid ] < key) low = mid + 1;
        else if( key < array[ mid ]) high = mid -1;
        else return mid;
    }
    return NOT_FOUND;
}
```

Since the input of the values is not significant in this example, we will "hard-wire" into our code the list of integers using the *.word* directive. The line

```
array:  .word      2,5,11,23,47,95,191,383,767,998
```

both reserves 10 words in memory labeled by the name "array", but also initializes those words to the given values.

```
# BinarySearch.s
#
# Demonstrates binary search on a fixed list of integers
        .data                      # Data declaration section
array:  .word      2,5,11,23,47,95,191,383,767,998
prompt: .asciiz    "\nInsert integer key (0 <= key): "
ymsg:   .asciiz    "\nKey was found at position "
nmsg:   .asciiz    "\nKey not found! "

        .text
main:                              # Start of code section
        la      $s0,array   # Put address of array in $s0
        li      $s1,10      # Put count of elements in $s1
        sll     $s1,$s1,2   # 4n byte = bytecount
input:  li      $v0,4       # Print_string function code
        la      $a0,prompt  # Prompt for key
        syscall
        li      $v0,5       # Get key
        syscall
        bltz    $v0,exit    # Look for sentinal (negative)
        move    $s2,$v0     # Put key in $s2
        li      $t0,0       # $t0 = low = 0
        sub     $t1,$s1,4   # $t1 = high = bytecount-4 (bytes)
loop:   bgt     $t0,$t1,fail# while( low <= high )
        add     $t2,$t0,$t1 # $t2 = mid = low + high
        sra     $t2,$t2,3   # mid = (low + high) / 8
        sll     $t2,$t2,2   # mid = (low + high) / 2 (aligned)
```

```
            add      $t3,$t2,$s0  # get
            lw       $t3,0($t3)   # array[mid]
            blt      $t3,$s2,LH   # if (array[mid] < key)
            blt      $s2,$t3,RH   # if (key < array[mid]
            j        found
    LH:     add      $t0,$t2,4    # low = mid + 4 (bytes)
            j        loop
    RH:     sub      $t1,$t2,4    # high = mid - 4 (bytes)
            j        loop
# found
found:      li       $v0,4        # Print
            la       $a0,ymsg     # Label
            syscall
            sra      $t2,$t2,2    # bytes to indexes
            add      $t2,$t2,1    # 1-based indexing
            move     $a0,$t2      # Print
            li       $v0,1        # Answer
            syscall
            j        input        # do it all again
# not found
fail:       li       $v0,4        # Print
            la       $a0,nmsg     # Label
            syscall
            j        input
# exit
exit:       li       $v0,10
            syscall
```

As often happens in moving from C/C++/Java to assembler, we must take special pains to distinguish between indexes in the high level language and memory addresses (4 bytes to each word). In addition, we have to watch for alignment problems. The calculation (low + high)/2 must not just be truncated to an integer, but must also be a multiple of 4 so we are accessing memory on word boundaries! As usual we have used shifts to multiply or divide by powers of two rather than bother with the HI and LO registers.

4.5 Insertion Sort

There are many algorithms for sorting arrays. Details can be found in any Data Structures text. The "best" ones run in asymptotic time proportional to $n \log n$, where n is the size of the array. That is, as n gets large, the time to sort the data grows as a constant times the factor $n \log n$. The criteria for being "best", however, differ widely. One can consider the worst case or the average case or other situations. In fact the entire idea of "best" is rather meaningless when the answer is given in terms of asymptotic time since real data sets, while large, are not infinite.

A particular example of a sorting algorithm that works well for small data sets is **insertion sort**. While its worst case behavior grows as n^2 (as does its average case behavior), for sets which are small its simplicity makes it better than complicated algorithms that require extensive machinery to work and the corresponding extra time needs to be amortized over large data sets to achieve their purported $n \log n$ behavior. In fact, insertion sort will achieve a performance proportional to *n* if the data happens to be almost sorted already (which is often the case).

Here is a complete program that takes input from the keyboard as usual, sorts it using the insertion sort algorithm, and then prints out the sorted array:

```
# insertion.s
# Demonstrates insertion sort
          .data                    # Data declaration section
array:    .space  100              # Room for 25 integers
prompt:   .asciiz "Input an integer (0 = EOF):"
result:   .asciiz "Sorted those integers were:\n"
LF:       .asciiz "\n"
##############
          .text
main:                              # Start of code section
# initializations
          li      $s0,0            # index is zero
          li      $a1,0            # count is zero
# input loop
getnxt:   li      $v0,4            # print_str function
          la      $a0,prompt       # what to print
          syscall
          li      $v0,5            # read_int function
          syscall
          beqz    $v0,donein       # branch if found zero
          sw      $v0,array+0($s0) # indexed array
          addi    $s0,$s0,4        # increment index by 1 word
          add     $a1,$a1,4        # increment count by 1 word
          j       getnxt           # go back for more input
donein:
# print the result string
          li      $v0,4            # print_str function
          la      $a0,result       # what to print
          syscall
## sort the integers ($a1 contains the count 4n bytes)
# C/C++/Java Code:
#     null insertion(int[] a, int n)
#     {      for (int i = 1;  i < n; i++)
#            {     temp = a[i];
#                  j = i-1;
#                  while (j >= 0 && temp < a[j])
#                  {     a[j+1] = a[j];
#                        j = j-1;
#                  }
#                  a[j+1] = temp;
#            }
#     }
##### Here is the actual sorting code ##########
          li      $s0,4        # use $s0 for i initalized to 1 word
iloop:    beq     $s0,$a1,idone  # test i loop (i < n)
          lw      $t0,array+0($s0)   # temp = a[i];
          sub  $s1,$s0,4  # use $s1 for j initalized to i-1 word
whilej:   bltz    $s1,jdone         # j >= 0 test
```

```
          lw      $t1,array+0($s1)   # put a[j] in $t1
          bge     $t0,$t1,jdone      # temp < a[j] test
          sw      $t1,array+4($s1)   # a[j+1] = a[j];
          sub     $s1,$s1,4          # j = j-1; bytes
          j       whilej             # continue while loop
jdone:    sw      $t0,array+4($s1)   # a[j+1] = temp;
          add     $s0,$s0,4          # increment i
          j       iloop
idone:
##### the integers are now sorted ##############
# print them
          li      $s0,0              # use $s0 as counter
ploop:    bge     $s0,$a1,exit       # test i < n (still in $a1)
          li      $v0,1              # print_int function
          lw      $a0,array+0($s0)   # put integer in place
          syscall                    # print it
          li      $v0,4              # print_str function
          la      $a0,LF             # put next on new line
          syscall                    # print it
          add     $s0,$s0,4          # increment counter
          j       ploop              # do it again
exit:
          li $v0, 10                 # exits program
          syscall
```

The actual assembler code follows the C/C++/Java code rather closely. The most frequent error in this type of program is to confuse indices with pointers. In particular, when using integer data one must carefully watch for places where an increment or decrement must be 4 (bytes) rather than 1 (word) as in *i++;*, *i+=1;*, or *i=i+1;* .

Exercises

1. Describe the differences between the *.space* directive and the *.word* directive. Test the *.byte* directive and contrast it to the *.space* directive.

2. Suppose we have the C/C++/Java code of

```
for( i == 25 ; i > 0 ; i--) {array[i] = i;}
```

   What code would be assembled for this statement and what would it do?

3. Modify the reverse program to test whether the input is a **palindrome;** *i.e.,* a string that reads exactly the same both forward and backward (*e.g.,* hannah).

4. Entire sentences may be considered palindromes when punctuation and case are ignored (e.g., "Able was I ere I saw Elba!"). Modify the palindrome program to remove punctuation (and spaces) and put all letters in upper case before testing to see if the input string is a palindrome in this sense.

5. Write a program that will test the random number generator described in this chapter. In particular, after generating the numbers as suggested, go through the array and print out how many are in each decade range (0-9, 10-19, ... ,90-99). You might modify the random number generator using different seeds, multipliers, or other changes (read Knuth's book).

6. Modify the random number generator to have it give you a random array of 100 characters ('a' = 0x61 through 'z' = 0x7a) with equal probabilities.

7. Analyze the insertion sort algorithm and determine its worst-case behavior, average case behavior, and best-case behavior as a function of n, the size of the array to be sorted. What are the worst and best cases?

8. Sorting a file is usually justified by the need to search the file efficiently. Write a binary search algorithm to find a specific character value in a sorted array of characters.

9. Show the results of each stage of using Insertion Sort on a random file of some 10 integers.

CHAPTER FIVE

Functions and Stacks

To a great degree, the C/C++/Java family of languages is based on functions or procedures and they are classified as "procedural" languages. Actually, the very ancient programming practice of **HIPO** (**H**ierarchical **I**nput **P**rocess **O**utput) fits our concepts very well. As we saw in earlier examples, we first input the data, then process it in whatever way the problem requires, and then output the results. In this chapter we will see how to think about programs in terms of a clear-cut input phase, a processing phase, and then an output phase. Further, once we see that the input and output phases are pretty much the same for almost all programs, we will be able to concentrate just on the processing phase.

A mathematical function is a rule which takes some input variables (arguments) and returns some output values. Computer functions are very similar. In C/C++/Java we might indicate the general form of a function by writing

```
return_type function_name(type₁ arg₁, … ,typeₙ argₙ)
  { <some_process>; }
```

In assembler we will have to find out how to define a function including where will be its arguments, where will be its returned values, and how it is to be activated.

5.1 Functions

The MIPS processor gives only minimal support to the programmer, in contrast to the importance of programming by writing functions which perform the needed processes. However, that simple support is all that is necessary.

Consider what must be done by the computer when processing an expression such as $y*sin(x)$ in an assignment statement. The value of x or a pointer to the location at which x is stored must be placed in an appropriate place (depending on earlier agreements between the compiler and the operating system). Then control of the computer must be transferred to the place where the actual code for the *sine* function has been placed. When that code is finished the operating system must return control to the very next place in the code after the call on the sine function; that is, it must now prepare to multiply the result of the function by the value of y. This short discussion leads us to understand that all that is needed are two instructions: one which changes control to another location but "remembers" where the next instruction in order is located, and a second which allows for the change in control back to the "remembered" place.

These two instructions are *jal* (**J**ump **A**nd **L**ink) and *jr* (**J**ump **R**egister). They are basically all that is needed to accomplish our goal. In each case the "Jump" part of the instruction does, indeed, transfer control to a different location. For the *jal* instruction, a label indicates the desired location while the *jr* instruction takes the name of a register as argument and its contents are to where it jumps. The "remember" part of *jal* (the "Link") is that the address of the very next instruction in order is placed in the *$31 = $ra* (**R**eturn **A**ddress) register[1]. When the function is finished it will return control with the command *jr $ra*.

In outline, our code will look like the following:

```
main: ...
      jal    sine
      ...

sine: ...
      jr     $ra
```

The other questions that must be answered before we code some functions are where one should place the arguments to a function and where the results should be placed. One hint is obtained by looking at the special *syscall* functions. We see that in the *print_int* (1) and *print_str* (4) calls register *$a0* is used to hold the integer or the pointer to the string. In *read_str* (8) *$a0* holds a pointer to the buffer and *$a1* holds the maximum length. This is characteristic of the convention used in SPIM programming. We usually use the four "argument" registers *$a0-$a3* to hold arguments (or pointers to arguments). Later we will discuss the procedure for handling the case when more than four arguments are necessary.

In the same way, we note that *syscall* function *read_int* (5) leaves the integer in register *$v0*. The convention in SPIM is that functions usually leave their result in register *$v0* (and *$v1* if there are two – such as the real and imaginary parts of a complex number) if they are integers or pointers. A single byte (or character) would also be left in the lower part of register *$v0*.

Note that these are merely conventional suggestions. The hardware does not require us to use these registers in that way. However, it is strongly recommended that programmers follow these conventions for many reasons. First, it allows others to understand one's code easily because things are as expected. Remember that most programmers work in an environment in which others must use and understand the code they write. In addition, assembler is difficult enough to read without making it any harder. Even an experienced programmer will forget what trick they used yesterday if it is not well commented in the code. Unusual usages of registers can be considered just another trick on the reader.

---

[1] There is also a *jalr* (**J**ump **A**nd **L**ink **R**egister) command that allows the programmer to choose a different register than *$ra* but defaults to *$ra* if only one register is given as argument. If two registers are given, the first is where the return address is to be stored and the second is to where the jump is to be taken.

Here is a very simple example of some code which counts the number of characters in a Null terminated string. It is assumed that *$a0* contains a pointer to (that is, the address of) the string and the result is to be returned in register *$v0*.

```
###############################################################
# The following SPIM code counts the number of characters in a
# Null terminated string pointed to by (whose address is in) $a0
# and returns the integer count in $v0.
#
# Equivalent C-type code:
#   int count(char*[] a0) {
#       int v0 = 0;
#       while (&a0[0] != '\0') { v0++; a0++; }
#       return v0;
#   }
###############################################################
count:                              # ← entry point
        li      $v0, 0              # initialize counter
loop:   lb      $t0, 0($a0)         # load one character from memory
        beq     $t0, $0, done       # done if Null character('\0')
        addi    $v0, $v0, 1         # increment counter
        addi    $a0, $a0, 1         # increment pointer
        j       loop                # repeat
done:   jr      $ra                 # $v0 contains answer
###############################################################
```

We could use this code by placing a cut-and-paste copy into any program. We would call on the function *count* by issuing the commands

```
la      $a0,string
jal     count
```

where the string whose length is desired has the label "*string*". Note, however, that we have created some problems; even with careful use of the registers!

First of all, register *$a0* no longer points to the beginning of the string. If that is not clear to the user of this code, errors may result. Of course the user can always issue another *la $a0,string* command but the need for that action was not obvious. Another problem is that we have used register *$t0* to hold the character being inspected. While the comments to this code probably would (and should) mention the change made to register *$a0*, one might easily forget to mention that *$t0* was also changed!

A general convention between MIPS programmers (indicated by the mnemonics) is that the registers *$s0-$s7* ("save" registers) must be preserved by any function when it returns from being called while registers *$t0-$t9* ("temporary" registers) need not be the same upon return and it is the **caller**'s responsibility to save them if they are needed. This is a very convenient convention as we see from our example. It would be acceptable to change *$t0* without a caller expecting it to be preserved. The changes made to *$a0* could have been easily avoided by first copying it into some other temporary register and then addressing the string characters using that other register.

We will actually avoid using this last convention so as to get more practice in preserving register values across function calls. In addition, many computer architectures have quite different requirements as to register preservation and we do not want to be too specific as to how computers are programmed. We will show how to preserve registers in the next section.

CONVENTION: In this text we will almost always assume that every function is required to preserve all registers not explicitly required to be changed (such as $v0 when returning a value) unless specifically stated otherwise.

From a purely efficiency standpoint, programming in this way is more trouble and the resulting code will be slower – possibly much slower. However, this is a beginning text and once the reader has gained sufficient experience with assembly language programming, he or she may write code in a more efficient way as long as the specifications do not require the preservation of registers.

Finally, the labels used in the function *count* may conflict with those used elsewhere in the code into which this is copied. Labels such as "*loop*" and "*done*" are ones that might appear in many functions. We have no good convention for fixing this problem. While students usually write fairly small programs and can check for duplication of labels (and the assembler will check for us, giving a "label is defined for a second time" message), in the real world large segments of code may be written by different members of a team and this becomes an even larger problem.

[Note: In some assemblers, numerical labels are allowed such as "1:" and "2:" and they may be repeated. Branches or jumps to these labels are indicated by "b 1b" or "j 2f". The suffix "f" means the compiler is to emit the code that branches to the very next usage of that numerical label Forward in the code, while the suffix "b" means to look Backwards in the code for the first use of that numerical label. This is a very useful naming convention since labels such as these are often useful for short jumps (*e.g.*, a simple translation of an if-then-else statement) which appear in many places in our code. Unfortunately, PCSPIM and MIPSter do not have such a convention.]

5.2 The Stack

The answer to where to save the registers we want to preserve is: on the **stack**. C/C++/Java programmers are already familiar with the stack data structure. When we bring up PCSPIM, we find in register $sp \equiv R29$ a number such as 0x7fffeffc. Since the mnemonic is "sp" standing for Stack Pointer, it is obvious that the system has given us a pointer to an area rather near the top (high values) of memory on our system which we may use as a stack. [Note that memory is divided in usage and higher addresses (above 0x80000000) are reserved for the operating system.] In fact, this stack will be assumed to grow downward (toward lower address values).

Higher-level languages often also include built-in "**push**" and "**pop**" commands. The MIPS processor does not have any such instructions but we can accomplish the results of those operations easily. We start with the assumption that all values on the stack are required to be one word (4 bytes) long. Note: Even when we are "pushing" bytes (characters) onto the stack, we will always use entire words. This is to keep alignment problems from arising. Remember that most instructions that operate on a word require that the value be word-aligned (its address is divisible by four).

The second assumption is that register *$sp* always points to the "top" (lowest address!) of the stack (the last value placed on the stack)[2]. All we need to do is to keep these assumptions true at all times.

First, let us "push" a value onto the stack. Since the stack pointer is assumed to be pointing at the top of the stack, we need to move it to the next available position and that is at an address 4 bytes lower (smaller) in value. *sub $sp,$sp,4* will accomplish that. Next, we may move (from some other register *$reg*) the desired value onto the stack (which is in memory) using *sw $reg,0($sp)* since this is a load-store machine. We now have the complete code for a "push" command:

```
sub         $sp,$sp,4
sw          $reg,0($sp)
```

Second, let us "pop" a value from the stack. Since *$sp* is pointing to the top of the stack, we need only retrieve that from memory and put it in some register *$reg* by the command *lw $reg,0($sp)*. Then we may fix the stack pointer by an *add $sp,$sp,4* command. The entire code for "pop" is then:

```
lw          $reg,0($sp)
add         $sp,$sp,4
```

As soon as we have added 4 to the stack pointer, we must assume that the value which used to be on the top of the stack may have been changed. In most operating systems, the hardware (for example, the clock) on a regular basis interrupts the processor and takes over long enough to perform some needed housekeeping (for example, updating the clock value) and may use the stack for its own purposes. All that is required is that the OS leaves the stack exactly the way it was when it interrupted us; that is, nothing at or above the stack pointer may be changed. No promise is made with regard to locations below the pointer. We will have the same requirement placed on us as programmers. When any part of our code that uses the stack finishes, it must leave the stack exactly the same as it was before.

---

[2] An alternate convention is to have *$sp* point to the first free location into which a value may be "pushed". When allocating our own memory for a stack this would be quite normal since otherwise we would have to initialize the pointer outside the allocated area! In the case where the system has given us a stack area and pointer, it is safer and will waste at most one memory location to keep our convention. The MIPS convention is to have *$sp* point to the "top" of the stack.

WARNING: The order of the above operations is critical. If, when we "push", we stored first and then moved the stack pointer as follows:

```
sw        $reg,-4($sp)        # WRONG ORDER!
sub       $sp,$sp,4           # NEVER DO THIS!!
```

it would seem to do the same thing. However, during the time between when the value from *$reg* is stored in its place 4 bytes below the stack pointer and the moving of that stack pointer, the operating system might have interrupted our program to do the above mentioned housekeeping and changed the value we stored. That would be permissible since the location is below the stack pointer. The same problem can occur with an incorrectly ordered "pop" operation.[3]

```
add       $sp,$sp,4           # WRONG ORDER!
lw        $reg,-4($sp)        # NEVER DO THIS!!
```

There is one small savings we can make when a number of successive pushes or pops are to be accomplished. For example, were we to want to push three values onto the stack as follows:

```
sub       $sp,$sp,4
sw        $reg1,0($sp)
sub       $sp,$sp,4
sw        $reg2,0($sp)
sub       $sp,$sp,4
sw        $reg3,0($sp)
```

we could do all the stack pointer manipulation at one time as follows:

```
sub       $sp,$sp,12  # note: this must be done first (see above)
sw        $reg1,8($sp)
sw        $reg2,4($sp)
sw        $reg3,0($sp)
```

[Draw the stack, showing the results of both methods of pushing.]

In a similar manner, popping these values could be done as follows:

```
lw        $reg3,0($sp)
lw        $reg2,4($sp)
lw        $reg1,8($sp)
add       $sp,$sp,12  # and this must be last!
```

Note that from a purely Data Structures point of view, these simplifications are illegal. That is, we are taught, quite correctly, that when using a stack in a high-level language we must never assume anything about the actual implementation of the stack. Thus, using the kind of pointer arithmetic we see here to address values within the stack, rather than

---

[3] Note that regardless of our convention regarding *$sp* (see previous footnote), it is always critical to move the stack pointer before a "push" and after a "pop"!

only the top of the stack, may not work. Of course the difference is that we are programming in assembler and we must know exactly how everything is implemented; in fact, we are the ones doing the implementation!

Because we know exactly how the stack is implemented, we may also introduce the frequently needed function *top*. Since the top element in the stack is located at address *0($sp)*, we can look at it without needing to *pop* it and then re-*push* it. We do not, however, have any error checking with regard to trying to *pop* a value from an empty stack. A test could be implemented for that case if desired (see Chapter 12).

[Note: Some assemblers allow the definition of **macros**; that is, short sequences of often repeated code with parameters that act like pseudo-instructions. Once defined, they are used just as if the pseudo-instruction were one of those originally recognized by the assembler. The definition, with values substituted for its parameters, is inserted directly into the code which is assembled in place of the new pseudo-instruction. The format of a definition for a macro whose name is "push" and that takes one parameter consisting of a register name might be something like the following:

```
.macro push(%R)
sub     $sp,$sp,4
sw      %R,0($sp)
.end_macro
```

Following this definition, we could push the return address onto the stack with the new pseudo-instruction *push($ra)*. While convenient, there are dangers in the use of macros. Since they work by text substitution, when reading the source code it is not always obvious exactly what instructions are being presented to the assembler. There are new possibilities for errors that many feel outweigh any advantages. In any event, our simulators do not support macros so it's not a problem for us.]

As an example of using the stack to preserve registers, consider the code to print a NewLine character using the *print_str* function. Since a pointer to the NewLine character must be put in register *$a0* and the *print_str* function number 4 must be placed in register *$v0*, we must save and then restore these values as shown in the following code:

```
                .data
NL:             .asciiz     "\n"
                .text
println:                    # subroutine to println saving registers
        sub     $sp, $sp, 8     #\
        sw      $a0, 0($sp)     # \
        sw      $v0, 4($sp)     #  \
        la      $a0, NL         #   \
        li      $v0, 4          #       > Print new line
        syscall                 #   /
        lw      $v0, 4($sp)     #  /
        lw      $a0, 0($sp)     # /
        add     $sp, $sp, 8     #/
        jr      $ra             # return
```

Now the only possible problem with copying this code into any program in which we want to be able to print a NewLine character is the potential for conflict between the two labels "NL" and "println" used here. Alternative code (which does not access memory but is not available in MIPSter at this time) will be shown in the next chapter.

5.3 Insertion Sort Revisited

In the previous chapter we gave the code for a complete program to input a sequence of integers, sort them using insertion sort, and then print them out in sorted order. We are now in a position to focus our attention just on the critical sorting part of the code and make it generic; that is, such that it may be copied into other programs as needed.

Recall that the insertion sort part of the code was as follows:

```
##### Here is the actual sorting code ##########
        li      $s0,4           # $s0 == i initalized to 1 word
iloop:  beq     $s0,$a1,idone       # test i loop (i < n)
        lw      $t0,array+0($s0)  # temp = a[i];
        add     $s1,$s0,-4   # $s1 == j initalized to i-1 word
whilej: bltz    $s1,jdone           # j ≥ 0 test
        lw      $t1,array+0($s1)  # put a[j] in $t1
        bge     $t0,$t1,jdone  # temp < a[j] test
        sw      $t1,array+4($s1)  # a[j+1] = a[j];
        add     $s1,$s1,-4        # j = j-1; bytes
        j       whilej            # continue while loop
jdone:  sw      $t0,array+4($s1)  # a[j+1] = temp;
        add     $s0,$s0,4         # increment i
        j       iloop
idone:
##### the integers are now sorted ##############
```

Let's modify this code so that it becomes an independent function. Some of our earlier choices were associated with the fact that the code was embedded in a complete program about which we knew all the details. For example, we knew we wanted to have not the number of items in the list to be sorted (n), but rather four times that ($4n$) since we would be addressing the integer values as words. Thus we added 4 to our count for every new element. It is much more natural to expect a user to increment the count by 1 for every item and we should require that $a1$ contains n, the exact number of elements in the list. When we need $4n$ we can just multiply by four ourselves (or, actually, shift the value left by two bits which is usually easier and faster on most machines).

This code also assumed that the label "array" labeled the list. According to our convention, we should rewrite this code to expect the address of the array to be in $a0$. The effect of that change is that we cannot use the $L+D(\$R)$ addressing scheme any more. That is, the $array+0(\$s0)$ and other addresses will have to be replaced by ones that are based on the contents of $a0$. What we would like would be the $D(\$B,\$I)$ scheme available on some machines – but not MIPS. What is easiest for us using the MIPS processor is to change *i* (*$s0*) and *j* (*$s1*) from being indexes starting at zero to being actual addresses based on the contents of *$a0*.

Here are some other design decisions. We will leave the address of the list unchanged in *$a0* throughout (and so will not have to save and restore it). Next, we will take the count in *$a1*, multiply by 4 (shift left 2 bits), and add the contents of *$a0* to it; thus, we will have in *$a1* a pointer to the next location in memory after the list and that will serve as a value which we may test instead of the count *i<n*. We will test whether the address in *$s0* is no longer less than the address in *$a1* to terminate the *i*-loop.

```
# Insertion Sort
# Call with address of array in $a0 and number of elements in $a1
# Returns with array sorted in place
Isort:                           # ← entry point
        sub     $sp,$sp,20       #\
        sw      $a1,0($sp)       # \
        sw      $s0,4($sp)       #  \ save registers
        sw      $s1,8($sp)       #  / on stack
        sw      $t0,12($sp)      # /
        sw      $t1,16($sp)      #/
        sll     $a1,$a1,2        # replace n by 4n (bytes)
        add     $a1,$a1,$a0      # put address of a[n] in $a1
        add     $s0,$a0,4        # init $s0 == i ptr to 1 word
Iiloop:
        beq     $s0,$a1,Iidone   # test i ptr loop (i<n)
        lw      $t0,0($s0)       # temp = a[i];
        sub     $s1,$s0,4        # init $s1 == j ptr to i-1 word
Iwhile:
        blt     $s1, $a0, Ijdone # j ≥ 0 ptrs test
        lw      $t1,0($s1)       # put a[j] in $t1
        bge     $t0,$t1,Ijdone   # temp < a[j] values test
        sw      $t1,4($s1)       # a[j+1] = a[j]
        sub     $s1,$s1,4        # decrement j bytes
        j       Iwhile           # continue while loop
Ijdone:
        sw      $t0,4($s1)       # a[j+1] = temp;
        add     $s0,$s0,4        # increment i bytes
        j       Iiloop           # continue i loop
Iidone:
        lw      $a1,0($sp)       #\
        lw      $s0,4($sp)       # \
        lw      $s1,8($sp)       #  \ replace registers
        lw      $t0,12($sp)      #  / from stack
        lw      $t1,16($sp)      # /
        add     $sp,$sp,20       #/
        jr      $ra              # return
```

Now the only problem we may have with copying this code is the possible conflict with labels in either our main program or other functions. We use the above code by issuing the commands such as

```
la  $a0,array # assuming the list to be sorted is labeled "array"
lw  $a1,n     # assuming the actual count is labeled "n"
jal Isort
```

5.4 Programming

We have seen how to translate some of the simplest control structures of C/C++/Java into assembler. For example, the *if-then-else* statement

```
if (<condition>) <statement-true> else <statement-false>;
```

is easily seen to be equivalent in pseudo-assembler to

```
<test condition leaving 0=false or 1=true in $R>
    beqz     $R,false_case
true_case:    <do statement-true>
    j         next
false_case:    <do statement-false>
next:
```

Of course there are many other ways to accomplish the same goal. A different test might lead to the following branch statement being *bnez $R1,$R2,true_case* where we have assumed that the "false_case" immediately follows the branch statement and the "true_case" is listed later.

In a similar way, the various looping constructs can be translated into assembler. First of all we note that the *for* statement

```
for (<initialize>;<test>;<modify>) <statement>;
```

and the *while* statements

```
<initialize>;
while(<test>) {<statement>; <modify>;}
```

are exactly the same. The pseudo-assembler for both would be

```
<initialize>
loop: <test condition leaving 0=false or 1=true in $R>
    beqz   $R, next
    <do statement>
    <do modifications>
    j       loop
next:
```

The *else_if* construct is obviously just a convenient simplification of repeated if-then statements and can be programmed as such. A frequent replacement for that construct is the *switch* statement. The form in C/C++/Java is

```
switch ( <integer_expression> )
{    case <constant_expression_1>: <statement_1>; break;
     case <constant_expression_2>: <statement_2>; break:
       ...
     default:                      <default_statement>;
}
```

In assembler we will use a **jump table**. That is, a list of addresses to be used by a *jr* (**J**ump **R**egister) instruction to go to the correct point in our code. We recall that the *.word* assembler directive such as

> *label: .word   value1,value2,...*

not only reserves space in memory as does the *.space* directive, but also initializes the words to the given values. For example,

> *table: .word 1,2,3*

reserves three consecutive words of memory, the first of which may be referenced by the label "table", containing the integers 1, 2, and 3. The "values", however, can be anything that the assembler can figure out such as actual addresses within our code.

As an example of the help the assembler can be to the programmer, let us consider the code for a calculator function. We will suppose the user has placed two integers in registers *$a0* and *$a1* and a code in *$a2* indicating (1=Add, 2=Subtract, 3=Multiply, and 4=Divide). As usual we will return the answer in register *$v0* but we will make no attempt to look for errors in the arguments or results. That is, we assume the user has checked that the only legal values in *$a2* are 1 through 4 and, if division is required, the value in *$a1* is not zero. We will also not worry about overflow; that will be left to the user in this example.

```
# calculate.s
#
# $a0 = first integer
# $a1 = second integer
# $a2 = operation (1=Add, 2=Subtract, 3=Multiply, 4=Divide)
# returns result of (first OP second) in $v0
# NO error checking
#
        .data           # Data declaration section
JumpTable:  .word   ADD,SUB,MUL,DIV # SPIM figures out where
        .text
calculate:                          # ← Entry point
        sub     $sp,$sp,8           # \  Push registers
        sw      $t0,0($sp)          # > which are changed
        sw      $t1,4($sp)          # /  onto the stack
        la      $t0,JumpTable       # Get address of JumpTable       *
        sub     $t1,$a2,1           # Zero-based addressing          *
        sll     $t1,$t1,2           # Multiply by 4 (bytes)          *
        add     $t0,$t0,$t1         # Address's location address     *
        lw      $t0,0($t0)          # Got actual address             *
        jr      $t0
# switch labels
ADD:    add     $v0,$a0,$a1         # Do the addition
        j       DONE
SUB:    sub     $v0,$a0,$a1         # Do the subtraction
        j       DONE
MUL:    mul     $v0,$a0,$a1         # Do the multiplication
```

```
                j       DONE
    DIV:    div     $v0,$a0,$a1              # Do the division
                j       DONE                    # (See below)
    # finished; return
    DONE: lw      $t1,4($sp)              # \  Pop registers
            lw      $t0,0($sp)              # > which were changed
            add     $sp,$sp,8               # / off the stack
            jr      $ra                     # return
```

What the assembler does is calculate exactly where the instruction labeled "*ADD*" is located within the *.text* segment and, knowing where the *.text* segment will be placed in memory, is able to load the first word of the jump table with that address. These steps can be done by hand but the assembler makes that unnecessary. On a machine with varying lengths for its instructions, the calculation requires translating every instruction in order to find out what it is and so how long it is. On the MIPS processor, every instruction is one word (4 bytes), an important design decision, and we can easily see that there are nine instructions between the beginning of the *.text* section and the "*ADD*" label. Clearly the assembler need only add $36_{DEC} = 0x24$ to the address of *.text* and place that in the first position of the jump table. There are two instructions between each of the labels so the other values must differ by eight bytes and so their addresses are also easy to calculate.

It is an easy exercise to write a program to input data and call on this function under PCSPIM and see what is put into the jump table. Let us give a more detailed explanation of the five instructions with "*" following them since they are complicated.

First we load into *$t0* the address of the jump table itself. There are the four addresses described above. We have asked our user to designate the operation with an integer between 1 and 4 but arrays are zero based in assembler (and C/C++/Java). Therefore we subtract one from the user's response and so have 0 to 3 in *$t1*. The actual addresses are four bytes long so we must multiply these values by 4 (by shifting left two bits) resulting in one of the numbers 0, 4, 8, or 12 now in *$t1*. Adding that to the jump table's address in *$t0* gives the address of the correct word in that table. Finally, we retrieve the actual address of the code we want from memory pointed to by that word.

It is obvious that this is an incredibly silly way to do programming unless you are trying to introduce the notion of a jump table. Note, however, that we have a *j DONE* statement right before the label "*DONE*". Normally one might, correctly, recognize that the jump statement is not required. Good programming practice is to put the extra jump there (just as putting an extra break statement at the end of a switch statement in C/C++/Java) because we might later change the number of cases and forget to insert the needed jump (or break) if it's not there to begin with. In the real world, code is often changed and looking in advance for places where errors can occur is a good idea.

5.5 Breakpoints

Now that our examples are getting more complicated, we find that the Single Step (F10) method of debugging has become inadequate. Going through even a simple loop one

operation at a time is too slow to help in many cases. Fortunately, our PCSPIM simulator
(as with real hardware usually) allows us to interrupt the execution of our program at any
predetermined point. The procedure is to set a **breakpoint** before running the code.

If we go to the "Simulator" pull-down menu we find "*Breakpoints… Ctrl+B*" as an
option. When we choose that option we get a pop-up window with which we may add
addresses.

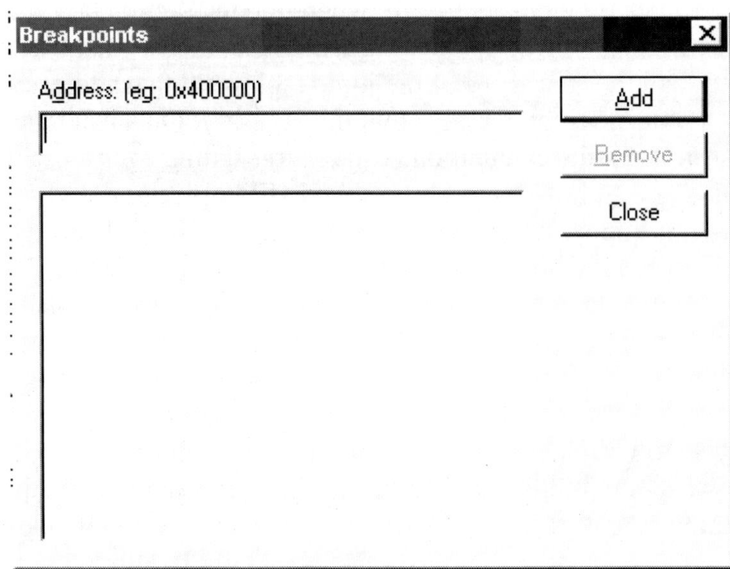

Let us try out this new ability with a program with a loop in it that might go on for
hundreds of iterations. Since early processors sometimes did not even have a hardware
multiply operation, programmers had to do the job in software. Here is an easy complete
program that takes two integers and multiplies them together by repeatedly adding.

```
# multiply.s
# integers without using the multiplication
# instruction but repeated addition instead
######  REGISTER USE:   #################
#
##     $s1    first integer - constant (or negated)
##     $s2    second integer - decreasing (made positive)
##     $s4    current answer
#
#######################################
        .data
promp1: .asciiz "Input first integer value: "
promp2: .asciiz "\nInput second integer value: "
answer: .asciiz "\nThe product is "
newln:  .asciiz "\n"
#######################################
```

```
                .text
                .globl main
main:
## Get input
# prompt for first value
        li      $v0, 4          # system call for print_str
        la      $a0, promp1     # address of string to print
        syscall
# read and echo first value
        li      $v0, 5          # system call for read_integer
        syscall                 # x in $v0
        move    $s1, $v0        # put in register
        li      $v0, 1          # system call for print_int
        move    $a0, $s1        # echo
        syscall
# prompt for second value
        li      $v0, 4          # system call for print_str
        la      $a0, promp2     # address of string to print
        syscall
# read and echo second value
        li      $v0, 5          # system call for read_integer
        syscall                 # y in $v0
        move    $s2, $v0        # put in register as constant
        li      $v0, 1          # system call for print_int
        move    $a0, $s2        # echo
        syscall
        bltz    $s2, twoneg     # if 2nd negative, change both
################################
# initialize
init:   li      $s4, 0          # inital value
##### Loop with test at beginning (while)
loop:   blez    $s2, endloop    # end of loop
        add     $s4, $s4, $s1
        sub     $s2, $s2, 1
        j       loop            # <= Breakpoint
endloop:
################################
##### Print answer
        li      $v0, 4          # system call for print_str
        la      $a0, answer
        syscall
        li      $v0, 1          # system call for print_int
        move    $a0, $s4
        syscall
#### Exit
exit:   li      $v0, 10
        syscall                 # Return control to the OS
#### Second argument negative - negate both
twoneg: neg     $s2, $s2
        neg     $s1, $s1
        j       init
####
```

The idea is that we add the value of the first number to the answer, which is initialized to zero, as many times as the value of the second number. Since we count down using the second number, if it were to be negative the program would not stop (or, at least, run too

long). Negating both of the numbers when the second is negative, since the program
works fine when the first number is negative, solves that problem.

We have placed an obvious comment where we might want to put a breakpoint: right at
the end of the loop. We now start PCSPIM and load the file. By scrolling down the code
we can easily find the line with the comment:

```
[0x00400084]    0x0810001e j 0x00400078 [loop]  ; 49: j  loop   # <= Breakpoint
```

The address of this code is 0x00400084 and we will insert that into the "Breakpoint" pop-
up window. The line now becomes

```
*[0x00400084]   0x00810001e j 0x00400078 [loop] ; 49: j  loop   # <= Breakpoint
```

and we are ready to try out the program. Running it as usual (starting at 0x00400000 as
always), the program gives us the prompts and takes our replies. Then it stops at location
0x00400084 and a pop-up window asks us whether we wish to continue or not. We may
first look at the registers or memory and see if their contents are what we expect.

In this case, if we tell the system to continue it will immediately again halt at the same
breakpoint and ask us again. Continuing in this way we can watch the counter $s2
decrease and the sum change. If we want to scroll through memory or see registers that
are not displayed, we may answer the continuation question "No" and look at whatever
we wish. We may start the program again by just using the usual "Go" command.

We will demonstrate the process again with our *insertion.s* file from the previous chapter
as follows. Open PCSPIM and choose the file *insertion.s* as expected. Now we may scroll
through the code section until we find a location at which we would like to see what is in
the registers. For example, the comment "continue while loop" might help us find the end
of the inner loop as described in the C/C++/Java code. The instruction we have chosen is
j whilej. The line we are looking for is:

```
[0x004000b0] 0x08100022 j 0x00400088 [whilej] ; 53: j whilej
                                              # continue while loop
```

When we find the address of that instruction (*0x004000b0*), we add it to the list of
breakpoints. When we close the window, the code now shows

```
* [0x004000b0] 0x08100022 j 0x00400088 [whilej] ; 53: j whilej
                                                # continue while loop
```

Now when we run the program, after the prompts and our responses, the system stops at
the instruction at 0x004000b0 and shows us a pop-up window asking us whether we wish
to continue or not. At this time we may look at the registers or memory and see if what
we expect to appear actually does appear.

Exercises

1. Add the appropriate error checking to the *calculate* code. Test it!

2. Test the *calculator* in PCSPIM and see what is in the *JumpTable*.

3. Modify *ISORT* to take an additional input of 1=increasing or 2=decreasing in $a2. Be sure to check for errors in that value (it must be 1 or 2). Test it!

4. Test the *count* function by writing a "driver" program; i.e., a program that reads any input needed, calls on the function to test it, and prints out any results for checking.

5. Insert breakpoints into some of our earlier complete programs with loops and watch the registers and memory change.

6. Compile the C/C++/Java statement *if (t0 == 0) s1 = 5; else s1 = 6;* into MIPS assembler language.

CHAPTER SIX

File and Character I/O

The latest version of PCSPIM includes system calls that allow file manipulation and character input and output. The ability to read and write files allows us to use large data sets to test our programs.

While high-level languages such as C++ and Java have extensive file manipulation capabilities, in SPIM we only have the equivalent of our keyboard for input and our monitor for output. These may be replaced by files that are sequential-access (one character after another) just as those devices are.

The new *syscall* functions available for file manipulation in PCSPIM (but not under MIPSter at this time) are as follows:

Code	Name	Argument and Result Registers
13	file_open	$a0→full path (zero terminated string with no LF), $a1=flags* $a2=permission (R=0x100,W=0x80); $v0=file descriptor (-1=error)
14	file_read	$a0=file descriptor, $a1→buffer, $a2=amount; $v0=result**
15	file_write	$a0=file descriptor, $a1→buffer, $a2=amount; $v0=result**
16	file_close	$a0=file descriptor

```
*flags: Read=0x0, Write=0x1, Read/Write=0x2
OR     Create=0x100, Truncate=0x200, Append=0x8
OR     Text=0x4000, Binary=0x8000

**result: Amount of data in buffer to/from file (-1=error, 0=EOF)
```

These allow us to create new files, read or write existing files, and close files. Let us demonstrate file manipulation first with a complete example. This will be a long program with much new material - made longer by careful checking for errors at each stage. We will intersperse the code with extra comments since it is so complicated.

6.1 A complete example

First we have comments that explain the purpose of the program.

```
################################################################
# fileio.s
#
# Demonstrates file manipulation system functions in PCSPIM
#
# Prompts for a (full path) file name
# Creates a file with that name (will overwrite existing file)
# Writes the file's own name in the file
# Closes and then reopens the file for reading
# Reads from the file and echoes the contents
# Closes the file and exits
################################################################
```

Next we have the *.data* section with buffers to hold the input and output strings. In addition, we have a prompt and various error messages.

```
            .data                   # Data declaration section
ibuffer: .space    80
obuffer: .space    80
prompt:  .asciiz   "Enter full file name: "
oerrmsg: .asciiz   "Error opening file"
werrmsg: .asciiz   "Error writing file"
rerrmsg: .asciiz   "Error reading file"
LF:      .asciiz   "\n"
```

Finally we have the *.text* section with our actual code. We start with a prompt for a file name and place the response in the input buffer. Another thing that makes the program long was our decision to prompt the user for a file name and use that as the name of the file to be created. Creating a new file is done with *syscall* function code 13 and it requires *$a0* to point to a zero terminated string containing the full path file name but no line feed at the end. When we read a string from the terminal using *syscall* function 8, it waits for the *<Enter>* key to be pressed but then appends a line feed (0x0a) to the string before the zero terminator.

```
.text
main:                               # Start of code section
# prompt for and get file name
        li      $v0,4
        la      $a0,prompt
        syscall
        li      $v0,8
        la      $a0,ibuffer
        li      $a1,80
        syscall                     # file name & LF now in ibuffer
```

That makes our first step to be removing that line feed. We start at the end of the buffer and work backwards until we find the offending line feed.

```
# remove LF
        la      $a0,ibuffer # \
        add     $a0,$a0,79  #  \
rLFloop: lb     $v0,0($a0)  #   \ Strip off
        bnez    $v0,rLFdone #   / Line Feed
        sub     $a0,$a0,1   #  /
```

```
            j         rLFloop      # /
# change LF to zero
rLFdone: sb          $0,0($a0)     # file name now in ibuffer
```

Now that we have replaced the line feed by a zero byte, we are ready to point $a0 to that string. In $a1 we place some flags telling the system what kind of file we wish to open. The various flags may be logically *OR*ed together. Since we want to create a new file, we will include 0x100 in the flag. Assuming it is a text file leads us to put 0x4000 in the flag. Finally, just for example, we can open it for both reading and writing by putting 0x2 in the flag. The result of *OR*ing these is 0x4102 and that is what we place in $a1.

Finally, we need to describe the permissions we give to the user in $a2. Again we may either allow reading (0x100) or writing (0x80) or both (0x180) and we chose both. The *syscall* then returns a **file descriptor** to the created (or opened) file in $v0. This is an integer with which we may refer to the file while it is open. Should there be an error in opening the file (for example, trying to open for reading, not creating, a non-existent file), the value in $v0 will be -1.

```
# file_open (create)
        li        $v0,13       # file open function code
        la        $a0,ibuffer  # → string with full path of file
        li        $a1,0x4102
            # flags: Text=0x4000 OR Create=0x100 OR R/W=0x2
        li        $a2,0x180
            # permissions: Read=0x100 OR Write=0x80
        syscall   # returns file descriptor or -1 if error
        beq       $v0,-1,oerror
        move      $s0,$v0      # good file descriptor in $s0
```

If all has gone well we are now ready to write into the file. The input to a file is taken from a buffer in memory and must consist of a string of characters, null terminated as usual. If we wish to take input from the user we must place it in a buffer every time. In our example we will just write the name of the file (already available as a null terminated string of ASCII characters) into the file. This program is long enough without any more complications.

The comments describe the contents of $v0 (the file write function code 15), $a0 (the file descriptor returned by the system when the file was created), and $a1 (a pointer to the buffer containing the string). In $a2 we put the maximum amount we want to write (which may be more than is actually written). Again the *syscall* returns -1 in $v0 if there is an error. Otherwise, in $v0 we will find the actual amount written (which may be zero if we were at the EOF=End Of File position). The system keeps a pointer to where in the file we are at all times and after this write that pointer will be at the EOF.

```
# file_write
        li        $v0,15       # file write function code
        move      $a0,$s0      # file descriptor
        la        $a1,ibuffer  # address of buffer
        li        $a2,80       # amount to write
        syscall   # returns amount written or -1 if error (0=EOF)
        beq       $v0,-1,werror
```

While we could continue to write at the position of the pointer (had we opened it with the "append" flag), we have decided to stop writing and read back what is now in the file. Although we did open the file for reading, trying to read immediately would return the EOF information since that's where the pointer is. It is necessary to return the pointer to the beginning of the file again. For that we will close the file and then reopen it for reading.

Closing the file merely requires using *syscall* function 16 with the file descriptor in *$a0*. Next we reopen the file using *syscall* function 13 again, but this time we will use the flags 0x4000=Text and 0x0=Read so in *$a1* we place $4000. Since we will only read we will make the permissions 0x100=Read in *$a2*. In *$a0* we make sure we have a pointer to the null terminated string giving the full path name of the file and issue the syscall. Again a (possibly new) file descriptor will appear in *$v0* and it will be -1 if there was an error.

```
# close / reopen for reading (since file pointer at EOF)
        li       $v0,16       # file close function code
        move     $a0,$s0      # file descriptor
        syscall  # closed, now reopen (file ptr at beginning)
        li       $v0,13       # file open function code
        la       $a0,ibuffer # → string with full path of file
        li       $a1,0x4000   # flags: Text=0x4000 OR Read=0x0
        li       $a2,0x100    # permissions: Read=0x100
        syscall  # returns file descriptor or -1 if error
        beq      $v0,-1,oerror
        move     $s0,$v0      # good file descriptor in $s0
```

If all has gone well we are now ready to read from the file from its beginning. We use *syscall* function code 14 in an obvious way for that. Everything else in this long program is self-explanatory.

```
# file_read
        li       $v0,14       # file read function code
        move     $a0,$s0      # file descriptor
        la       $a1,obuffer # address of buffer
        li       $a2,80       # amount to read
        syscall  # returns amount read or -1 if error (0=EOF)
        beq      $v0,-1,rerror
# echo                        # echo the file name
        li       $v0,4
        la       $a0,LF
        syscall
        li       $v0,4
        la       $a0,ibuffer
        syscall                  # write from ibuffer
        li       $v0,4
        la       $a0,LF
        syscall
        li       $v0,4
        la       $a0,obuffer
        syscall                  # write from obuffer
# file_close
        li       $v0,16       # file close function code
        move     $a0,$s0      # file descriptor
```

```
            syscall                 # file closed
exit:
            li          $v0,10
            syscall
oerror:                             # open error
            li          $v0,4
            la          $a0,oerrmsg
            syscall
            j           exit
werror:                             # write error
            li          $v0,4
            la          $a0,werrmsg
            syscall
            j           exit
rerror:                             # read error
            li          $v0,4
            la          $a0,rerrmsg
            syscall
            j           exit
```

It is important to note that creating a file with the same name as one that already exists is
quite legal and results in destroying the old file. There is no warning from the system if
this is about to happen so it is an important exercise to rewrite this program so that it asks
the user to confirm the creation (and destruction) when the file already exists!

6.2 Random Numbers Revisited

Now that we can create a file, we may use the random number generator developed
earlier to place a file with 100 pseudo-random numbers between 0 and 99 inclusive onto
our disk so we can use it for testing later. Of course the name of the file could be
prompted for as in the previous example but that has nothing to do with this function so
we will omit it. In addition, the seed and number of numbers could be treated as
parameters, but, again, we will not bother at this time.

```
# randomfile.s
#
# Puts 100 pseudo-random numbers between 0 and 99 inclusive
# into file called "c:random.dat"
#
# X[n+1] ← (a*X[n] + c) mod m
#
# using m = 2^16 = 65536
# using a = 32445 so that a mod 8 = 5 and 99m/100 > a > m/100
# using c = 1
# using X0 = 31416 in $s0
#
# based on Knuth
#
            .text
main:
            li      $s0, 31416      # X0 - initalized (could be input)
            li      $t0, 32445      # a - initialized
```

```
        li      $t1, 0x0000FFFF     # mask to modulo - initialized
        li      $t2, 396            # counter - initialized 4*100-4
        li      $t3, 100            # limit so values 0-99
# Create file
        li      $v0, 13             # file open function code
        la      $a0, fname          # → string with full path of file
        li      $a1, 0x4101 # flags: Text=0x4000, Create=0x100, W=0x1
        li      $a2, 0x80           # permissions: Write=0x80
        syscall                 # returns file descriptor or -1 if error
#
        beq     $v0, -1, oerror
        move    $s1, $v0            # good file descriptor in $s1
Loop:   bltz    $t2, Store          # end loop when counter passes zero
        mul     $s0, $s0, $t0       # X = aX
        addi    $s0, 1              # now X = aX+c
        and     $s0, $s0, $t1       # now X = (aX+c) mod m
        move    $a0, $s0            # keep X stored in $s0
        srl     $a0, $a0, 8         # divide by 256 (use upper 8 bits)
        bge     $a0, $t3, Loop      # only want those < 100
        sw      $a0, buffer+0($t2)  # save it (in reverse order)
        sub     $t2, $t2, 4         # decrease counter (4 bytes)
        j       Loop
# file_write
Store:  li      $v0, 15             # file write function code
        move    $a0, $s1            # file descriptor
        la      $a1, buffer         # address of buffer
        li      $a2, 400            # amount to write
        syscall                     # returns amount written
        beq     $v0,-1,werror       # or -1 if error (0=EOF)
# file_close
Exit:   li      $v0, 16             # file close function code
        move    $a0, $s1            # file descriptor
        syscall
        li      $v0, 10             # standard return to OS
        syscall
#
oerror: la      $a0, oerrmsg        # file open error
        li      $v0, 4
        syscall
        j       Exit
werror: la      $a0, werrmsg        # file write error
        li      $v0, 4
        syscall
        j       Exit
#
        .data
fname:    .asciiz   "c:random.dat"
oerrmsg:  .asciiz   "Error opening file\n"
werrmsg:  .asciiz   "Error writing file\n"
          .word     0xEEEEEEEE  # aligns to word boundary
buffer:   .space    400         # 100 words
          .word     0xFFFFFFFF  # also easy to find in PCSPIM
```

We have placed the words 0xEEEEEEEE and 0xFFFFFFFF on either side of the buffer so the list of pseudo-random numbers will be easy to find in the *data* segment when run under PCSPIM. The list will be in hexadecimal format with values between 0x00 and

0x63, inclusive. Note that if we reload this program and run it again, we get the same "random" numbers as before (we expected that) and we write over the old file with no notice. Of course we can't see that happening since the numbers end up the same, but it is important to emphasize that there is no warning that a file already exists when creating a file. That's why the exercise to write such a notification and verification is so important!

6.3 Sorting the Random Numbers

Now that we have a file of pseudo-random numbers, we can write a program that will read them into memory, call on the insertion sort function of section 5.3, and then write them to a new file and/or print them out in sorted order.

6.4 Character I/O

PCSPIM (but, again, not MIPSter) also has two more *syscall* functions that allow for I/O of individual characters. They are the following:

Code	Name	Argument and Result Registers
11	print_char	$a0=character (low 8 bits)
12	read_char	;$v0=character (no LF) echoed

Unlike function 4 (*print_string*), the actual character to be printed is placed in the low 8 bits of register *$a0* (not a pointer) for function 11 (*print_char*). In addition, unlike functions 5 through 8, function 12 (*read_char*) does not wait for the *<Enter>* key to be pressed before responding to the input of a character. Note that *<ConTRoL-C>* still interrupts the execution of the program, even though other control characters are accepted.

Here is an example using these functions in a way that we may copy in other programs.

```
        # characterio.s
        #
        # Demonstrates character I/O functions 11 and 12
        #
            .data                       # Data declaration section
prompt: .asciiz     "Proceed? (y/n): "
yes:        .asciiz     "\nYES!\n"
no:         .asciiz     "\nNO!!"
echo:       .asciiz     "\nYou entered: "
            .text
main:                                   # Start of code section
            li          $v0,4
            la          $a0,prompt
            syscall                     # Print prompt
            li          $v0,12
```

```
        syscall                    # Read 1 character (without LF)
        move        $s0,$v0        # Save it
        beq         $v0,0x79,OK    # Test for lc "y"
        beq         $v0,0x59,OK    # Test for uc "Y"
# Anything but 'y' or "Y"
        li          $v0,4
        la          $a0,no
        syscall                    # Print "NO!!" message
        la          $a0,echo
        syscall
        li          $v0,11
        move        $a0,$s0
        syscall                    # Print the actual character
        j           exit
# It was 'y' or "Y"
OK:     li          $v0,4
        la          $a0,yes
        syscall                    # Print "YES!" message
exit:
        li          $v0, 10        # exits program
        syscall
```

Here we have decided to accept only either 'y' or 'Y' to mean acceptance. Any other character (not just 'n') is failure. With this as an example, we can now take care of the problem associated with creating a file which already exists. We may also check for control characters other than *<ConTRoL-C>*. Of course the echo of the entered character is not necessary in most cases and is put here for demonstration purposes.

6.5 Memory Mapped I/O

Although most computer systems contain many input and output devices, our SPIM simulator is written to emulate just one of each. We will assume that the keyboard is our input device (called the **receiver** or reader) and the display our only output (called the **transmitter** or writer). As in many real computers, the interface with these devices appears to be by "memory-mapping"; that is, certain virtual memory locations are actually directly connected to I/O devices. Reading from the appropriate location actually reads a character from the keyboard; writing to the appropriate location actually prints a character on the display terminal.

Although we have noticed that the stack pointer $sp starts out around 0x7FFFFFFC, it was not clear why it was not up at $FFFFFFFC, the highest possible address for a word. The reason is that there is an agreement between the Operating System (OS) and SPIM that any user's program is limited to the first half of memory while the OS itself makes use of the upper half (all addresses from 0x80000000 up). In some systems there are hardware checks to be sure that a user cannot directly access the operating system's code or data areas; they can only be accessed by calling on the OS to do the desired operations and the system can check whether it is permissible or not.

In the case of SPIM's I/O, it is assumed that the four words located at 0xFFFF0000 are used for the purpose of memory mapping and are accessible in limited ways by the user. In the first word (offset 0), called the **Receiver Control Register** (RCR), bit 0 is the "ready" bit telling whether a character has been transmitted from the keyboard but has not been read yet (it is "read-only"). The character appears in the low order byte of the second word (offset 4), called the **Receiver Data Register** (RDR). When a character has been typed, the ready bit is changed to 1 and when the character has been read from the RDR it is changed back to 0.

The situation is similar but a little more complicated for output. The third word (offset 8), called the **Transmitter Control Register** (TCR), has in bit 0 a "ready" bit to indicate that it is available to accept a character to be displayed. The character itself appears in the low order byte of the fourth word (offset 12), called the **Transmitter Data Register** (TDR). When the ready bit is on (1), it is able to accept a character; when off (0), it is still busy transmitted the previous character. The fact that it should take some time to print out a character is emulated by PCSPIM in that it will turn off the ready bit for some time to emulate that delay. (See Figure 7 in Appendix D.)

The following program demonstrates the use of memory mapped I/O where the devices are "polled". That is, the program continually tests the "ready" bits until they are the correct value for the program to continue. The result is, of course, that the computer can do no other work while these "tight-loops" are running. A better method would have the device itself have enough compute power to be able to report back when it is ready while allowing other processing to be done by the central computer. We will study this "Interrupt Driven" programming in Chapter Twelve.

Be sure that the "Mapped I/O" box is checked in the "Settings" of PCSPIM to try the following program.

```
# PolledIO.s
#
# Demonstrates memory mapped I/O
#    Repeatedly prompts for a character with '>'
#    Echos printable characters until <Control-Z>
#    Prints '$' and exits (<Control-C> breaks)
#
# Function getChar puts character into $v0
# Function putChar takes character in $a0
#
# Takes the place of syscall functions 11 & 12
#
        .text
main:                            # Start of code section
        li      $a0,0x0a        # Line feed
        jal     putChar
        li      $a0,'>'         # Prompt character
        jal     putChar
        jal     getChar
        beq     $v0,0x1a,exit   # <Control-Z>
        move    $a0,$v0
        jal     putChar
```

```
             j       main
exit:
        li      $a0,'$'
        jal     putChar
        li      $v0,10          # exits program
        syscall
#
### gets character from keyboard into $v0
getChar:                        # ← entry point
        sub     $sp,$sp,4       # push changed register
        sw      $t0,0($sp)      # onto stack
        la      $t0,0xFFFF0000  # MEMORY MAPPED I/O
rrloop:
        lw      $v0,0($t0)      # read ready status (RCR)
        and     $v0,$v0,0x01# mask the ready bit
        beqz    $v0,rrloop      # keep polling
# ready to read
        lw      $v0,4($t0)      # read the data byte (RDR)
        lw      $t0,0($sp)      # pop changed register
        add     $sp,$sp,4       # from stack
        jr      $ra             # return from getChar
#
### prints character in $a0 onto display
putChar:                        # ← entry point
        sub     $sp,$sp,8       # push changed
        sw      $t0,0($sp)      # registers
        sw      $t1,4($sp)      # onto stack
        la      $t0,0xFFFF0000  # MEMORY MAPPED I/O
beloop1:
        lw      $t1,8($t0)      # buffer empty status (TCR)
        and     $t1,$t1,0x01# mask buffer empty bit
        beqz    $t1,beloop1 # keep polling
# ready to write
        sw      $a0,12($t0) # write to port (TDR)
beloop2:
        lw      $t1,8($t0)      # buffer emptied status (TCR)
        and     $t1,$t1,0x01# mask buffer emptied bit
        beqz    $t1,beloop2 # waiting until empty again
# done writing
        lw      $t1,4($sp)      # pop changed
        lw      $t0,0($sp)      # registers
        add     $sp,$sp,8       # from stack
        jr      $ra             # return from putChar
#
## End of polledIO.s
```

As we see, the writing function *getChar* requires a tight-loop and *putChar* requires two tight-loops to complete its work since it takes a while for the character to be written.

Exercises

1. We have used *syscall* function 4 with the ASCIIZ string "\n" in memory to print a new line (see Section 5.2). Show that we can avoid a reference to memory (which usually slows a program down) by using the following commands in PCSPIM:

```
li      $a0,0x0a
li      $v0,11
syscall
```

2. Write functions which replace *syscall*s 4 and 8 by using repeated calls on these new functions 11 and 12. Note that those *syscall*s require a terminating *<Enter>* ; your code should do the same. For extra credit, look for a backspace character (0x08) and treat it correctly.

3. Sort the file of random numbers as described in Section 6.3.

4. Test out the statement about only the low eight bits being used in function 11.

5. Test the input in our *characterio* example for control characters. Echo them by printing, for example, the actual string "*<Control-A>*" when 0x01 is entered.

6. Demonstrate code that warns the user when trying to create a file that already exists.

7. Extend the memory-mapped I/O example by labeling the program.

8. Investigate what happens with function 13 when the flags in *$a0* and the permissions in *$a1* seem to be inconsistent.

CHAPTER SEVEN

Recursion

The idea of a **recursive function**, one that may call on itself, is paradoxical for many reasons. Many programmers consider recursion a difficult concept but actually it is often so simple that it should be used for rapid prototyping (quickly writing some possibly poor code which can be used to demonstrate a system). Some of the most basic methods of software engineering are based on recursion. We will treat Binary Search Trees and Quicksort as important examples of recursion later. Let us first demonstrate recursion with some simple examples.

7.1 Factorials

The well-known **factorial** function is defined on the non-negative integers by the mathematical formula

$$0! = 1 \text{ and}$$
$$n! = n * (n-1)! \text{ for } n > 0$$

The C/C++/Java form of this definition immediately becomes

```
public int factorial(int n)
{
    if (n == 0) return 1;
    return n*factorial(n-1);
}
```

This example is characteristic of recursive function translation from mathematical definition to high-level language. If a function is given in recursive form the translation is almost automatic. Of course one should be careful to check that the original definition is correct and should note restrictions on the type and range of input variables. In our factorial example the function is only correctly defined for non-negative integers.

A recursive definition of a function always includes some **"base" cases** which, for some reason, are so trivial that their values are known or can be calculated without further recursion. The recursive cases, on the other hand, must make some progress toward the base cases. This means that the arguments for the recursive call are usually smaller in some sense (possibly smaller sets rather than always smaller integers). All our examples will be such that they are independent of the language we use.

Now we will translate this high-level language function into assembly language. Again much of this process will become automatic.

```
# factorial.s
#
# recursive implementation
######  INPUT:   ##########
#
## non-negative integer n in $a0
## (no check so caller must test)
#
######  OUTPUT: ##########
#
## value of n! in $v0
#
#########################
factorial:                      # ← entry point
# save registers
        sub     $sp,$sp,12  # \  push on the stack
        sw      $ra,0($sp)  # \  return address
        sw      $a0,4($sp)  # /  argument n (will be changed)
        sw      $s0,8($sp)  # /  changed register
# check for base case
        beqz    $a0,basecase # n == 0
# adjust input parameter
        sub     $a0,$a0,1   # n-1 new argument
        jal     factorial   # recursive call puts answer in $v0
        lw      $s0,4($sp)  # load this call's n into $s0
        mult    $v0,$s0     # assume $v0 has (n-1)!
        mflo    $v0         # put (small) n! into $v0
        j       return
basecase:
        li      $v0,1       # 0! = 1
return:
        lw      $s0,8($sp)  # \  put everything back
        lw      $a0,4($sp)  # \  the way it was including
        lw      $ra,0($sp)  # /  the return address
        add     $sp,$sp,12  # /  done popping
        jr      $ra
```

Almost every recursive program will start with pushing onto the stack all the registers
that must be saved including, in particular, the return address. We must save *$ra* since
this function may call on some other (or the same) function and write over that register.
Then we check to see if we have reached one of the base cases. If so, we do whatever is
necessary to return the base case value. Otherwise we prepare the arguments for the
recursive call. Upon return from the recursive call we just assume that the function has
performed properly. Of course it is the programmer's duty to ensure that fact. Finally, we
restore all the registers that were stored on the stack and return to the original return
address.

Calculating the value of $pow(n,k) = n^k$ for positive n and k is almost exactly the same
process and is requested in the exercises.

7.2 Sum of Vector Elements

Although it is unnatural to do so, we may use recursion to add up the values of all the integers stored in an array. Here is our C/C++/Java code:

```
public int sumvector(int[] a, int n)
{
    if (n <= 0) return 0;
    return sumvector(a, n-1) + a[n-1];
}
```

Again this can be translated into MIPS assembly language directly.

```
# sumvector.s
#
# recursive implementation
####### INPUT:   ########
#
##    address of the array a in $a0
##    length (actual count) n of the array in $a1
##    if n ≤ 0, returns zero (only check)
#
####### OUTPUT: ###########
#
##    sum of the elements in $v0
#
####### TO USE: ###########
#
#      la    $a0, a        // Put address of a in $a0
#      lw    $a1, n        // Put the count in $a1
#      jal   sumvector     // Returns with sum in $v0
#
sumvector:                 # ← entry point
# save registers
        sub   $sp,$sp,12   # \  push on stack
        sw    $a1,0($sp)   # \  argument n (will be changed)
        sw    $s0,4($sp)   # /  changed register
        sw    $ra,8($sp)   # /  return address
# check for base case
        blez  $a1,basecase # n == 0
# adjust input parameter
        sub   $a1,$a1,1    # count n-1 new argument
        jal   sumvector    # recursive call puts answer in $v0
        lw    $s0,0($sp)   # get this call's n
        sub   $s0,$s0,1    # zero based array
        sll   $s0,$s0,2    # multiply by four (bytes)
        add   $s0,$a0,$s0  # address of a[n-1]
        lw    $s0,0($s0)   # get a[n-1] itself
        add   $v0,$s0,$v0  # new $v0
        j     return
basecase:
        li    $v0,0        # nothing to add
return:
        lw    $ra,8($sp)   # \  put everything
        lw    $s0,4($sp)   # \  back the way
```

```
lw      $a1,0($sp)   # / it was
add     $sp,$sp,12   # /  done popping
jr      $ra
```

The only complicated thing in this example is to keep straight the difference between the count of the number of elements and the array indices which are zero-based.

7.3 Fibonacci Numbers

Unlike our last example which is somewhat unnatural, we will now consider one of the most famous naturally recursive functions. Introduced around 1202 by Fibonacci, they arose first in calculating how many rabbits there would be in succeeding generations under a simple rule of birth. These same numbers appear in many applications. Their mathematical definition (in one simple form) is:

$$Fib(0) = 0$$
$$Fib(1) = 1$$
$$Fib(n) = Fib(n-1) + Fib(n-2) \text{ for } n \geq 2$$

Again the translation into C/C++/Java is automatic:

```
public int Fib(int n)
{
     if (n == 0 || n == 1) return n;
     return Fib(n-1) + Fib(n-2);
}
```

This example is somewhat more complicated since there must be two recursive calls when calculating the result. Nevertheless, the assembly language translation is rather straightforward.

```
# Fib.s
#
# recursive implementation
###### INPUT:   ########
#
##    non-negative integer n in $a0
##    (no test - returns any negative integer)
#
###### OUTPUT: ##########
#
##    nth Fibonacci number in $v0
#
###### TO USE: ##########
#
#      lw    $a0,n        // Put the n in $a0
#      jal   Fib          // Returns with sum in $v0
#
Fib:                      # <- entry point
# save registers
```

```
        sub     $sp,$sp,12  # \  push on stack
        sw      $a0,0($sp)  # \  argument n (will be changed)
        sw      $s0,4($sp)  # /  changed register
        sw      $ra,8($sp)  # /  return address
# check for base case
        li      $s0,1
        ble     $a0,$s0,basecase # tests n <= 1
# adjust input parameter
        sub     $a0,$a0,1   # n-1 new argument
        jal     Fib         # first recursive call
        move    $s0,$v0     # save result
        sub     $a0,$a0,1   # now use n-2 as argument
        jal     Fib         # second recursive call
        add     $v0,$v0,$s0 # new $v0
        j       return
basecase:
        li      $v0,$a0     # Fib(n) = n for n <= 1
return:
        lw      $ra,8($sp)  # \  put everything
        lw      $s0,4($sp)  # \  back the way
        lw      $a0,0($sp)  # /  it was
        add     $sp,$sp,12  # /  done popping
        jr      $ra
```

Of course there are many variations of this and our other examples that will work equally well. For example, one might test for the base cases before saving the registers, but then it is necessary to return to the caller without any clean-up process of restoring the registers (and the return address in particular). As always, which registers we use is not really important and the order of pushing and popping the stack does not matter (but must be consistent). The point is that it is trivial to write recursive functions, especially if the function's definition is, or can be made to be, recursive.

7.4 Combinations

As a final example we will take a result from combinatorial analysis that prepares us for printing the Pascal Triangle. It will also require a double recursion and so will, at first glance, look complicated. Nevertheless, it will turn out to be very straightforward in its development.

The number of combinations of n identical objects taken k at a time, denoted by $C(n,k)$, can be calculated using the recursive formula given in C/C++/Java code by

```
public int C(int n, int k)
{
    if (n == 0 || k == 0 || k == n) return 1;
    return C(n-1,k) + C(n-1,k-1);          // 0 < k < n
}
```

In our study of Discrete Mathematics we will see that $C(n,k)$ is the kth coefficient in the expansion of the expression $(x + y)^n$. These numbers are called the **binomial coefficients**.

Again it is easy to translate this directly into MIPS assembly code.

```
# C.s
#
# Recursive implementation
####### INPUT:   ########
#
##    non-negative integers n in $a0 and k in $a1
##    (no test for 0 <= k <= n; returns 1 otherwise)
#
####### OUTPUT: ###########
#
##    C(n,k) in $v0
#
####### TO USE: ###########
#
#       lw      $a0,n           // Put the n in $a0
#       lw      $a1,k           // Put the k in $a1
#       jal     C               // Returns with C(n,k) in $v0
#
C:                              # ← entry point
# save registers
        sub     $sp,$sp,16      # \   push on stack
        sw      $ra,0($sp)      # \   return address
        sw      $a0,4($sp)      # > argument n
        sw      $a1,8($sp)      # /   argument k
        sw      $s0,12($sp)     # /   also changed so save
# check for base cases
        blez    $a0,basecase    # base case n <= 0
        blez    $a1,basecase    # base case k <= 0
        bge     $a0,$a1,basecase  # base case k >= n
# adjust input parameters
        sub     $a0,$a0,1       # decrease argument n
        jal     C               # recursive call C(n-1,k)
        move    $s0,$v0         # returned value in $v0, save it
        sub     $a1,$a1,1       # decrease argument k
        jal     C               # recursive call C(n-1,k-1)
        add     $v0,$v0,$s0     # now final answer in $v0
        j       return
basecase:
        li      $v0,1           # return 1 for all base cases
return:
        lw      $s0,12($sp)     # \   put back everything
        lw      $a1,8($sp)      # \   the way it was
        lw      $a0,4($sp)      # > before the call
        lw      $ra,0($sp)      # /   including return address
        add     $sp,$sp,16      # /   done popping
        jr      $ra             #
```

The only problem with this code (as with the Fibonacci example) is that it runs very
slowly for large values of *n*. That is the biggest complaint about recursive functions in
general. In addition, they take up stack space. On those computers in which it is normal
to save all the registers (there might be a *sar* [**S**ave **A**ll **R**egisters] command – but <u>not</u> in
MIPS), that can add up to more memory than is available. We will address these
problems in the next section.

7.5 Tail-recursion

Once we have written, tested, and demonstrated some quick prototype code using recursion, we must turn to optimizing the code that we will actually deliver for production. The example above for calculating factorials will show us one type of optimization that is possible.

Let us consider what return addresses are pushed onto the stack as we run a test program using our code. The test program will call on *factorial* once passing *n* as its argument and we store the address of the next instruction of the test program away on the stack. After that there will be many recursive calls on *factorial* with decreasing arguments from *n-1* down to *0* but in every case the return address will be the same: the instruction *lw $s0,4($sp)* which follows the *jal factorial* within *factorial*. In a way the repeated return addresses on the stack are little more than counters telling us how many times the function has been called.

Each time we return from the *factorial* function we must then multiply the result by the corresponding argument *n*. In particular, we have something else to do. The same situation occurred with the *sumvector* recursive function. When we returned from the recursive call we had something else to do (add *a[n-1]*).

If the recursive call is the very last thing we need to do we call the function **tail-recursive**. In such a case we can directly turn our recursive calls into simple jumps and so have a loop (which is faster since we would not be using the stack at all). Even when a function is not itself tail-recursive, with the aid of an **auxiliary function** we can often obtain the same benefit. Again, this technique may be used with high-level languages just as well. Here is our improved factorial function in C/C++/Java.

```
public int factorial(int n)
{
   return factorialAux(n,1);
}
int factorialAux(int n, int ans)
{
   if (n == 0) return ans;
   factorialAux(n-1, n*ans);
}
```

If we follow the behavior of this code when we test our program with a small number like 5 as input, we see that there would be one call on *factorialAux(5,1)* by the main *factorial* function. Then there would be the succession of recursive calls *factorialAux(4,5)*, *factorialAux(3,20)*, *factorialAux(2,60)*, *factorialAux(1,120)*, *factorialAux(0,120)*. Finally, the base case test of *n == 0* would return "true" and we would immediately return the answer of *120* to *factorial*.

A smart compiler (and we) may realize that we do not need to keep all the return information since each call on the auxiliary function need not do any additional work or return its value to the preceding caller. When we reach the base case, we may return the value directly to the actual function. We may code this so that it is a loop rather than a function call!

```
# factorial.s
#
# tail-recursive loop implementation
######  INPUT:  ##########
#
## non-negative integer n in $a0
## (no check - infinite loop if negative)
#
######  OUTPUT: ##########
#
## value of n! in $v0
## (changes $a0 and $a1)
#
########################
factorial:                  # ← entry point
        li     $a1,1        # start with ans = 1
Aux:                        # $a0 = n, $a1 = ans
       beqz  $a0,return    # test for base case
       mult  $a1,$a0       # n*ans
       mflo  $a1           # new ans value
       sub   $a0,$a0,1     # new n value
       j     Aux           # just a loop! Don't change $ra!!
return:
       move  $v0,$a1       # put final answer in $v0
       jr    $ra           # return to original caller
```

The important thing about this example is not that we can program *factorial* as a loop; we would probably have done that anyway. The point is that we can see how a recursive program can so easily be changed to a loop program. For this reason it is even more likely that originally using recursion would not be a waste of effort. It is an easy exercise to change this code so that *$a0* and *$a1* are restored to their original values without losing the speed of a loop.

Let's now do the same thing to our *sumvector* function. The C/C++/Java code using an auxiliary function would simply be

```
public int sumvector(int[] a, int n)
{
   return sumvectorAux(a, n, 0);
}
int sumvectorAux(int[] a, int n, int ans)
{
   if (n == 0) return ans;
   sumvectorAux(a, n-1, ans + a[n-1]);
}
```

Clearly, this is the same situation. We may now translate this into MIPS assembler language directly.

```
# sumvector.s
#
# tail-recursive loop implementation
####### INPUT:   ########
#
##    address of the array a in $a0
##    length (actual count) n of the array in $a1
##    if n ≤ 0, returns zero (only check)
#
####### OUTPUT: ###########
#
##    sum of the elements in $v0
##    ($a1,$a2,$s0 changed)
#
####### TO USE: ###########
#
#      la    $a0, a              // Put address of a in $a0
#      lw    $a1, n              // Put the count in $a1
#      jal   sumvector           // Returns with sum in $v0
#
sumvector:                  # ← entry point
       li    $a2, 0         # $a2 will hold sum starting at 0
Aux:                        # $a0 → a, $a1 = n
       blez  $a1,return     # test for base case: n <= 0
       sub   $a1,$a1,1      # next time n-1
       move  $s0,$a1        # find a[n-1]
       sll   $s0,$s0,2      # (bytes) so times 4
       add   $s0,$s0,$a0    # in the array
       lw    $s0,0($s0)     # that's it
       add   $a2,$a2,$s0    # sum + a[n-1]
       j     Aux            # just a loop! Don't change $ra!!
return:
       move  $v0,$a2        # put sum in $v0
       jr    $ra            # return to original caller
```

Once again it is an easy exercise to modify this code so that no registers are changed (other than *$v0*, of course).

7.6 Dynamic Programming

Another form of optimization is possible in the cases above where we used double recursion. For example, let us analyze the work done in calculating a Fiboncci number using the straightforward recursive code. Following the mathematical description, $Fib(10) = Fib(9) + Fib(8) = (Fib(8) + Fib(7)) + (Fib(7) + Fib(6)) = \ldots$ for $n = 10$. We see that some values will be calculated repeatedly. In fact, the Fibonacci numbers grow in size exponentially with *n* and so does the number of recursive calls.

A very simple solution to this problem is to keep a table of those values that have already been calculated and so evaluate each Fibonacci number only once. The table lookup method is called **dynamic programming** and proceeds from small cases to larger.

Let us apply this technique to the Fibonacci numbers. We will use an array that can hold 50 integers since for larger n the corresponding number will overflow anyhow. Since SPIM initializes space to the value zero, we will not put in any code to do that initialization but it might be necessary in other systems or languages. Another concession will be to use zero as an indication that the value has not been calculated yet. That forces us to note that Fib(2) = 1 and use that in addition to the usual base cases since Fib(0) = 0 would not look like a previously calculated value.

```
        # Fib.s
        #
        # Dynamic Programming implementation
        ####### INPUT:   ########
        #
        ##    non-negative integer n in $a0
        ##    (no test - negative values address locations outside array)
        #
        ####### OUTPUT: ###########
        #
        ##    nth Fibonacci number in $v0
        #
        ####### TO USE: ###########
        #
        #     lw    $a0,n                  // Put the n in $a0
        #     jal   Fib                    // Returns with sum in $v0
        #
        Fib:                       # ← entry point
        # save registers
               add   $sp,$sp,16
               sw    $a0,0($sp)
               sw    $s0,4($sp)
               sw    $s1,8($sp)
               sw    $ra,12($sp)
        # check FibArray for answer
               move  $s0,$a0       # take n
               sll   $s0,$s0,2     # multiply by 4 (bytes)
               la    $s1,FibArray# get array address
               add   $s1,$s1,$s0 # actual location address
               lw    $v0,0($s1)   # what's there
               bnz   $v0,return   # if not zero, found it already
        # otherwise we have to actually do the calculation
        # adjust input parameter
               sub   $a0,$a0,1    # n-1 new argument
               jal   Fib          # first recursive call
               move  $s0,$v0       # save result
               sub   $a0,$a0,1    # now use n-2 as argument
               jal   Fib          # second recursive call
               add   $v0,$v0,$s0 # new $v0
               sw    $v0,0($s1)   # save it in FibArray
        # restore registers
        return:
               lw    $ra,12($sp)
               lw    $s1,8($sp)
               lw    $s0,4($sp)
               lw    $a0,0($sp)
               sub   $sp,$sp,16
```

```
        jr      $ra
        .data
FibArray:
        .word       0           # Fib(0) = 0
        .word       1           # Fib(1) = 1
        .word       1           # Fib(2) = 1
        .space   188            # room for 47 more
```

Even on a fairly fast processor we can finally do so large a calculation that the time lag will be quite noticeable. The recursive *Fib* function will take a significant amount of time to run when given, for example, an *n* value of 40. With most of the recursive calls removed by Dynamic Programming, it should be instantaneous.

Finally, let us print out the Pascal Triangle of values of *C(n.k)* where we use Dynamic Programming to reduce the number of recursive calls. Since this is a two-dimensional array, there has to be a complicated calculation to find the index within the one-dimensional storage. Here is the complete program based on the recursive C function:

```
# Pascal.s
#
# SPIM code to print out the Pascal triangle
# using recursion and DYNAMIC PROGRAMMING.
#
# if (n==0 || k==0 || k == n) return 1;
# else // 0 < k < n
# return C(n,k) = C(n-1,k) + C(n-1,k-1);
#
######  REGISTER USE:   #################
#
#       $a0     pass n to C
#       $a1     pass k to C
#       $v0     C returns result
#
##      $s3     constant N
##      $s4     counter i   //for(i=1;i<=N;i++)
##      $s5     counter j   //for(j=0;j<=i;j++)
#
#       Note: index = (i*i+i+j+j)/2 (words; *4 bytes!)
#
###########################################
        .data
prompt: .asciiz "Pascal(int N);\nInput non-negative integer: "
output: .asciiz "\nThe Pascal Triangle\n"
newln:  .asciiz "\n"      # Can't use MIPSter if we use …
tab:    .asciiz "\t"      # function 11 to print a character
        .align  8
table:  .space  10000    # room for more than 50 levels
###########################################
        .text
main:
## Get input
## prompt for value of N
        li      $v0, 4          # system call for print_str
        la      $a0, prompt     # address of string to print
        syscall
```

```
        # read and echo N
                li      $v0, 5          # system call for read_integer
                syscall                 # N in $v0
                move    $s3, $v0        # put fixed value in $s3
                li      $v0, 1          # system call for print_int
                move    $a0, $s3        # echo
                syscall
                jal     println
        # label output
                li      $v0, 4          # system call for print_str
                la      $a0, output     # address of string to print
                syscall
        #
        # Right here should check for negative N
        #
        # Print N=0 case:
                li      $v0, 1
                la      $t0, table
                sw      $v0, 0($t0)     # start array
                li      $a0, 1
                syscall
                jal     println
        # setup outer loop (i)
                li      $s4, 1          # i=1; initialized
        iloop:  bgt     $s4, $s3, done# while(i<=N)
        # setup inner loop (j)
                li      $s5, 0          # j=0; initialized
        jloop:  bgt     $s5, $s4, next# while(j<=i)
                move    $a0, $s4
                move    $a1, $s5
                jal     C               # returns with C(i,j) in $v0
                move    $a0, $v0
                li      $v0, 1
                syscall                 # print it
                li      $v0, 4          # print
                move    $t0, $a0        # (save $a0)
                la      $a0, tab        # tab
                syscall
                move    $a0, $t0        # (replace $a0)
                addi    $s5, 1          # j+=1;
                j       jloop
        next:   addi    $s4, 1          # i+=1;
                jal     println
                j       iloop
        done:
        ####
                li      $v0, 10         # Put the integer 10 into $v0
                syscall                 # Return control to the OS
        ####
        println:                # subroutine to println saving registers
                sub     $sp, $sp, 8     #\
                sw      $a0, 0($sp)     # \
                sw      $v0, 4($sp)     #  \
                la      $a0, newln      #   \
                li      $v0, 4          #    > Print new line
                syscall                 #   /
                lw      $v0, 4($sp)     #  /
```

```
            lw      $a0, 0($sp)    # /
            add     $sp, $sp, 8    #/
            jr      $ra            # return
    ##### Recursive function C(n,k) returned in $v0 <== The main idea
    C:
            sub     $sp,$sp,20     # save $a0 = n and $a1 = k
            sw      $ra,0($sp)     #
            sw      $a0,4($sp)     #
            sw      $a1,8($sp)     #
            sw      $s1,12($sp)    # also change s1 so save
            sw      $s2,16($sp)    # also change s2 so save
            blez    $a0,basecase       # base case n ≤ 0
            blez    $a1,basecase       # base case k ≤ 0
            bge     $a0,$a1,basecase   # base case k ≥ n
    # calculate index
            move    $s1, $a0       # \
            mult    $s1, $s1       #   \
            mflo    $s1            #     \
            add     $s1, $s1, $a0  #      > CALCULATE THE INDEX
            add     $s1, $s1, $a1  #     /
            add     $s1, $s1, $a1  #    /
            sll     $s1, $s1, 1    #   /
            la      $t0, table     # \ calculate
            add     $s1, $s1, $t0  # / pointer
            lw      $v0, 0($s1)    # look in table
            bnez    $v0, return    # if found - done
            sub     $a0,$a0,1      # decrease argument n
            jal     C              # recursive call C(n-1,k)
            move    $s2,$v0        # returned value in $v0
            sub     $a1,$a1,1      # decrease argument k
            jal     C              # recursive call C(n-1,k-1)
            add     $v0,$v0,$s2    # now final answer in $v0
            sw      $v0, 0($s1)    # put it in the table
            j       return
    basecase: li    $v0,1          # return 1 for base cases
    return:
            lw      $s2,16($sp)    # put back everything
            lw      $s1,12($sp)
            lw      $a1,8($sp)
            lw      $a0,4($sp)
            lw      $ra,0($sp)
            add     $sp,$sp,20
            jr      $ra            # return
```

EXERCISES

1. Write and test a function to calculate $pow(n,k) = n^k$ for positive integers n and k.

2. Extend your function for $pow(n,k)$ so as to allow for any integer inputs (and check for 0^0 which is an error).

3. Modify the tail-recursive version of *sumvector* so that only *$v0* is changed. Also, add check for negative input, return 0xFFFFFFFF in that case.

4. Write and test a program to reverse an input string using recursion.

5. Explain the index calculation used in storing the Pascal triangle for use in Dynamic Programming.

6. Write and test a tail-recursive function to calculate the product of two integers *product(n,m)* = *n* * *m* using only addition and subtraction as if there were no multiply hardware and it must be done in software.

7. Write and test a tail-recursive function to calculate the sum of two integers *sum(n,m)* = *n* + *m* using only increment (adding 1) and decrement (subtracting 1) as if there were no adding hardware and it must be done in software using only increment and decrement hardware.

8. Rewrite *Pascal.s* to test for negative values of *n*.

9. Add checks for incorrect input in *Fib.s*, return -1 if $0 \leq k \leq n$ fails in any way.

10. Using the function *c(n,k)* as a model, write SPIM code to calculate the recursive function *J* defined by *J(0)* = *0*, *J(1)* = *1*, and

$$J(n) \;=\; 2nJ(n\text{-}1) - J(n\text{-}2)$$

for $n \geq 2$. Assume, as usual, that *$a0* contains *n* and the answer is returned in *$v0*. Write a driver program to print out the values of *J(n)* for *n* = *0* to *n* = *25*. (Also, assume the values are small integers.)

11. Rewrite the following C/C++/Java code into MIPS assembler and with the aid of a driver program print out the values of the mystery function for *a0* = *0* to *a0* = *25*. Do you recognize the function?

```
int mystery (int a0)
{      int t0 = 0;
       int t1 = 1;
       while (a0 >= 2)
       {      t2 = t0 + t1;
              t0 = t1;   t1 = t2;   a0 -= 1;
       }
       return t1;
}
```

CHAPTER EIGHT

Data Structures

There is no question that the data structures used in programming are closely related to and as important as the choice of algorithms. Early in our study of C/C++/Java we must treat arrays (as we did earlier). Later we examine lists, trees, and other more complicated structures. The basis for many of the interesting data structures studied earlier was the concept of nodes, pointers, and linked lists. Assuming that the reader has seen these concepts in some high-level language, we will demonstrate a complete singly linked list program and most of a binary search tree program. We will also introduce a simple hash function example. There is also no question, however, that assembler is not the language to use for manipulation of data structures unless it is absolutely necessary. Unfortunately, it is necessary when writing important code such as for operating systems, assemblers and compilers, and almost all embedded systems.

8.1 Linked Lists

In the following example we will use **nodes** consisting of two words. The first will contain the **data** field and the second the **pointer** field that contains the address of the next node in the list. We will use a Null (zero) pointer to indicate the end of the list. In more realistic examples the data field might contain a pointer to rather complex records of information such as name, address, telephone number, *etc*. Of course with small records there might be a few data fields at each node rather than one; it is not necessary that the data field consist of only one field, just our choice. In addition, we choose to use an entire word as the data field even though in this program only single characters (one byte) are being stored. We have done that to avoid any alignment problems.

Another decision was to have only one pointer at each node, thus having a singly linked list. For many purposes two and even multiple pointer fields may be used. One advantage of the doubly linked list where the second pointer contains the address of the previous node in the list is that one can find that previous node immediately. With our singly linked lists we must carefully keep track not only of which node we are working with, but also what was the previous node in the linked order (as we shall see).

The purpose of this simple program is to demonstrate inserting into, deleting from, and printing a singly linked list of characters. It is actually very straightforward but it leaves many possibilities for improvement. We have decided to use a "header" node for our linked list so that there is always a valid address for the list, even when it is empty. (It is not necessary to do it this way but it avoids any "creation" problem.) Although we allocated 8 bytes for the header and put -1 in its data field, it was not necessary to have

the header of the same type as the nodes. Wasting a little space, however, is often a way
to make one's code more consistent and easier to write correctly. It is not at all significant
in this particular example, however.

Another decision was to always insert each character value at the beginning of the list.
Since we naturally wanted to print them in linked-list order (any other choice is
extremely difficult), which means they will appear in LIFO (Last-In First-Out) order.
Note that this format can be used to implement a stack when needed.

Since we did not bother to keep them in alphabetic order (it is a moderately difficult
exercise to do so), it is not easy to look for duplicates and print a warning when trying to
insert a value already present. (It can be done even with the lack of ordering – another
exercise). Hence, we will allow duplicate entries.

On the other hand, when trying to delete an alphabetic value, we expect to go all the way
through the linked-list until we find a particular value, and so we also expect to find out
when a particular value does not appear at all. In that case we can and do print out a
warning message.

Another reason for this example is to show how to use another of the PCSPIM and
MIPSter system calls, number 9. In the toolbox listing under "Instruction/Calls" we find
it titled "sbrk" but we will label it "malloc" since it is just like the **M**emory **alloc**ation
function *malloc()* in C. In C++ or Java we would use the **new** operator to dynamically
allocate memory.

Code	Name	Argument and Result Registers
9	malloc	$a0=amount; $v0=address

In register *$a0* we place the amount of memory (in bytes) that we wish to allocate and it
returns the beginning address of that amount of contiguous memory in register *$v0*.

Each time we insert a character, we will allocate two words of memory (8 bytes) using
this system call. There is no call corresponding to the *free()* operator and no garbage
collection as in Java, so when deleting a character we will simply leave the node
unreferenced.

Here is the complete program:

```
# LinkedList.s
#
        .data                       # Data declaration section
title:  .asciiz "\nLinked List Demonstration"
prompt: .ascii  "\nLinked List: "
        .ascii  " 'P' = Print; "
        .ascii  " 'I' = Insert;"
        .ascii  " 'D' = Delete;"
        .asciiz " 'E' = Exit:   "
```

```
errmsg: .ascii   "\nYou must reply with 'P', 'I', 'D', or 'E'! "
        .asciiz "Try again"
imsg:   .asciiz "\nWhat letter do you want inserted? "
dmsg:   .asciiz "\nWhat letter do you want deleted? "
pmsg:   .asciiz "\nThe Linked List now is as follows: \n\t"
header: .word   -1,0
emsg:   .asciiz "\nThe List is Empty"
noinmsg:.asciiz "\nThat letter does not appear in the list!"
exitmsg:.asciiz "\n\nGoodbye!"
#
        .text
main:                              # Start of code section
        li      $v0,4
        la      $a0,title
        syscall
        la      $s0,header         # Constant pointer to header
loop:                              # Main loop
        li      $v0,4
        la      $a0,prompt
        syscall
        li      $v0,12             # No MIPSter
        syscall
        beq     $v0,'P',Pcode
        beq     $v0,'p',Pcode      # accept lower case also
        beq     $v0,'I',Icode
        beq     $v0,'i',Icode      # accept lower case also
        beq     $v0,'D',Dcode
        beq     $v0,'d',Dcode      # accept lower case also
        beq     $v0,'E',Ecode
        beq     $v0,'e',Ecode      # accept lower case also
        li      $v0,4
        la      $a0,errmsg         # Not P, I, D, or E
        syscall
        j       loop
#
# PRINT
Pcode:  lw      $t0,4($s0)         # Get pointer from header
        beqz    $t0,Empty          # Empty list
        li      $v0,4              # Label output
        la      $a0,pmsg
        syscall
Ploop:  li      $v0,11             # Print_char (no MIPSter)
        li      $a0,0x09           # Tab
        syscall
        lw      $a0,0($t0)         # Next data
        li      $v0,11             # Print_char (no MIPSter)
        syscall
        lw      $t0,4($t0)         # Get next pointer
        bnez    $t0,Ploop          # If not zero pointer continue
        j       loop               # Zero pointer, start over
Empty:  li      $v0,4
        la      $a0,emsg
        syscall
        j       loop
#
# INSERT
Icode:  li      $v0,4              # Prompt for input
```

```
            la        $a0,imsg
            syscall
            li        $v0,12          # Read_char (no MIPSter)
            syscall
            move      $s1,$v0         # save it
            li        $v0,9           # Malloc (Memory Allocation)
            li        $a0,8           # 8 bytes desired
            syscall                   # $v0 now contains the address
            lw        $t0,4($s0)      # Former header pointer
            sw        $s1,0($v0)      # Char saved in new first position
            sw        $t0,4($v0)      # Old header pointer in new 1st
            sw        $v0,4($s0)      # New pointer in header
            j         loop            # Insert done, start over
#
# DELETE
Dcode:      li        $v0,4           # Prompt for input
            la        $a0,dmsg
            syscall
            li        $v0,12          # Read_char (no MIPSter)
            syscall
            move      $s1,$v0         # save it
            lw        $t0,4($s0)      # Get pointer from header
            move      $t3,$s0         # Use $t3 for previous
# $t3 -> previous element; $s1 = character; $t0 -> next element
# find character in list:
floop:      beqz      $t0,NotIn       # End of list
            lw        $t1,0($t0)      # get next character
            beq       $t1,$s1,found
            lw        $t3,4($t3)      # move pointer
            lw        $t0,4($t0)      # move pointer
            j         floop
found:      lw        $t2,4($t0)      # character's pointer
            sw        $t2,4($t3)      # previous points past now
            j         loop
NotIn:      li        $v0,4
            la        $a0,noinmsg
            syscall
            j         loop
#
# EXIT
Ecode:
            li        $v0,4
            la        $a0,exitmsg
            syscall
            li        $v0, 10         # exits program
            syscall
# End of LinkedList.s
```

Here is a detailed explanation of the above code. The *.data* section contains the usual prompts and messages. In addition, the header node referred to above is declared.

In the *.text* section, after printing the title, we load into *$s0* the address of the header and will keep it in that register throughout the program. Another approach to this need for the address of the header is to load it every time we need to use it. As long as we have sufficient registers available, this is quicker and easier.

The main loop of the program repeatedly prompts the user for which function is desired. The decision was made to prompt for upper case letters but to accept the corresponding lower case letters. Control passes to the appropriate code.

The printing function checks for and prints out an informative message when it finds that the linked list is actually empty. Otherwise, there is a print loop that prints a tab and then the character at the node and prepares to continue using the pointer at the node. This continues until (just as with an *until* loop in C/C++/Java) it finds a Null (zero) pointer.

The inserting function prompts for the character to be inserted and calls on the new memory allocation *syscall* function 9 to obtain the 8 bytes required. Following the decision to insert always at the beginning of the list, it is easy to adjust the pointers to have the new pointer field point to the node that the header pointed to and the header to point to this new node. The character is inserted into the other field of the node. As pointed out before, this method is very easy to implement but it allows for duplicate entries in the linked list. It is an exercise to look for the value to be inserted in the list (which means traversing the entire list if it is not found) and then placing only a new value at the end of the list instead of the beginning. As long as we are treating single character data, we could also insist that the insertion be done in alphabetical order (which requires keeping track of the node after which the value is to be inserted).

The comments about keeping track of a previous node become significant during the deleting process. In the deleting code we must traverse the linked list until we find a node with the desired value in it or reach the end of the list as indicated by a Null (zero) pointer. If we find the character, we must have a pointer to the previous node so that we can change its pointer to take us past the deleted node to the one to which it pointed. The find-loop, therefore, keeps updating two pointers during each iteration.

8.2 Binary Trees

Another basic data type is the tree. It is easy to define a tree recursively. A **tree** is a collection of nodes that is either empty (the base case for recursive programs) or a special node called the **root** from which zero or more subtrees (which are themselves trees) descend. We usually call the subtrees the "children" of the "parent" node and use other words that remind us of the descendants of an individual.

One simple tree is the **binary tree** in which each node has exactly two children (of course one or the other or both may be an empty tree). We will comment later that while binary trees may be useful as simple examples of trees, in most cases having many children will lead to more efficient programs. We will call the two subtrees the **left** and the **right** children and assume that a data field is also available in each node.

As with linked lists, if there is a great deal of data to be associated with a node, we might store a pointer to a large record. In the case of little data, there might be a few fields to contain the data. Also, we might store additional pointers at each node including, for example, a pointer to the node's "parent" node. We will assume that each node contains a field with a **key** in it; that is, some data that uniquely identifies the node.

Finally, we will consider a special type of binary tree: a **binary search tree (BSTree)**. In this case the key at each (non-empty) node is greater than the key at any node of its left child and less than the key at any node of its right child. On average, if we build a binary search tree, finding the node with a particular key in it can be done efficiently; just as in the case of binary search described in Section 4.4.

We will give an example of a complete program that inserts, finds, and prints out values of a binary search tree in which the key (and data) at each node is, again, a single character. We will leave deletion for an exercise (and a major project). Since this is a long program we will intersperse additional comments. As usual the code begins with comments and the *.data* segment which contains prompts and messages.

```
# BSTree.s
#
# Binary Search TREE
#
# Node: 3 words:
#        Left (pointer), Data (character), Right (pointer)
#
# Header (pointer) initialized to 0; points to root
#
        .data                           # Data declaration section
title:  .asciiz    "Binary Search Tree Demonstration"
head:   .word      0                # (could have been a register)
prompt: .asciiz    "\nBSTree OP: F, I, D, P, or E: "
error:  .asciiz    "\nUndefined Operation; try again: "
value:  .asciiz    "\nWhat (character) value? "
nofmsg: .asciiz    "\nThat value is not in the BSTree "
fmsg:   .asciiz    "\nThe value was found "
noI:    .asciiz    "\nThat value is already in the BSTree "
Emsg:   .asciiz    "\nThe tree is empty "
Pmsg:   .asciiz    "\nBSTree: "
bye:    .asciiz    "\nGoodbye! "
```

Note that we have again decided to use a "header" but this time not to have it in the same format as the nodes (just to show that it is not necessary to do so). The comment explains the format of each node. We have again used an entire word for the character data section of the node in order to avoid alignment problems.

The *.text* segment contains the main loop which repeatedly prompts the user for the function desired.

```
        .text
main:                               # Start of code section
        li      $v0,4
```

```
            la        $a0,title
            syscall
loop:       li        $v0,4
            la        $a0,prompt
            syscall                   # Print prompt
            li        $v0,12          # No MIPSter
            syscall                   # Get reply
            andi      $v0,$v0,0xFF    # Mask character
# Condensed tests for legal character (save source space)
  beq $v0,'F',F; beq $v0,'f',F; beq $v0,'I',I; beq $v0,'i',I
  beq $v0,'D',D; beq $v0,'d',D; beq $v0,'P',P; beq $v0,'p',P
  beq $v0,'E',E; beq $v0,'e',E
# Not a legal request
            li        $v0,4
            la        $a0,error
            syscall
            j         loop            # main interface loop
```

Just to show that it is possible, we have demonstrated how to put more than one
assembler language statement on a line. One separates them by a semi-colon (";"). While
it is usually very bad practice to do this, one might feel it worth the possible problems
just to save a little space on one's program listing. The code generated is just the same so
there are no real savings as far as length of code is concerned.

Since we defined a binary search tree recursively, we will give the code corresponding to
the "print" command in recursive form. As emphasized in Chapter 7, one almost does not
have to think about the transformation from definition to code. The only decision we
have made is to print the data at each node after all the data in its left child is printed and
before all the data in its right child. The only special case is the one when the tree is
totally empty (the header pointer is zero) and we will print out a special message when
that happens.

```
            # PRINT
            P:
            la        $a0,head
            lw        $t0,0($a0)      # what's in header
            beqz      $t0,Pempty      # special empty tree case
            la        $a0,Pmsg        # \
            li        $v0,4           #  > print heading
            syscall                   # /
            move      $a0,$t0         # $a0 → root
            jal       PFrec           # call the recursive function
            j         loop
Pempty:     li        $v0,4           # make this a special case
            la        $a0,Emsg        # so recursive function can
            syscall                   # always expect the root node
            j         loop
#
# Print Function (recursive)
# $a0 → root node [not header since it is not a node]
# Recursive implementation
# Inorder traversal (Left-Node-Right)
#
PFrec:                                # ← entry point
```

```
            sub       $sp,$sp,16       #\
            sw        $a0,0($sp)       # \
            sw        $v0,4($sp)       #   > save registers
            sw        $ra,8($sp)       # /
            sw        $t0,12($sp)      #/
# Basecase
            beqz      $a0,PFret        # root pointer zero
# Left
            move      $t0,$a0
            lw        $a0,0($a0)
            jal       PFrec            # recursive call
            move      $a0,$t0
# Node
            move      $t0,$a0
            lw        $a0,4($a0)       # print the character
            li        $v0,11           # at the node
            syscall
            move      $a0,$t0
# Right
            move      $t0,$a0
            lw        $a0,8($a0)
            jal       PFrec            # recursive call
            move      $a0,$t0
# Return
PFret:      lw        $t0,12($sp)      #\
            lw        $ra,8($sp)       # \
            lw        $v0,4($sp)       #   > restore registers
            lw        $a0,0($sp)       # /
            add       $sp,$sp,16       #/
            jr        $ra
```

Writing the recursive function *PFrec* is so straightforward just because it is recursive. In the exercises we will also consider printing (traversing) the tree in different orders.

Another operation the user may desire is to find out whether a key appears in the tree. We will use an auxiliary function *FF* to perform this chore since we will need to find out where to place a new key when we come to the insert operation.

Although we could write *FF* easily as a recursive function, we will only give the result of changing a tail-recursive version into a loop. Note that finding a key in a binary search tree only requires using at most one of the two pointers at each node and so is like traversing a linked list. Here is the code for the find operation.

```
    # FIND
    F:
            li        $v0,4
            la        $a0,value
            syscall                    # prompt for (char) value
            li        $v0,12           # no MIPSter
            syscall                    # puts (char) value in $v0
            move      $a1,$v0
            la        $a0,head
            jal       FF               # call on FF function
            bltz      $v0,Fempty       # empty tree
```

```
                lw        $v0,4($v0)
                bne       $v0,$a1,notin # wrong character
# found
                li        $v0,4         # for debug purposes
                la        $a0,fmsg      # usually just return
                syscall                 # pointers
                j         loop
# not found
notin:  li        $v0,4         # for debug purposes
                la        $a0,nofmsg    # usually just return
                syscall                 # flag like -1
                j         loop
# empty tree
Fempty: li        $v0,4         # for debug purposes
                la        $a0,Emsg      # usually just return
                syscall                 # a special flag
                j         loop


#
# Find Function (not recursive)
# $a0 → Header; $a1 = key (character)
# returns address of Node containing character in $v0
# or whose child it should be or -1 if empty tree
# In $v1 will be put the parent of $v0 if it exists
# (for "delete" purposes only)
#
FF:                                     # ← entry point
                sub       $sp,$sp,4     # save register
                sw        $t0,0($sp)    # just $t0 changed
                li        $v0,-1        # initialize return
                li        $v1,-1        # initialize return
                lw        $t0,0($a0)    # what's in header
                beqz      $t0,FFreturn  # empty tree
                move      $v0,$t0       # $v0 → root ($v1=-1)
FFloop: lw        $t0,4($v0)    # get character
                blt       $a1,$t0,FFleft
                bgt       $a1,$t0,FFright
                b         FFreturn      # equal, so found
FFleft: lw        $t0,0($v0)    # get left pointer
                beqz      $t0,FFreturn
                move      $v1,$v0       # fix parent
                move      $v0,$t0       # go down
                b         FFloop
FFright: lw        $t0,8($v0)    # get right pointer
                beqz      $t0,FFreturn
                move      $v1,$v0       # fix parent
                move      $v0,$t0       # go down
                b         FFloop
FFreturn:sw        $t0,0($sp)    # restore register
                add       $sp,$sp,4     # just $t0
                jr        $ra
```

As noted in the comments, in addition to returning a pointer to the node containing the desired character, we also treat the case when the character does not appear but we want to know where to place it during the insertion operation. The additional information concerning a pointer to the parent of the node is needed when deleting a node.

Remember, the parent is pointing to the node that is to be removed and it must be changed. Unless we have extra back pointers (just as with linked lists), we cannot find the parent node easily.

The insertion operation can now take advantage of the FF function as follows.

```
# INSERT
I:
            li      $v0,4
            la      $a0,value
            syscall                 # prompt for value
            li      $v0,12          # no MIPSter
            syscall                 # puts value in $v0
            move    $a1,$v0         # $a1 has value to insert
            la      $a0,head
            jal     FF              # use find (FF) function
            bltz    $v0,Iempty      # was empty tree
#
            lw      $t0,4($v0)      # get character at $v0
            blt     $a1,$t0,IL      # into left child
            bgt     $a1,$t0,IR      # into right child
# equal, so already there
            li      $v0,4           # print already
            la      $a0,noI         # there message
            syscall
            j       loop
# insert into right child
IR:         move    $t1,$v0         # save old node pointer
            li      $v0,9           # getmem
            li      $a0,12          # 3 words (initially 0)
            syscall                 # $v0 → new node
            sw      $a1,4($v0)      # put char in proper place
            sw      $v0,8($t1)      # right pointer fixed
            j       loop
# insert into left child
IL:         move    $t1,$v0         # save old node pointer
            li      $v0,9           # getmem
            li      $a0,12          # 3 words (initially 0)
            syscall                 # $v0 → new node
            sw      $a1,4($v0)      # put char in proper place
            sw      $v0,0($t1)      # left pointer fixed
            j       loop
# empty tree
Iempty:     li      $v0,9           # getmem
            li      $a0,12          # 3 words (initially 0)
            syscall                 # $v0 → new node
            sw      $v0,head        # head → root
            sw      $a1,4($v0)      # put char there
            j       loop
```

The insertion function uses the new *syscall* we labeled "malloc" as expected. The final parts of the complete *BSTree.s* program are the (unimplemented) delete operation:

```
# DELETE
# NOT implemented yet (exercise project)
```

```
            .data
notimp:     .asciiz    "\nDelete function not implemented\n"
            .text
D:
            li         $v0,4
            la         $a0,notimp
            syscall
            j          loop
```

and the usual exit operation:

```
# EXIT
E:          li         $v0,4
            la         $a0,bye
            syscall
            li         $v0, 10         # exits program
            syscall
```

Now that we have given a complete example of a Binary Search Tree, let us take a moment to consider why a "multi-way" tree would be even more useful rather than the "2-way" tree demonstrated here. The nodes of a multi-way tree would be larger, containing many (16, 32, 64, or more) pointers rather than just 2 and many (15, 31, 63, or more) keys.

At each node, we would think of the format being

$$P_0 \, K_1 \, P_1 \, K_2 \, P_2 \, ... \, K_n \, P_n$$

where each P_i is a pointer and each K_i a key where the values of the keys increase from left to right. Each pointer P_i points to a subtree containing only keys between K_i and K_{i+1} (with P_0 pointing to the subtree with keys all less than K_1 and P_n pointing to the subtree with keys all greater than K_n). Not every node will have all its possible keys and pointers.

The advantage comes from the fact that getting data from secondary storage (and even memory) is much slower than the time needed to do calculations within the processor. In particular, if trying to read data from a computer's hard drive, there is a tremendous amount of latency time involved. That is, time that must be spent even before any data is transferred. Ignoring any calculation time in the processor, the reading head must be moved over the disk until it is over the correct track (*i.e.*, at the correct distance from the center). That's a mechanical movement that must be done extremely accurately and takes ages compared to the nanosecond times of the processor. After that, the system must wait until the desired data has rotated to be under the reading head; on average, one-half turn of the disk. Only after all that can reading actually start and that goes quite quickly compared to the other operations. For that reason, most systems actually read much more than is requested and put the results in a buffer from which other values can be taken if further requests come for them.

The effect for trees is that an entire large node can usually be read at one time (even if hidden from the programmer) and it takes almost no more time for nearby data to be made available. We will investigate this in Chapter Eleven.

Exercises

1. Make a linked list containing deleted nodes and look in that list first for a new node when inserting.

2. Write programs to demonstrate "post order" (Left-Right-Node) and "pre order" (Node-Left-Right) traversals of a Binary Search Tree.

3. Describe what happens if one inserts letters in alphabetical order into a Binary Search Tree.

4. For data that is very static (few insertions or deletions), a **Hash Table** can be even more efficient than a Binary Search Tree. One must devise an easily calculated function (the **hash function**) taking keys into addresses (or indices into an array) that can be used to find a key in a table directly. Examples of static data would be the periodic table or the list of planets. Devise a (perfect) hash function taking the names of the 10 planets into 10 different integers 0-9. In most cases a less-than-perfect hash function that is very quick is used and various methods are devised to deal with the cases of two or more keys having the same hash value (called a "collision").

5. Implement the "Delete" function for a BSTree.

CHAPTER NINE

Floating-point Numbers

So far we have only treated numbers that are integers. As we saw, their size (assuming a 32-bit 2's-complement representation) is limited to the range of -2,147,483,648 to +2,147,483,647. For scientific purposes, even larger numbers are necessary. At the other end of the scale, very small numbers (anything less than one in absolute value!) play an equally important role. While there are many possible ways to obtain a wider range and finer accuracy than considering only the nearest integer, we will concentrate on the representation standardized by the IEEE in 1985 and rather universally used.

9.1 IEEE-754 Standard

We should be used to what is called "scientific notation" from courses in chemistry and physics. For example, Avogadro's number is about 6.023×10^{23} atoms/mole and Planck's constant is near 6.62×10^{-27} erg-seconds. The general rule in decimal notation is to pick a power of 10 for which there is exactly one non-zero digit to the left of the decimal point. Such numbers are called "**normalized**." Thus, from the choice of

$$\ldots, 6023 \times 10^{20}, 602.3 \times 10^{21}, 60.23 \times 10^{22}, \underline{6.023 \times 10^{23}}, 0.6023 \times 10^{24}, 0.06023 \times 10^{25}, \ldots$$

we will pick the representation used above.

The same rule will be applied to binary numbers. Each non-zero number will be written as a 1 to the left of the binary point, a binary fraction to its right, all multiplied by a power of two. For example, 25.75_{DEC} would be 11001.11_{BIN} or $1.100111_{BIN} \times 2^4$ in normalized form. Conversions between base 10 and base 2 are quite straightforward.

The next question is how to represent these numbers in a computer. Much careful analysis was made about that problem and in 1985 a standard was agreed to under the direction of the IEEE. Assuming a 32-bit word, the decision must be made as to what the various bits stand for. As with integers, one bit must be used to indicate the sign of the number and, again, bit 31 will be used for that purpose. Now the other 31 bits must be assigned.

Clearly, the choice must be how many are to be assigned to the exponent of 2 and how many (the remainder) to the binary fraction part of the number, often called the **mantissa**. The more we allow in the exponent, the larger and smaller the numbers can be. The more we allow in the mantissa, the more accurate our approximations will be. Obviously, we must trade off between range and accuracy.

The choice made by the numerical analysts was to use 8 bits for the exponent part and the remaining 23 bits for the fractional part. Just to show how important each bit is, it was noted that every non-zero number had a single 1 to the left of the binary point. Since it must be there, it need not actually appear in the word. Thus, bits 22 down to 0 are the binary fractional part of the number with "1." understood before it. Thus there is the equivalent of 24 bits of accuracy rather than just 23 bits!

The choice just made affects the other 8 exponent bits from 30 down to 23, however. There are just 256 different bit patterns for those bits and again we must decide on their meanings. Both positive and negative exponents are needed and two's complement representation would have worked, but that wasn't the decision for various reasons. As unsigned integers, those 8 bits would be representations of numbers from 0 to 255. In order to allow negative exponents, a **bias** of -127 is applied to these numbers. That is, 127 is subtracted from the unsigned value giving a range of exponents of the base 2 from -127 to +128.

In summary, the form of a non-zero floating-point number will be

$$(-1)^S \times 2^{E-127} \times (1.M)$$

where S is the sign bit (31), E is the exponent field (30-23) as an unsigned integer, and M is the mantissa (22-0).

The number zero does not have a 1 before the binary bit and so could not be expressed in this way. Another detail was added to the rules. The unbiased exponents of 0 and 255 were reserved for special cases. For example, a zero exponent is associated with the floating-point number 0.0 and some "unnormalized" numbers smaller than those that can be expressed in normalized form. They have the general form $(-1)^S \times 2^{E-127} \times (0.M)$. The exponent 11111111_{BIN} is associated with such special values as "infinity" and "NotANumber" (0/0, for example). We will not go into these special values in any detail since the regular numbers are interesting enough. They are the "floats" of C/C++/Java.

In case the 24-bit accuracy is not sufficient, **double precision** numbers were also defined. They use two consecutive words (64 bits) in a similar way. The high order bit of the first word is the sign bit as before. The next 11 bits of the first word are the exponent of 2 biased by -1023. Finally, the remaining 52 bits consisting of the last 20 bits of the first word and all the 32 bits of the second word are the fractional part with an understood "1." in front as before. The unbiased exponents of 0 and 1024 are reserved for special cases as with single precision numbers. The general form of these numbers is

$$(-1)^S \times 2^{E-1023} \times (1.MW_2)$$

where S is the sign bit (31) from the first word, E is the exponent field (30-20) from the first word as an unsigned integer, M is the mantissa field (19-0) of the first word which is concatenated with W_2, the entire second word. These are the "doubles" of C/C++/Java.

9.2 Examples

The number $25.75_{DEC} = 1.100111_{BIN} \times 2^4$ described above has an exponent of $4 = 131 - 127$ and a fractional part of $.100111_{BIN}$. Since $131_{DEC} = 10000011_{BIN}$ and the number is positive, the full representation of that floating-point number would be

$$25.75_{DEC} = 0\ 10000011\ 10011100000000000000000_{BIN} = 0x41CE0000$$

Starting with the floating-point representation of a number such as

$$1\ 01111100\ 01011000000000000000000_{BIN} = 0xBE2C0000$$

we see that the sign bit is on and so the number is negative. The exponent bits form the unsigned integer 124 and so, after subtracting 127, the exponent of 2 is -3. Putting the understood "1." in front of the fractional part we get 1.01011_{BIN}, which means $1 + 1/4 + 1/16 + 1/32 = 43/32$. Multiplying by $2^{-3} = 1/8$, we get the fraction $43/256$ or the decimal number -0.16796875_{DEC} as our final answer. PCSPIM can do these calculations for us so we will not practice many of them by hand.

An important example we should consider immediately is the decimal value $1/10 = 0.1_{DEC}$. A simple method for converting base ten fractions to base two is to repeatedly double the fractional part of the value and take the integer part (0 or 1, obviously) as the next bit. Thus, we obtain (0).2, (0).4, (0).8, (1).6, (1).2, (0).4, (0).8, (1).6, (1).2, (0).4, (0).8, (1).6, etc. The binary fraction, then, is

$$0.000110011001..._{BIN} = 2^{-4} \times 1.10011001..._{BIN}\ ,$$

obviously a repeating fraction. When we try to represent this number we must truncate it to as many bits are available. In normalized IEEE-754 form we would have

$$+2^{123-127}(1 + .10011001..._{BIN}) = 0\ 01111011\ 10011001100110011001110?_{BIN}$$

where the last place is in question since there must be round-off error when truncating a repeating fraction of this type. The bit in the question mark place is a zero but the next bit would be a one. That means that the remainder would be more than one-half and so we should round the value to a one in the last place. Our final answer would be

$$0.1_{DEC} \approx 0\ 01111011\ 10011001100110011001101_{BIN} = 0x3DCCCCCD$$

This number is slightly more than $1/10$ but $0x3DCCCCCC$ is slightly less than $1/10$. We cannot express the simple fraction $1/10$ exactly in our binary system! We have, however, exactly expressed the fraction $13421773/134217728$ (check this!).

In many computers there are additional bits carried along with the stated 32 to improve the accuracy of computations. That is a subject of more advanced study. For us the important thing is that no matter how many bits are used, there will be errors in our values since not all numbers can be exactly represented. Indeed, only at most 2^{32} different numbers could possibly be represented with only 32 bits. Doing everything in double precision may be more accurate (and slower), but is not the entire answer since, again, not all values can be represented.

9.3 Extremes

Since one of the reasons for using floating-point numbers rather than just integers was to extend the range of values which could be described, we will now consider exactly what the largest and smallest values available are. Using the 32-bit IEEE-754 standard, we must remember that the unbiased exponents of 0 and 255 are reserved so the smallest we may use is 1 and the largest 254.

The smallest (positive) number would have an unbiased exponent field of 00000001_{BIN} and a mantissa of all zeros. The true exponent of 2 would be $1-127 = -126$ while the fractional part would be just the virtual "1." we assume present. In other words, the decimal value of the smallest positive number would be $2^{-126}(1.0) \approx 1.175494351 \times 10^{-38}$.

It is interesting to also consider what would be the very next larger positive number that can be represented. The unbiased exponent would still be 1 but the fraction would have a 1 in the last place, corresponding to a term of 2^{-23}. The result, then, is

$$2^{-126}(1 + 2^{-23}) = 2^{-126} + 2^{-149} \approx 1.175494211 \times 10^{-38},$$

the numbers differing by about $1.401298464 \times 10^{-45}$. Notice that the smallest and the next larger number agree in their first seven digits (1175494). We would say that they are the same to seven[1] "significant figures."

At the other end of the range of values, the largest positive number would have an unbiased exponent of 254 so the true exponent would be $254-127=127$. The fractional part would have all ones and the number would look like

$$0\ 11111110\ 11111111111111111111111_{BIN} = \text{0x7F7FFFFF}$$

Recognizing the positions in the fraction stand for negative powers of two, we see that if we add one in the last or least significant position (2^{-23}) to the number, we would get a sum of 2 (since there is already a virtual "1." in front of the fraction). Putting these facts together we have the value

$$2^{127} \times (2 - 2^{-23}) = 2^{128} - 2^{104} \approx 3.402823669 \times 10^{38} - 2.028240960 \times 10^{31}$$

and that is approximately $3.402823466 \times 10^{38}$.

---

[1] Since $\log_{10} 2 \approx 0.30103$, the number of bits available (24) times that is just over 7 and that's an easy way to estimate the decimal accuracy of any such calculation. Thus, the 53 bits available in double precision means we should have almost 16 significant figures in our calculations.

Now let us find the very next (smaller) number in this representation. It would look like 0x7F7FFFFE, differing by having a zero in the last place. The calculation we just did tells us that the change will be the value of 2^{104} found above or about $2 \times 10^{31,}$ which is a very large number. The fact that any number in the entire range of over 10^{31} reals from one number to the next must be rounded-off to one of these numbers differing by so much is surprising. On the other hand, we note that we still have the same seven significant figures as we had before!

While there can be no exact representation of all the integers between the largest and the next largest number, it is interesting to note that every integer less than 16,777,216 has an exact IEEE-754 representation. It is an exercise to show why that is true.

9.4 Exceptions

Although we now can express numbers over a very large range, it is still possible to have the same **overflow** problem we had with integers. If the result of a calculation (or any of its intermediate steps) is larger in size than the $3.402823466 \times 10^{38}$ we found above, the system must take some special action. As with integers, the behavior of a system depends on the hardware and software involved. In some cases an exception is raised (as in Java's *try-catch* statements) and can be handled by special code written by the programmer. In other cases the hardware may automatically transfer control to code in the operating system that may or may not allow the program to continue.

With floating-point numbers there is another problem that can arise. The result of a calculation (or, again, any of its intermediate steps) may be smaller in size than the $1.175494351 \times 10^{-38}$ we calculated above. If that happens, we say that **underflow** has occurred. Again the behavior of the system depends on both the hardware and the software involved.

A very frustrating situation can occur when one's program contains a loop in which better and better approximations to the correct answer are being calculated. The error term is getting smaller and smaller. On some systems the language/compiler/OS/hardware combination is such that if the approximation gets too good, the error term causes underflow and the program is aborted without any way for the user to retrieve that excellent approximation. (See Chapter 12 for more on exceptions.)

9.5 Accuracy

Unlike integers in which their arithmetic is exact, the operations of addition, subtraction, multiplication, and division will usually yield only approximations to the correct answer. As we saw above, we cannot represent 0.1_{DEC} exactly and so adding it to itself 10 times will probably not yield 1.0_{DEC} exactly. Consider the simple *for-loop*s in C/C++/Java pseudo-code:

```
for (float x = 0.0; x < 1.0; x + 0.1) {do something involving x}
```

versus

```
for (int i = 0; i < 10; i++) {do something involving x=i/10.0;}
```

While the second will definitely loop ten times, the first might not! In fact, an even more dangerous idea is to test two float numbers for equality. While we could replace $i < 10$ by $i != 10$, the expression $x != 1.0$ would probably always be true and give us an infinite loop! As a general rule in C/C++/Java, never test floats for equality!

As mentioned before, we will not spend time now on hand calculations that involve floating-point numbers since the MIPS processor actually supports them and the SPIM simulator allows us to use them quite easily. However, even before writing programs which use floating-point numbers in the next chapter, we can consider another major problem that can occur with them.

Suppose we are doing decimal calculations involving $\pi = 3.141592654\ldots$ and also a very accurate fractional approximation $355/113 = 3.14159292\ldots$. [Note: That's a lot better than 22/7.] If we actually have, as calculated above, just 7 significant digits, these two values would be stored as 3.141593 and 3.141593 – exactly the same! Indeed, if we were able to store them to 8 significant figures, they would be 3.1415927 and 3.1415929. Their difference would be 0.0000002 a figure with just 1 significant digit in it!

This behavior is called **catastrophic cancellation**. When we take the difference between two numbers of approximately the same size, we lose significant digits in the answer. The ill-conditioned Hilbert matrices are an excellent example of this problem. The n-th Hilbert matrix is defined to be

1	1/2	1/3	...	1/n
1/2	1/3	1/4	...	1/(n+1)
1/3	1/4	1/5	...	1/(n+2)
...	...	...	...	...
1/n	1/(n+1)	1/(n+2)	...	1/(2n-1)

Expanding the determinant of such a matrix we find it has $n!$ terms, half positive and half negative, and all about the same size. Trying to calculate the determinant of even small cases of the Hilbert matrix is difficult.

A common behavior is using $22/7 = 3.142857143\ldots$ and keeping all those figures past the third when approximating π. The problem is that a computer will print out the same large number of digits, even if most of them are meaningless. That leads people to believe in their accuracy quite unjustifiably.

Let us look at the simple act of adding two floating-point numbers together. If their sizes are nearly the same, we saw above that subtracting can cause loss of precision. Now suppose that the two numbers are quite different in size and we wish to add them. Since they are assumed to be different in size, their exponents will be very different. In order to add them we must first shift the smaller one (with the smaller exponent) to the right, thus "un-normalizing" it, until it has the same exponent as the larger. Only then can we add the fractional parts. That result may need renormalization but that is easy to do. The problem is that when we shifted the smaller number right we may have lost some of the important information those lower bits contained. Obviously, if the numbers differ by more than the seven significant decimal digits we have, the smaller will look just like zero!

*9.6 Fixed-point Numbers

While the floating-point numbers have the advantage in range, the integers we considered earlier had the advantage of allowing for exact calculations. Our integers in two's complement form are just one example of another general way in which we may represent numbers in a computer. **Fixed-point** numbers are used in many Digital Signal Processing (DSP) systems [but NOT the MIPS processor we are studying].

Since they are not really part of our use of MIPS as an example for the study of assembler and computer architecture, we will introduce them as they would appear on a 16-bit machine just to emphasize this point. A general notation for a fixed-point format is $m.n$ ($mQ.n$ and Qn are also used in the literature) where m is the number of bits (including a sign bit) assumed to the left of the binary point and n is the number of bits to the right. Thus, $m+n$ always equals the total number of bits available (we will use 16 here).

For negative numbers we will still use the two's complement method of representation. Thus, the 16-bit integers may be considered fixed-point numbers with format 16.0; all sixteen bits appear before the virtual binary point. Were we to need to consider exact calculations concerning dollars and cents, we might use the equivalent of a 14.2 format in a decimal computer, carrying two digits after the decimal point.

In many cases, we know that our data is of absolute value less than one (sine or cosine, maybe). An interesting format for such numbers would be 1.15 (also called Q15); one sign bit and 15 fractional bits. Let us consider the details of such numbers.

The largest 16-bit positive fixed-point number expressible in 1.15 format would be 0111111111111111_{BIN}. That is, the sign bit of zero followed by a binary point and the fractional part consisting of all ones. The value of this number would be $1 - 2^{-15} \approx .9999694824_{DEC}$, very close to 1. On the other hand, the smallest positive number would be 0000000000000001_{BIN} whose value is $2^{-15} \approx .00003051757812_{DEC}$.

These numbers act like integers in that each successive number differs by exactly that 2^{-15} we found above and their arithmetic is exact. For many purposes, particularly in DSP calculations, fixed-point numbers fit the problem very well and the hardware should be made available to support such numbers and their calculations. All that we have discussed concerning 16-bit numbers applies to our usual 32-bit numbers. A point to notice is that there are just 65536 different 16-bit patterns and it is up to us to decide how to interpret them.

Exercises

1. Justify the doubling method described for converting decimal fractions to binary.

2. Express 1.0_{DEC} in IEEE-754 form. What is the next larger number expressible in that representation?

3. What integers can be exactly expressed in IEEE-754 form?

4. What is the decimal value of the floating-point number 0xD52C0000?

5. What are the values of the two approximations to 0.1_{DEC} found above?

6. What are the largest and smallest positive numbers in double precision?

7. In C/C++/Java, add up the terms of the infinite series $1 + 1/2 + 1/3 + 1/4 + \ldots$ until the partial sums no longer change. At what point did that happen? What value for the partial sum did you get? What is the correct sum of this infinite series? Try starting at the place you found above and adding them together in reverse order. Is the answer the same?

8. What are the largest and smallest 32-bit fixed-point numbers in 1.31(or Q31) format?

9. Calculate the determinant of some of the small cases of the Hilbert matrices.

CHAPTER TEN

Real Computations

In the early days of computers, there was no hardware support for floating-point computations. If they were needed, software routines had to be written to perform any operations desired. The 8087 chip which was added later and served as a coprocessor to the 8088 processor in the original PC was extremely powerful and demonstrated the advantages of having floating-point numbers fully supported in hardware. Nevertheless, many DSP chips today, although fantastically powerful, only support fixed-point numbers.

The MIPS processor has a floating-point coprocessor with it and so does an excellent job of supporting such computations. In fact, a glance at the "Floating Point" toolbox in MIPSter shows us a long list of built-in operations. Almost all appear in pairs with ".s" and ".d" as suffixes, standing for single-precision and double-precision operations. It is clear that the MIPS coprocessor supports both type operations.

10.1 Floating-point Registers

The floating-point coprocessor, called **coprocessor one** (coprocessor zero is the control processor handling interrupts and exceptions), consists of 32 registers completely distinct from the 32 general-purpose registers described previously. These 32 floating-point registers each contain 32 bits and so can contain one single precision number. They are referred to in assembler as $f0-$f31. These registers may be accessed in pairs in order to have the 64 bits necessary for double-precision numbers. When used in that way, only the even numbered registers $f0, $f2, ... , $f30 may be addressed. Thus, $f0 refers to the 64 bit combination of registers $f0 and $f1 when using them to hold a double-precision number.

When we bring up PCSPIM and scroll down the first window, we find listed the 16 double-precision registers followed by the 32 single-precision registers:

```
                Double Floating Point Registers
    FP0  = 0.000000 FP8  = 0.000000 FP16 = 0.000000 FP24 = 0.000000
    FP2  = 0.000000 FP10 = 0.000000 FP18 = 0.000000 FP26 = 0.000000
    FP4  = 0.000000 FP12 = 0.000000 FP20 = 0.000000 FP28 = 0.000000
    FP6  = 0.000000 FP14 = 0.000000 FP22 = 0.000000 FP30 = 0.000000
                Single Floating Point Registers
    FP0  = 0.000000 FP8  = 0.000000 FP16 = 0.000000 FP24 = 0.000000
    FP1  = 0.000000 FP9  = 0.000000 FP17 = 0.000000 FP25 = 0.000000
    FP2  = 0.000000 FP10 = 0.000000 FP18 = 0.000000 FP26 = 0.000000
    FP3  = 0.000000 FP11 = 0.000000 FP19 = 0.000000 FP27 = 0.000000
```

```
FP4   = 0.000000 FP12 = 0.000000 FP20  = 0.000000 FP28  = 0.000000
FP5   = 0.000000 FP13 = 0.000000 FP21  = 0.000000 FP29  = 0.000000
FP6   = 0.000000 FP14 = 0.000000 FP22  = 0.000000 FP30  = 0.000000
FP7   = 0.000000 FP15 = 0.000000 FP23  = 0.000000 FP31  = 0.000000
```

Notice that by default these registers are displayed as decimal numbers. Should we want to see them in hexadecimal form we may use the "Simulator" pull-down menu to select "Settings…" and check "Floating point registers in hexadecimal". We then see:

```
            Double Floating Point Registers
FP0 =00000000,00000000 FP8 =00000000,00000000
FP16=00000000,00000000 FP24=00000000,00000000
FP2 =00000000,00000000 FP10=00000000,00000000
FP18=00000000,00000000 FP26=00000000,00000000
FP4 =00000000,00000000 FP12=00000000,00000000
FP20=00000000,00000000 FP28=00000000,00000000
FP6 =00000000,00000000 FP14=00000000,00000000
FP22=00000000,00000000 FP30=00000000,00000000
            Single Floating Point Registers
FP0 =00000000 FP8 =00000000 FP16=00000000 FP24=00000000
FP1 =00000000 FP9 =00000000 FP17=00000000 FP25=00000000
FP2 =00000000 FP10=00000000 FP18=00000000 FP26=00000000
FP3 =00000000 FP11=00000000 FP19=00000000 FP27=00000000
FP4 =00000000 FP12=00000000 FP20=00000000 FP28=00000000
FP5 =00000000 FP13=00000000 FP21=00000000 FP29=00000000
FP6 =00000000 FP14=00000000 FP22=00000000 FP30=00000000
FP7 =00000000 FP15=00000000 FP23=00000000 FP31=00000000
```

With nothing loaded, all are zero fields but there is room for exactly 8 hexadecimal characters in the appropriate positions as expected. Notice how the double-precision registers are addressed using only the even register names.

As usual, these 32 registers are also referred to as "general purpose" but, just as in the case of the other 32 registers, some have special meanings. There are *syscall*'s that refer specifically to some of these registers. Here are the final system calls available in PCSPIM and MIPSter for reading and printing floating-point numbers.

Code	Name	Argument and Result Registers
2	print_float	$f12 = float
3	print_double	$f12 (and $f13) = double
6	read_float	;$f0 = float
7	read_double	;$f0 (and $f1) = double

We see that register *$f0* is where a float is placed when read (and in both *$f0* and *$f1* is where a double is placed). Similarly, we must have a float in *$f12* to print it (and in both *$f12* and *$f13* when printing a double).

10.2 Operations

In order to see what instructions are available to the programmer using these registers, we might look in the pull-down toolbox labeled "Floating Point" in MIPSter. Strangely enough, some of the listed instructions are only pseudo-instructions while the actual machine instructions may not be listed. We will consider both types of instructions here. For simplicity, we will treat the single precision operations and leave the corresponding double precision operations for the exercises. The operations may be grouped into a few functional classes.

10.2.1 Load/Store Instructions

Coprocessor 1 of a MIPS computer also has the Load/Store architecture. That is, the only operations that access memory are the load and store ones. In the MIPSter toolbox we find listed the two operations "l.s" and "s.s" which, when double clicked, give

```
l.s   $f, $
s.s   $f, $
```

for single precision numbers (there are double precision versions with ".*d*" suffixes also). The *l.s* is a mnemonic for **Load.Single** and *s.s* stands for **Store.Single**. The "*$f*" indicates that a floating-point register is used in that position while the "*$*" indicates that an *L±D($R)* memory address is expected as the second operand.

In order to test these instructions, let us use MIPSter to write some elementary code. In the *.data* segment we will place the following:

```
        .data
s:      .word      0x41CE0000
x:      .word      0x3DCCCCCD, 0x3DCCCCC7, 0x3DCCCCC6
```

We have chosen some values that we saw in the previous chapter. Now to place them in the floating-point registers we will write in our *.text* segment just a few instructions. It is not necessary to have a complete program that would run in order to use PCSPIM to see the results of some instructions.

```
        .text
l.s        $f0, s
l.s        $f1, x
l.s        $f8, x+4
l.s        $f9, x+8
```

Let us single step (**F10**) through these four instructions and see the results (as always there are six instructions placed by the system preceding our *main* code). The first load places 25.75 in register *$f0* (if the floating-point register is displayed in hexadecimal, go to the "Simulator" pull-down menu and click on "Settings …" to uncheck that box). This show that our calculations in the previous chapter were correct: $25.75_{DEC} = $ 0x41CE0000.

The next single step places 0.100000_{DEC} in register *$f1*. We recall that 0x3DCCCCCD was found to be the closest approximation to the decimal value of 1/10, again checking our work. It is now clear why extensive hand computations were not required in the previous chapter since it is so easy to have the PCSPIM emulator do them for us. Additional single steps load the next two values into registers *$f8* and *$f9*. The display now shows

```
            Single Floating Point Registers
FP0   = 25.7500  FP8  = 0.100000  FP16 = 0.000000 FP24 = 0.000000
FP1   = 0.100000 FP9  = 0.0999999 FP17 = 0.000000 FP25 = 0.000000
```

These last two values are interesting. We mentioned that 0x3DCCCCCC was less than 1/10 and further from it than 0x3DCCCCCD which is larger than 1/10. Just to see what happens we can try still smaller values down to 0x3DCCCCC7 and the system will still find 0.100000_{DEC} as the closest decimal value with six significant digits (all after the decimal point). However, when we try 0x3DCCCCC6, we obtain 0.0999999_{DEC} which is the closest decimal with six significant figures.

It is surprising that the actual code generated by our first statement (*l.s $f0,s*) is assembled into two different instructions. One of them is familiar. The *lui $1,4097* is the usual first step to addressing an address in our data segment which always starts at 0x10010000 and so we **Load** the **Upper** half of *$1* with the **Immediate** 4097_{DEC} as always. Next the assembler calculates how far from the beginning of data segment the specific word begins (zero in the case of *s* and four in the case of *x*). Thus the *D($R)* form of the address of *s* is *0($1)* and of *x* is *4($1)*.

The actual code is

```
[0x00400024]  0x3c011001  lui $1, 4097   ; 32: l.s      $f0, s
[0x00400028]  0xc4200000  lwc1 $f0, 0($1)
```

and this shows that the machine instruction built into the MIPS processor is *lwc1* (Load a **Word** into **Coprocessor 1**). We do not find *lwc1* in the MIPSter list under the "Floating Point" pull-down menu, but it appears under "Load/Store/Move" in the form

```
lwcz $, $
```

where we must replace the "z" by the number "1" of our coprocessor. The first "$" must be filled in by the name of the floating-point register desired while the second "$" is replaced by a legal *L±D($R)* memory address.

When we attempt to use it directly in MIPSter, we can tell that it is not recognized as an operation by the color-coding environment since it remains black. Nevertheless, we may use that instruction directly in PCSPIM or MIPSter and it works fine. Thus, we may add the line

```
lwc1     $f16, s
```

to our code and single step through one more instruction and see

```
                    Single Floating Point Registers
   FP0 = 25.7500   FP8 = 0.100000   FP16 = 25.7500   FP24 = 0.000000
   FP1 = 0.100000  FP9 = 0.0999999  FP17 = 0.000000  FP25 = 0.000000
```

and we have loaded s into $\$f16$, as expected.

The corresponding instructions for storing into memory are available. In fact, the *s.s* (Store.Single) command is actually performed by a *swc1* (Store a **W**ord from **C**oprocessor **1**) instruction. This instruction also appears in the MIPSter toolbox under the "Load/Store/Move" pull-down menu in the form *swcz* where the "z" must be replaced by "1" to indicate coprocessor 1.

For double precision versions of load and store (*l.d* and *s.d*), we find they are accomplished by two calls on *lwc1* or *swc1* and so there are no explicit operations, only those pseudo-operations.

10.2.2 Move Instructions

The "mov.s" instruction listed in the toolbox, when double clicked, places

```
mov.s $f, $f
```

in the code for us to use. The two place holders, "$\$f$", indicate that the move is between two of the floating-point registers. This is equivalent to the instruction used to move values between the general purpose registers in the CPU and has obvious application.

In addition, we need to be able to move values between coprocessor 1 where floating point operations are handled and the CPU's general purpose registers where integer and other operations are handled. The only command like that in the "Floating Point" toolbox is *mfc1.d* and that turns out to be based on one of the two actual move instructions of that form that are implemented:

```
mfc1 $R,$f # Move From Coprocessor 1 register $f to CPU register $R
mtc1 $R,$f # Move To Coprocessor 1 register $f from CPU register $R
```

These are quite obvious in their applicability but be careful of the unusual order of the operands in *mtc1*! Again MIPSter does not color code these as instructions but they do work in PCSPIM and MIPSter. When we experiment with these instructions with commands such as

```
mfc1        $a1, $f0
mtc1        $sp, $f18
```

we find that there is no conversion from a floating point number to or from its integer (2's complement) form. The hexadecimal forms are exactly the same in each processor. We clearly need conversion instructions.

10.2.3 Conversions

In the MIPSter "Floating Point" toolbox we find many conversion instructions. For example there is

```
cvt.w.s $f, $f
```

where the message in the status line of MIPSter tells us that this command will take a (single precision) floating point number in the second floating point register and **ConVerT** it into its corresponding integer (word) format in the first floating point register. It is natural that

```
cvt.s.w $f, $f
```

will convert an integer (word) in a floating point register into a (single precision) floating point number in a floating point register.

There are also conversions involving double precision values that work as expected. On the other hand, there are no "immediate" instructions so any such operand must be placed in one of the floating point registers by loading it into one of the CPU's registers, moving it, and finally converting it.

10.2.4 Arithmetic

There are add, subtract, multiply, and divide three address instructions for floating point numbers similar to those for integers. One of the main differences is that there is no need for extra registers such as HI and LO for multiplications since the value, unless there is overflow, can be held in one register (although with no more precision than the operands). Of course there is also no need for (or meaning that can be given to) a remainder during division.

Negate and absolute value instructions, just as with integers, also are available with two addresses needed.

10.2.5 Branches

While there are many branch instructions based on values in the CPU's general purpose registers (as see in the pull-down menu in MIPSter), there are only two branch instructions based on values in the floating-point registers. In the MIPSter toolbox we find only the following:

```
bc1t label
bc1f label
```

They are based on the fact that there is a bit (usually called a "**flag**") in the control part of the coprocessor (often not directly accessible by the programmer) which is set by any one of a list of compare instructions. The value of that bit – either "true" or "false" depending on the result of the comparison – is used to determine whether or not the branch is to take place. The branch, when taken, means the next instruction is at the position designated by the "*label*". The mnemonics are as follows:

```
bc1t = Branch if the flag in Coprocessor 1 is True
bc1f = Branch if the flag in Coprocessor 1 is False
```

The list of comparisons is not long either. As usual there are two forms, one for single precision and another for double precision, distinguished by the suffixes ".s" and .d". The single precision comparisons we use are as follows in the MIPSter toolbox:

```
c.eq.s $f, $f        # true if first = second, false otherwise
c.le.s $f, $f        # true if first ≤ second, false otherwise
c.lt.s $f, $f        # true if first < second, false otherwise
```

As described, the comparison returns a Boolean: true or false. Of course we really do not need any more than these comparisons. We do not need *c.ne.s* since we could use *bc1f* rather than *bc1t*. In the same way, *c.gt.s* is the negative of *c.le.s* and *c.ge.s* is the negative of *c.lt.s*.

Note: In many computers every arithmetic operation sets some bits in the control part of the processor and they may be used to determine whether to branch or not. In such machines it is vitally important to test for a condition immediately after doing the operation since any other operation will overwrite the previous value. We do not have that problem in MIPS since only the explicit comparison instructions change the bit.

10.3 Examples

10.3.1 Geometric Series

The following code prints out the elements of a geometric series with floating point values for the initial value and the ratio, both of which are supplied by the user.

```
# geoseries_f.s
#
# SPIM code to print out the elements of a geometric series with
# the floating point values of initial value a, ratio r and
# number of terms n read in.
#
# The series is a, ar, ar^2, ar^3, ... , ar^(n-1), a^n
#
####
#       REGISTER USE:
#       $f12   current element - initalized to a and printable
#
#       $f0    input area for syscall 6
#
#       $f2    ratio r
#
#       $s0    number n to be printed (actually n+1)
#
```

```
####
        .data
promp1: .asciiz "Input initial real (float) value: "
promp2: .asciiz "Input ratio real value: "
promp3: .asciiz "How many values to print: "
newln:  .asciiz "\n"
tab:    .asciiz "\t"
#
        .text
main:
#
# Get input
#
# prompt for initial value
        li      $v0, 4          # system call for print_str
        la      $a0, promp1     # address of string to print
        syscall
# read initial value
        li      $v0, 6          # system call for read_float
        syscall                 # a in $f0
        mov.s   $f12, $f0       # put a in register $f12
# prompt for ratio value
        li      $v0, 4          # system call for print_str
        la      $a0, promp2     # address of string to print
        syscall
# read ratio value
        li      $v0, 6          # system call for read_float
        syscall                 # r in $f0
        mov.s   $f2, $f0        # put r in register $f2
# prompt for number value
        li      $v0, 4          # system call for print_str
        la      $a0, promp3     # address of string to print
        syscall
# read number value
        li      $v0, 5          # system call for read_int
        syscall                 # n in $v0
        move    $s0, $v0        # put in register $s0
# initialize counter
        li      $t0, 0
# print initial value
        li      $v0, 1
        move    $a0, $t0
        syscall                 # print count
        li      $v0, 4
        la      $a0, tab
        syscall                 # print tab
        li      $v0, 2          # print_float function
        syscall                 # a is in $f12
        jal     println
        j       loop
####
# Loop with test at beginning (while)
loop:
        bge     $t0,$s0,endloop  # end of loop
        add     $t0,$t0, 1      # increment counter
        li      $v0, 1
        move    $a0, $t0
```

```
                syscall                 # print count
                li      $v0, 4
                la      $a0, tab
                syscall                 # print tab
                mul.s   $f12,$f12,$f2 # next value in $f12
                li      $v0, 2          # print_float function
                syscall
                jal     println
                j       loop
endloop:
####
                li      $v0, 10
                syscall                 # Return control to the OS
####
println:                # subroutine to println saving registers
                sub     $sp,$sp,8       #\
                sw      $a0,0($sp)      # \
                sw      $v0,4($sp)      #  \
                la      $a0,newln       #   \
                li      $v0,4           #    > Print new line
                syscall                 #   /
                lw      $v0,4($sp)      #  /
                lw      $a0,0($sp)      # /
                add     $sp,$sp,8       #/
                jr      $ra             # return
####
```

This simple example uses few of the floating-point instructions but the results are interesting. Note that if we run it under MIPSter we are given six decimal digits after the decimal point, even if the number is stored with greater accuracy (try $a = 1.0$ and $r = 0.5$). Under PCSPIM we get 18 decimal digits printed (try the same values for a and r).

On the other hand, if we put in large values of a and r such as 65536.0 for both, we find 20 significant figures printed by MIPSter and then "*Inf*" for "Infinity" when they are too large to be expressed in IEEE-754 format. In PCSPIM we get 18 significant figures and then the string "*1.#INF00000000000000*" to indicate "Infinity" again.

10.3.2 Calculator

In Section 5.4 we introduced a simple integer calculator to demonstrate the use of a jump table. The limitations on the size of numbers can be avoided by using float (real) numbers. The changes are very simple to implement. We will write the actual calculator function to take floats in registers *$f2* and *$f4* and return the answer in register *$f12* (so it is immediately available for printing). Here is the code:

```
        # calculate-f.s
        #
        # $f2 = first float
        # $f4 = second float
        # $a0 = operation (1=Add,2=Subtract,3=Multiply,4=Divide)
        # NO error checking
        #
                .data
```

```
prompt1: .asciiz    "\nInput a real (float): "
prompt2: .asciiz    "\nInput another real (float): "
help:    .asciiz    "\n 1=ADD, 2=SUB, 3=MUL, 4=DIV, 5=EXIT: "
         .align     4
JumpTable:
         .word      ADD,SUB,MUL,DIV # SPIM figures out where
#
         .text
##################################################################
calculate:                          # ← Entry point
         sub        $sp,$sp,8        # \  Push registers
         sw         $t0,0($sp)       #  > which are changed
         sw         $t1,4($sp)       # /  onto the stack
         la         $t0,JumpTable    # Get address of JumpTable
         sub        $t1,$a0,1        # Zero-based addressing
         sll        $t1,$t1,2        # Multiply by 4 (bytes)
         add        $t0,$t0,$t1      # Place in table
         lw         $t0,0($t0)       # Actual address
         jr         $t0
# switch labels
ADD:     add.s      $f12,$f2,$f4     # Do the addition
         j DONE
SUB:     sub.s      $f12,$f2,$f4     # Do the subtraction
         j DONE
MUL:     mul.s      $f12,$f2,$f4     # Do the multiplication
         j DONE
DIV:     div.s      $f12,$f2,$f4     # Do the division
         j DONE                      # (see below)
# finished; return
DONE:    lw         $t1,4($sp)       # \  Pop registers
         lw         $t0,0($sp)       #  > which were changed
         add        $sp,$sp,8        # /  off the stack
         jr         $ra              # return
##################################################################
main:                               # ← main entry point
         li         $v0,4
         la         $a0,prompt1
         syscall
         li         $v0,6            # read_float
         syscall
         mov.s      $f2,$f0          # 1st in $f2
         li         $v0,4
         la         $a0,prompt2
         syscall
         li         $v0,6            # read_float
         syscall
         mov.s      $f4,$f0          # 2nd in $f4
# calculator calls
loop:    li         $v0,4
         la         $a0,help
         syscall
         li         $v0,5
         syscall
         beq        $v0,5,exit
         move       $a0,$v0          # which operation in $a0
         jal        calculate
         li         $v0,2            # answer is in $f12
```

```
                syscall
                j          loop
    exit:       li         $v0,10
                syscall
```

Since we did not have to move any values between coprocessor 1 and the general purpose registers, and we did not need any conversions, this was a simple exercise.

Note also that the usual convention for passing parameters is to put the arguments in floating point registers $f12 and $f14 and return results in $f0 and $f2. As always, one need not follow the convention but violates it at one's own risk.

10.3.3 Random Numbers

Our treatment of random numbers can also be improved by the availability of real numbers. Required reading for all scientists and engineers should be the article by Park and Miller[1] and the references there. Here is a pseudo-random number generator that gives us 1000 values in the interval (0,1) based on the recommendation of L'Ecuyer.

```
# URAND.s
#
# Uniformly distributed Random Number Generator of L'Ecuyer
# for 32-bit computers. See "Efficient and Portable
# Combined Random Number Generators", CACM 31 (June 1988).
#
            .data                       # Data declaration section
title:      .asciiz    "1000 Random Numbers\n\n"
const:      .float     4.656613e-10
LF:         .asciiz    "\n"
#
            .text
main:                                   # Start of code section
            li         $a1, 31415926 # Initialize
            li         $a2, 27182818 # Seeds Randomly
#
            li         $v0, 4
            la         $a0, title
            syscall                     # Print title
#
            li         $s0, 1000        # How many numbers to print
loop:       beqz       $s0, exit
            jal        urand            # Get next random
            li         $v0, 2           # print_float code
            mov.s      $f12,$f0         # It was in $f0
            syscall                     # Print it
            la         $a0, LF
            li         $v0, 4           # Print Line Feed
            syscall
            sub        $s0, $s0, 1      # Decrement counter
            j          loop
```

---

[1] Stephen K. Park and Keith W. Miller, "Random Number Generators: Good Ones Are Hard To Find," **Communications of the ACM**, vol. 31 # 10 (October 1988), pp. 1192-1201.

```
#
exit:    li        $v0, 10
         syscall
###
urand:                                   # <- Entry point
# Takes two seed values in $a1 and $a2.
# Modifies both of them and returns the
# next random number in $f0 as expected.
# Does not save $t0, $t1, $t2, or $f12.
         div       $t0, $a1, 53668
         mul       $t1, $t0, 53668
         mul       $t2, $t0, 12211
         sub       $a1, $a1, $t1
         mul       $a1, $a1, 40014
         sub       $a1, $a1, $t2
         bgez      $a1, L1
         add       $a1, $a1, 2147483563
L1:      div       $t0, $a2, 52774
         mul       $t1, $t0, 52774
         mul       $t2, $t0, 3791
         sub       $a2, $a2, $t1
         mul       $a2, $a2, 40692
         sub       $a2, $a2, $t2
         bgez      $a2, L2
         add       $a2, $a2, 2147483399
L2:      sub       $t0, $a1, $a2
         blez      $t0, L3
         b         convert
L3:      add       $t0, $t0, 2147483562
#
convert:
         mtc1      $t0, $f0
         cvt.s.w   $f0, $f0
         l.s       $f12, const
         mul.s     $f0, $f12, $f0
#
         jr        $ra
```

All the "magic numbers" used in this program are explained in the articles referenced. Note that almost all the calculations are done with integers and the only use of floating point numbers is in the final "convert" stage. This was all based on the following C/C++/Java-type code:

```
int s1; // Initialized to 1..2147483562
int s2; // Initialized to 1..2147483398
real urand()
{    int z,k;
     k = s1 % 53668;
     s1 = 40018 * (s1 - k * 53668) - k * 12211;
     if (s1 < 0) s1 += 2147483563;
     k = s2 % 52774;
     s2 = 40692 * (s2 - k * 52774) - k * 3791;
     if (s2 < 0) s2 += 2147483399;
     z = s1 - s2;
     if (z < 1) z += 2147483562;
```

```
        return (z * 4.656613e-10);
    }
```

The *urand* function should return a pseudo-random number in the interval $(0,1)$, not repeating itself for over 10^{12} values.

Exercises

1. Rewrite all examples in this chapter to work in double precision.

2. Another recommended generator[2] giving pseudo-random numbers in the range $(0,1)$ starting with a given seed value between 1 and $2^{31}-2 = 2147483646$ has C/C++/Java-type code as follows:

```
real Uniform(int* seed)
{       int a = 16807;
        int m = 2147483647;               // 2^31 - 1
        int q = 127773;                   // m div a
        int r = 2836;                     // m mod a
        int hi, lo, temp;
        lo = seed/q;                      // lo = seed div q
        hi = seed%q;                      // hi = seed mod q
        temp = a* hi - r * lo;
        if (temp > 0) seed = temp;
        else seed = temp + m;
        return( (float) seed / (float) m) ); // integer div gives 0
}
```

    Translate this code into assembler (albeit with lots of code) and test it.

3. Write code to calculate the determinant of some of the small cases of the Hilbert matrix.

4. Note the differences in your results when you use fractions and when you use real numbers in your calculations of the Hilbert matrix or in Problem 7 of Chapter 9.

5. Modify earlier programs such as *Pascal.s* and *Fibonacci.s* to work with real values.

---

[2] Thanks to Dr. Charles "Pete" Bernardin of UT-Dallas for modern random number generator references.

CHAPTER ELEVEN

Caches and Pipelines

The Central Processing Unit (CPU) of today's computers is so fast that a number of problems have arisen in an attempt to take advantage of their speed. For one thing, the access time of memory has not kept pace with the speed of the CPU and so bringing data and instructions from memory has become a bottleneck[1]. The use of cache memory has become absolutely essential in trying to make use of the very fast processor. We will describe that later. First we will consider the other major method of improving performance: pipelining. The basic idea of pipelining is that while the CPU may perform one instruction at a time, different parts of the circuitry may well do the steps of each instruction and so sit idle most of the time. By breaking up each instruction into its component parts, it may be possible to have many instructions being worked on at the same time by a single CPU.

11.1 Pipelining

The usual view of the simple MIPS processor we study is that it has a five-stage **pipeline**. That is, each instruction can be broken up into five separate stages in which specific parts of executing the instruction take place. They are:

IF) Instruction Fetch: The 32 bit instruction is brought from memory into the CPU and decoded. Remember that we pointed out in Section 2.4 that all instructions are the same length so no additional time is needed to figure out exactly what instruction it is so as to be able to calculate where to find the next instruction. In addition, we saw that the first field (bits 31 down to 26) of six bits contains the actual operation code so, again, no time is lost trying to find out exactly what operation is required.

RR) Read from Registers: The five bits needed to address a register are always in the same location so easy to find in both R-type and I-type instructions. J-type instructions do not need this step but the time will be taken so as to keep everything synchronized.

AL) Use the Arithmetic-Logical Unit: Here is what we usually think of as the CPU, but is only a part of the processor. For instructions that do arithmetic or logical operations, they are performed at this time.

---

[1] According to "Moore's Law", processor speeds are doubling every 18 months and this has held true for over twenty years. Memory access time, however, seems to be increasing by a factor of only about 1.2 every 18 months.

MA) Memory **A**ccess: Since the MIPS processor is a Load-Store machine (see Section 2.3), the only operations that access memory are the load and store ones. For all other instructions this step is not necessary but, again, has the time reserved.

WR) Write back to **R**egister: In our 3-address machine, the result of a calculation needs to be written into the appropriate register and that is the last part of the execution of an instruction.

The wiring of the CPU is such that each of these five steps takes place in a different part of the processor. Thus, once an instruction has been fetched, the circuitry for that step is free to start fetching the next instruction in sequence immediately; it does not have to wait until the entire first instruction has been executed. Similarly, the second instruction can start reading from the register file as soon as the first has finished that part of its operation.

A diagram of this pipeline is as follows:

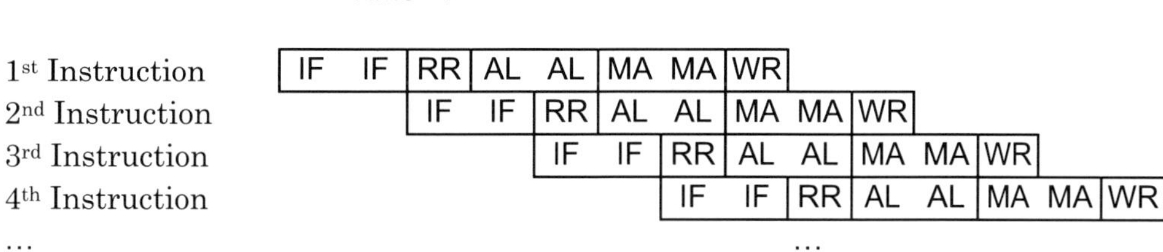

The implication of the figure is that we seem to have increased our performance by a factor of four, but that is unlikely to be the case. Clearly every jump instruction causes the pipeline to have to halt, as the next instruction in sequential order (already fetched) is not the one to be performed. For conditional branches the problem is even more difficult. Until a calculation has been made it is not clear whether the branch is to be taken or not.

Long sequences of code without branches are then best for pipelining. Some processors have even longer pipelines that would seem to multiply their performance by an even larger number but they are then even more likely to encounter a branch instruction that "breaks" the pipeline. As with almost everything in computer design, a balance must be taken between the desire for a longer pipeline and the occurrences of branches.

11.2 Delayed Branches

There are many methods used to improve the pipeline performance of processors when faced with branch instructions. Complicated prediction hardware and software may try to determine the likelihood of the branch being taken from past experience. One very simple method is used in the MIPS processor and emulated in PCSPIM so we can experiment with it. When the MIPS processor comes to a branch instruction the next instruction in sequence has already been fetched. The decision was made to have that instruction executed regardless of whether the branch is to be taken or not! The instruction after a branch instruction is said to be in its **Branch Delay Slot (BDS)**. If the branch is to be taken, the branch is delayed until after that instruction is executed. Of course the instruction after the branch instruction is certainly executed if the branch is not taken.

Consider the following simple code:

```
# BDS.s   Branch Delay Slot example

        .data                   # Data declaration section
title:  .asciiz   "\nBranch Delay Slot test\n"
strt1:  .asciiz   "\n$t1 = "
strt2:  .asciiz   "\t$t2 = "

        .text

main:                           # Start of code section
        li        $v0,4         # print_str
        la        $a0,title
        syscall

        li        $t1,0         # Initialize
        li        $t2,0         # Initialize
        li        $t3,10        # Limit test

loop:
        bge       $t1,$t3,exit
        nop                     # BDS
        la        $a0,strt1
        li        $v0,4         # print_str
        syscall
        move      $a0,$t1
        li        $v0,1         # print_int
        syscall
        la        $a0,strt2
        li        $v0,4         # print_str
        syscall
        move      $a0,$t2
        li        $v0,1         # print_int
        syscall

        add       $t1,$t1,1     # increment $t1
        b         loop          # Next is BDS
        add       $t2,$t2,1     # increment $t2 ?

exit:
        li        $v0,10        # exits program
        syscall

# END OF BDS.s
```

When this is run under PCSPIM with the check box "Delayed Branches" not marked, the register *$t2* is never incremented (as one would expect) since the *add* instruction is preceded by an unconditional branch instruction. However, if we check off "Delayed Branches" in the "Settings" menu, we see that the *add* instruction is executed!

This odd behavior is how the real MIPS processor actually works! When programming for it, we must be careful to rearrange our code so that we want the instruction immediately after a branch to be executed regardless of whether or not the branch is taken. If we cannot find anything useful to do in that BDS, we must insert a *nop* (**N**o **OP**eration) pseudo-instruction in that spot. The common term for this *nop* is a **bubble** or a **pipeline stall** and the hardware itself often is designed to insert such delays when necessary.

Of course the *nop* takes up time in the pipeline and accomplishes no real work. It should be avoided if possible. One more difficult problem for the compiler writer is to look for ways to use the BDS. Indeed, the best MIPS assemblers have directives *.reorder* and *.noreorder* available to ask it to try to rearrange our code (or not to) so as to take advantage of any BDS's rather than always inserting a *nop* instruction.

Notice that we have introduced many *nop* instructions in our *PGAexceptions.s* code in Appendix C so that it will work regardless of the "Delayed Branches" setting.

In order for the time of this one instruction to be helpful, additional hardware must be inserted into the processor. While the first instruction has been fetched and decoded in its first stage, its registers must be accessed during its second stage but then the system cannot wait until the third stage to use the ALU to calculate the result. This problem is termed a **control hazard** and again may require the system to insert "bubbles" into the pipeline. One solution is for extra comparison hardware separate from the ALU to be added to immediately decide whether to take the branch or not and so what to fetch for the third instruction (while the second executes in the BDS).

11.3 Caches

In order for the pipelining to be successful in speeding up processing, the architecture of the machine must be such as to allow some simultaneous operations to take place. One of the decisions made early in the design of the MIPS processor is to have separate data paths for the instructions and for the data[2]. Since the instructions to be performed also must be loaded from memory, we would not want to delay the accessing of data from memory. We can see the possibility of this **structural hazard** in our diagram of the pipeline. When the fourth instruction is fetching the actual instruction from memory, the first instruction is in its memory access mode.

Even that is not nearly enough to allow a pipeline to work efficiently. We must arrange for both instructions and data to be accessible very quickly. Very fast memory is both expensive and consumes much power. Only a small amount of it can be afforded. There is a direct relationship between the speed and the cost of memory. We can afford a great deal of slow memory, somewhat less of faster memory, and little very fast memory.

---

[2] If there are separate memories and data busses for instructions and data we say that the processor has the "Harvard Architecture". The "Von Neumann Architecture" has one memory for both instructions and data.

The solution used universally is to have **cache** memory. There are often a few levels of cache (referred to as L-1 cache, L-2 cache, etc.) and they correspond to the various speeds described above. There would be a very small amount of very fast memory, more somewhat slower memory, and quite a lot of slow memory. The very fast memory used for caches is so important that more than one half the area on a chip may now be allocated to it.

When a program is to be run it may reside on the system's hard disk (rather slow memory). It may then be loaded into what we usually think of as the computer's "memory", now often measured in gigabytes. When it begins execution, code and data are brought into registers but also into smaller areas of much faster memory. These areas are called "caches" and there are separate ones for instructions (I-cache) and data (D-cache). As long as there is room in the caches, instructions and data may be inserted into them and then fetched very quickly from them by the CPU when needed again. Thus it avoids additional accesses to regular memory. Execution is accelerated when an entire loop, for example, or successive elements of data are already in the cache. When trying to fetch the next instruction or needed data, the system first looks into the cache (a rather complicated operation) and, if it is there, may retrieve it very quickly. It is then that the pipeline can progress at its maximum speed.

Whenever the next instruction is not in the cache, however, the pipeline must be stopped while the cache is filled with the correct instruction. If the cache is full, an algorithm must be used that decides what is to be removed from the cache to make room for the required instruction. This and other related subjects are studied in Operating Systems courses.

Similar problems occur with respect to the data used by a program. When data is to be used the system first looks into its data cache. Again a problem arises if the needed data is not in the cache. Again the details of how much slower accessing, for example, the hard disk is compared with memory access are discussed in Operating System classes. We should only note that with a mechanical device such as a disk, there is a tremendous amount of "latency" time involved. That is, the time it takes the device to be ready to transmit the required data. It includes the time to move the reading head over the correct track of data and the rotation time for the data to come under the reading head. In comparison to the nanosecond speeds of today's processors, these times are incredibly long. For that reason, once the head is over the requested data, it invariably reads an entire segment of data into a buffer (just like cache) so it is available more quickly if it is needed.

It is well known that "locality" is a very important feature of computer programs. With both instructions and data, experiments show that accesses are usually to "nearby" elements. If a pipeline is to proceed at maximum speed, we must find what is needed in the cache (called a "hit") rather than have to go out to slower systems (a "miss"). The ratio of "hits" to accesses turns out to often be in the high 90 per cent range. Unfortunately, it must be very high or else the pipeline fails to be useful.

When regular memory is accessed, the same "locality" feature leads to moving a larger amount of data into the cache than is actually needed immediately. Thus, a new word request probably is met by bringing in at least four words in sequential order.

11.4 Delayed Loads

Another problem can arise in regard to data access even from registers. We might have an instruction that is to write a new value into a register followed immediately by an instruction that uses that new value. Our diagram of the MIPS pipeline shows us that writing into a register is the last thing done (5th stage) and is much too late for the next instruction to read that value in its 2nd stage. This, and similar problems are called **data hazards**.

For example, the code

```
add $t0,$t1,$t2
add $t3,$t0,$t4
```

causes a data hazard. The second *add* instruction needs the new value of *$t0* to work properly.

A careful consideration of the pipeline, however, shows us that the value to be written into a register is actually known at the end of the 3rd stage (it cannot depend on any memory access). Rather than wait for it to be written, additional hardware can be inserted (**forwarding** hardware) so as to make it available for reading in the 3rd stage of the next instruction. That is still not early enough for that instruction but it is in time for the 2nd stage of following instruction. All that is necessary, then, is to delay any instruction following a register write that needs the new value. Inserting a nop or some instruction not needing that new value as with delayed branches can do this.

Here is another place for an intelligent compiler to help a programmer. It might rearrange our code so that as few data hazards occur as possible. Of course it is often up to the programmer to look for and avoid such problems.

Fortunately, the latest version of PCSPIM, by using the check box for "Delayed Load", does actually support the behavior of the MIPS processor so we can demonstrate it. The following program works differently if we allow for the real load delays that the MIPS processor uses.

```
# LDS.s   Load Delay Slot example

        .data               # Data declaration section
title: .asciiz  "\nLoad Delay Slot test\n"
strt1: .asciiz  "\nOld memory = "
strt2: .asciiz  "\tNew memory = "
memory: .word    100         # Initialize memory (100)
new:    .asciiz  "\nThey are the same so no delay"
old:    .asciiz  "\nThey are different which shows the delay"
```

```
        .text                    # Start of code section
main:
        li        $v0,4          # print_str
        la        $a0,title
        syscall
        la        $s0,memory     # Initialize memory ptr
        li        $t0,0          # Initialize register (0)
        la        $a0,strt1
        li        $v0,4          # print_str
        syscall
## Test the Load Delay Slot Here
        lw        $t0,0($s0)     # contents of memory (100)
        move      $s1,$t0        # **LDS** old value (0?)
        move      $s2,$t0        # new value by now (100)
## Now see the results
        move      $a0,$s1        # old value
        li        $v0,1          # print_int
        syscall
        la        $a0,strt2
        li        $v0,4          # print_str
        syscall
        move      $a0,$s2        # new value
        li        $v0,1          # print_int
        syscall
## Explain result
        beq       $s1,$s2,no
        la        $a0,old        # yes
        li        $v0,4
        syscall
        b         exit
no:     la        $a0,new
        li        $v0, 4
        syscall
exit:   li        $v0,10         # exits program
        syscall

        # END OF LDS.s
```

Still, we are lucky that we are not trying to program a complicated processor such as those used in Digital Signal Processing. In one such processor, the data from any load instruction is not available until five instructions later. A very smart compiler can keep track of when data is available, but human programming becomes very difficult.

11.5 Error Conditions

One of the most difficult problems related to the pipeline is what to do when error conditions occur. We have always implicitly assumed that every instruction ran to completion before the next began. What if, as we see in pipelining, instructions that occur after the one causing the problem have already begun? Clearly we must be sure that we can undo any changes to the system made by later instructions that actually might not ever need to be executed.

Once again we must design our hardware to prepare for that eventuality. We want to be able to "flush" the pipeline in a clean way. The details of hardware design are treated in Computer Architecture courses. See the paper by Wade Walker and Harvey G. Cragon[3] for an excellent discussion of this problem and possible solutions.

Exercises

1. Run earlier programs with "Branch delay" checked. For those that no longer work, try to rearrange the code to take advantage of the BDS. If nothing else works, insert *nop*'s as necessary.

2. In earlier programs, insert code to gather statistics on how often each branch is taken. In what cases might branch prediction help?

3. Obtain figures on your (or an advertised) computer system in regard to memory speed, cache speed and amount, etc. Calculate what kind of hit rate percentage is necessary for the cache to help processing time.

4. Obtain figures on your (or an advertised) hard disk. Calculate latency times for that hard disk and compare it with processor speed.

5. According to FORTRAN standards, two-dimensional arrays must be stored in column-major order (that is, down the columns). Most scientists write code that accesses such arrays in row-major order (that is, across the rows). Consider how that might effect processing time in a computer with D-cache.

6. Consider earlier programs and look for (and correct) data hazards. As always, use *nop*'s only if necessary.

7. Identify the data hazards assuming there is no "forwarding" in the following code:

```
add $2,$5,$4
add $4,$2,$5
sw  $5,100($2)
add $3,$2,$4
```

Which dependencies will be resolved by forwarding?

8. How would you modify the following code to make use of a branch delay slot?

```
Loop:    lw    $2,100($3)
         addi  $3,$3,4
         beq   $3,$4,Loop
```

---

[3] *Interrupt Processing in Concurrent Processors*, **Computer**, June 1995, pp. 36-46.

9. To capture the fact that the time to access data for both hits and misses affects performance, designers often use average memory access time (AMAT) as a way to examine alternative cache designs.

   a) Find the AMAT for a machine with a 2-ns clock cycle, a miss penalty of 20 clock cycles, a hit rate of 95%, and cache access time (including hit detection) of 1 clock cycle.

   b) Suppose we can improve the hit rate to 97% by doubling the cache size. This causes the cache access time to increase to 1.2 clock cycles. Using AMAT as a metric, determine if this is a good trade-off.

CHAPTER TWELVE

Exception Handling

Although we hope it never happens, we often have to "reboot" our computers. A simple *<Control-Alt-Delete>* restarts the machine. When we do that (and when we first power up the computer), the hardware in the computer is designed to start control at some specific location. At that location, which may be on a floppy disk, the hard drive, or elsewhere, is found a small amount of code usually called a "bootstrap loader." Since it is very small, it may reside in hardware (in "Read-Only" memory). Its job is usually to load a very small amount of code into memory and then transfer control to its location. That code will then load even more code into the appropriate locations in memory. After the entire operating system is loaded, control is transferred to the system that then waits for orders from the user.

Another thing we hope never happens is that some operation fails to work correctly. For example, we may try to divide by zero or perform an addition that overflows the size of the registers. While it is hard to do it in a high-level language, in assembler we may well try to execute an instruction code for which the machine has not been wired or we may try to access an address that is not available. When any of a number of problems arises we say that an **exception** has occurred. The operating system, working together with the hardware, must be prepared for handling these exceptional cases.

A special type of exception is when the system is interrupted (and we say that an **interrupt** has occurred) by a message from some hardware device. We mentioned that possibility when discussing memory mapped I/O. Another special type of interrupt is when we purposely issue a *syscall* instruction. While these exceptions are not due to errors or problems, the result is the same: control is transferred to some other appropriate location in memory rather than continuing with its normal flow of operations.

As pointed out earlier, certain areas of memory are reserved for the operating system and it is there we usually find the code that is to be performed when an exception occurs. The code is usually placed there when the operating system is loaded as described above. In some cases there is an array of memory locations in which addresses are placed (similar to the jump table introduced earlier) and the hardware automatically transfers control to the address it finds at the location associated with the cause of the interrupt. These are called "vectored interrupts" but they are not the way MIPS handles the problem.

In case the standard code given to us by the operating system is not adequate, in some systems it is possible to write **Terminate and Stay Resident** programs (TSR's) that change the behavior of the system. One writes a program which includes the desired code for the system to perform and changes the address in the special location for that interrupt to where the code is located. A TSR does what it sounds like: when it terminates it leaves some of its code (the part including the new behavior) resident in memory instead of it all being removed as happens when most programs are exited. Thus, when done, the operating system seems to have changed in regard to how it handles that interrupt. When the system is rebooted, the OS returns to its original form and the TSR needs to be run again if the new behavior is desired.

In our SPIM simulator we do not have TSR's but we may change the way in which the system responds to exceptions. In this chapter we will show how to make some of those changes.

12.1 Coprocessor Zero

Before we can treat the software that handles exceptions, we must consider what hardware features are available to us. This is characteristic of many computer-programming problems. Merely writing very good software if the hardware does not support some needed security features, for example, cannot solve concerns about security.

Of course we are using a simulator so we are even more limited in what we can do. The actual MIPS processors have extensive control capabilities but the PCSPIM simulator only emulates some of them. Fortunately, they are sufficient to allow us to do some interesting things.

The actual MIPS processor has (and PCSPIM simulates) another coprocessor similar to the floating-point processor (Coprocessor One) we treated in Chapter 10. The System Control Coprocessor, called **Coprocessor Zero (CP0)**, has exception and control registers (and memory management and other registers). Although the simplest MIPS processor has many registers, our simulator basically has five.

When we bring up PCSPIM we see at the top of the first window some special control registers. We have already noted the PC (Program Counter) and the HI and LO registers used in multiplication and division. There are four other registers displayed there and they are in CP0 and are the ones we may use in handling interrupts. The "BadVAddr" register (number 8 in CP0) is set when a bad virtual address is generated but we will not consider that problem here.

The three registers[1] we use most often are **Status** ($12 in CP0), **Cause** ($13 in CP0) and **Exception Program Counter - EPC** ($14 in CP0). The EPC is simple to explain: When an exception takes place the address of the instruction which caused it is placed in the EPC so the handler knows to where control should be returned.

---

[1] Registers 9 contains the value of a timer and register 11 contains an integer to which the timer value is compared. When they are equal, an exception is raised if enabled. The timer will be demonstrated in Section 12.6.

The instructions used to move data back and forth between CP0 and the CPU so that we may work with them are just like those for CP1 (the floating-point processor)[2]:

> *mfc0 $R, $CR # Move From Coprocessor 0 register $CR to CPU register $R*
> *mtc0 $R, $CR # Move To Coprocessor 0 register $CR from CPU register $R*

Just as in Section 10.2.2, we must be careful of the order of operands in the second instruction!

Finally, there is one additional instruction used as the last instruction in handling exceptions:

> *eret*

that is used when one does an **E**xception **RET**urn. The instruction returns control to the instruction pointed to by the EPC and sets a bit in the Status register. This is a new instruction (see below) that replaces the *rfe* (**R**eturn **F**rom **E**xception) instruction described in Appendix D.

12.2 Status and Cause Registers

The actual format of the two important registers, Status ($12) and Cause ($13) depends on the particular MIPS processor being used. In early versions of the simulator SPIM, forms patterned after the R2000 were made available to the programmer. Appendix D shows the old forms of those registers in Figures 3 and 4. Since Version 7 of SPIM, the forms of these registers are based on the MIPS32 architecture. This latest architecture includes many new instructions and somewhat different exception handling.

Status: <u>3130292827262524232221201918171 6**1514131211100908**0706**0504**0302**0100**</u>

The Status register shown above includes the **Interrupt Mask** (that really should be called the "Exception Mask" following our terminology) contained in bits 15-8. In our references there are said to be eight possible exception levels with the high 6 being hardware exceptions and the lower two software exceptions. When set (1) each bit allows exceptions at that level; when reset (0), that level exception is disabled. From experience, we will turn on bit 8 to enable interrupts in PCSPIM.

Bit 4 is the User Mode bit that, on the MIPS32 processor determines whether the system is operating in kernel (supervisor) mode or user mode. SPIM does not use this option and the bit is always set to 1.

Bit 1 is the Exception Level bit that is normally reset to 0. When an exception occurs, it is set to 1 so no other exception is allowed. Thus the EPC cannot be changed by a later exception. It should be reset when the exception handler finishes.

---

[2] Note that MIPSter may not color code all the instructions correctly.

Bit 0 is the Interrupt Enable bit that allows interrupts when set (1).

Cause: **31**302928272625242322212019181716**1514131211100908**07**0605040302**0100

The Cause register shown above includes the **Pending Interrupts** (Exceptions) field (15-8). Each bit corresponds to the same bit in the Status register and, when set, indicates that an exception has occurred at that level. These bits are set even if they have not been enabled in the Status register.

An important field is the **Exception Code** field in bits 6-2. These five bits tell the exception handler what caused the interruption to the system. Code zero corresponds to an <u>interrupt</u> and we will see some of the other possible codes in Section 5 and the exercises.

Bit 31 indicates that the exception took place in the Branch Delay Slot. Handling exceptions that occur in that slot is so complicated that we will ignore that problem.

The hardware of the latest MIPS processors is such that exceptions, when enabled, cause a jump to the address 0x80000180 and PCSPIM emulates that behavior. That address is in the upper half of possible memory and is not in the user's address space – it belongs to the operating system. When starting PCSPIM we may place in the kernel's data segment whatever we desire. Rather than *.data*, we use the assembler directive *.kdata* with whatever address we need to use as an argument. Thus, similarly,

> *.ktext 0x80000180*

indicates that we wish to place the following special code at the location to which the system goes for handling exceptions. We are now ready to look at the code used to initiate PCSPIM so that it can handle exceptions (it is called *exceptions.s*).

12.3 The Exception Handler

When we start PCSPIM the bottom window contains, in addition to copyright notices, a line similar to the following (depending on where the simulator was loaded):

```
Loaded: F:\exceptions.s
```

This file, supplied with PCSPIM by James R. Larus (see the copyright notice), contains the code that instructs the operating system on how to respond to exceptions. We may choose a different file by going to the "Simulator" pull-down menu and choosing "Settings…". The following pop-up window appears:

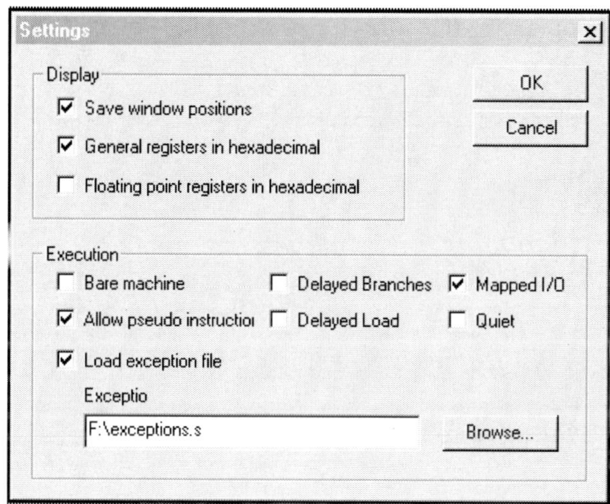

We have seen the "Mapped I/O" check box before and now we concentrate on the "Exceptio" box. As is obvious, we may place the address of a different file in what should be called the "Exception" area and the result will be that when PCSPIM starts, a different file will be used for this purpose.

Before using a different file, let us carefully investigate what the original file does. In Appendix C is a highly modified version of the *exceptions.s* file supplied in the 2005 version of PCSPIM. There are many added comments and editorial changes. In addition, there are new operations defined there including a timer and buffered I/O. In the comments we have added clear indications of where to modify the code further so as to handle exceptions differently and also make other changes. We titled our file *PGAexceptions.s*.

Note that near the end of the original file (at label __*start*) is the standard startup code that calls on the *main* function. Here we find the six instructions mentioned in Chapter Three that we have to single-step through before beginning our code. Clearly we can now easily change the code there and the execution will differ. This is where we will initialize the event handling by enabling interrupts and modify the memory mapped I/O described in Section 6.5.

Another place at which we will make changes is at the __*intrpt* label where we may place different code to handle interrupts that occur. Note the convention to use two underscore characters ("_") in these labels to emphasize that they refer to locations in the exception handler and initialization code. That is just one of the few special characters that are legal in labels (like variable names) but we should not try to remember or use them in our normal code. Note also that execution apparently begins at the label __*start*.

12.4 Clock Example

Consider the following simple program

```
# Clock.s              # Suggested by Dr. Herman Harrison

          .data        # Data declaration section
title:    .ascii       "\nTic/Toc Timing\n"
          .asciiz      "<Control-C> to stop\n"
Tic:      .asciiz      "\nTic"
Toc:      .asciiz      "\nToc"
pause:    .word        100000       # Adjust as needed

          .text

main:                  # Start of code section
          li           $v0,4
          la           $a0,title
          syscall
#
loop:
          lw           $t0,pause
loop1:    sub          $t0,$t0,1    # Count down
          bgez         $t0,loop1    # Test
          la           $a0,Tic      # Print
          li           $v0,4        # "Tic"
          syscall
          lw           $t0,pause
loop2:    sub          $t0,$t0,1    # Count down
          bgez         $t0,loop2    # Test
          la           $a0,Toc      # Print
          li           $v0,4        # "Toc"
          syscall
          b            loop         # Until <Control-C>

# END OF Clock.s
```

When we run this program using the supplied *exceptions.s* (adjusting the constant 100000 to fit the speed of our computer), we get "Tic" and then "Toc" printed repeatedly until we input *<Control-C>*. We find that it completely ignores all other inputs.

Let us now extend our treatment of memory mapped I/O by modifying the handler file to allow for interrupt driven I/O as suggested in Section 6.5. We will allow the system to respond to our input while continuing to run the *Clock.s* program.

In Figure 7 of Appendix D we see that bit 1 of the RCR (Receiver Control Register) and of the TCR (Transmitter Control Register) are used to enable interrupts. We must turn them on to allow for this interrupt driven I/O and we do that in the "Initialize Event Handling Here" location in the startup code. Bit 0 in the Status Register ($12) is set on (mask 0x1) so interrupts are enabled. We also enable interrupts in the Status Register by setting certain bits on (mask 0x8c11).

```
mfc0    $t0, $12              # Get Status Register
nop                           # LDS
ori     $t0, 0x00008c11 # Enable interrupts; Set Current values
mtc0    $t0, $12              # Set Status Register
```

```
la      $t0, 0xFFFF0000 # Memory-mapped I/O
li      $t1, 2          # Interrupt enable bit
sw      $t1, 0($t0)     # Enable ReceiverControlR
sw      $t1, 8($t0)     # Enable TransmitterControlR
```

Now this code will also be executed when the system starts and we may check that by single stepping through it when we start PCSPIM.

The other change we make is to put some code where we have "Interrupt Handler Here". Although we could do more interesting things (and we may in exercises), we will merely ask the system to echo the character input when the interrupt occurs. The code for that is very simple:

```
_interruptHandler:
andi $a0, $k0, 0x800  # Look in CauseR; was it output?
beqz $a0, int_ret     # Ignore if so
li   $a0, 0xFFFF0000  # Memory mapped I/O
lw   $v0, 4($a0)      # Read character from ReceiverDataR
lw   $v0, 12($a0)     # Write character to TransmitterDataR
b    int_ret          # Don't skip instruction as warned
```

When we reach this code, $k0 contains the Cause Register value and bit 11 indicates that the interrupt was caused by the output system. Otherwise, it was the keyboard and we wish to acknowledge that fact.

Associated with these two changes, we also insert the text

```
beqz  $a0, _interruptHandler  # Don't print about interrupts
```

just before the "Print information about interrupts" comment (line 97) since we do not want such information printed. We also insert a new label *int_ret* right before the "Restore resisters and reset processor state" comment so that we can jump over the code that skips the instruction that caused the interrupt.

Now, when we run *Clock.s* using the modified handler, we may type characters and the system immediately responds by echoing them but continues to "keep time" with the printing of "Tic" and "Toc". We did not need to tie up the processor in tight loops waiting for input or printing. This "asynchronous" behavior simulates having more than one processor: one for the "clock" and the other handling the I/O.

12.5 Emulation

As mentioned before, we are using an emulator, PCSPIM, not an actual MIPS processor and so the behavior may differ in various ways. For example, the divide instruction we introduced in Section 2.1 using the HI and LO registers does not cause the "[Divide By 0]" message to appear. There is another divide instruction with three operands that we see is available in MIPSter. In the "Arithmetic" toolbox it appears as

```
div Rdest, Rsrc1, Src2
```

with the comment

```
div: [signed, with overflow] Put the quotient of the integers
                              Rsrc1 and Src2 into register Rdest
```

Here is the result of using PCSPIM on code containing the two lines that show as comments:

```
[0x00400044]    0x0109001a  div $8, $9     ; 10: div $t0, $t1
[0x00400048]    0x15200002  bne $9, $0, 8 ; 12: div $t2, $t0, $t1
[0x0040004c]    0x0000000d  break $0
[0x00400050]    0x0109001a  div $8, $9
[0x00400054]    0x00005012  mflo $10
```

If we run this code with register *$t1* = $9 containing zero, the first statement causes no interrupt or error message. The second is expanded, as shown, to four instructions and if run with *$t1* equal to zero, causes the *break $0* instruction to be executed. This will give us the "[Breakpoint]" interrupt message, not the "[Divide by 0]" message!

This behavior encourages us to experiment with the simulator. In our main program we may put

```
mfc0        $a0, $12      # Status register
li              $v0, 1         # Print_int
syscall
```

and

```
mfc0        $a0, $13      # Cause register
li              $v0, 1         # Print_int
syscall
```

any place we wish and see what is contained in those registers. The same thing can be done in our *exceptions.s* code. We may insert these print statements while debugging to see exactly what those registers contain.

12.6 Buffered Input

As a further demonstration of our ability to change the operating system, let us look at a modified version of *exceptions.s*. In Section 4 we were able to keep the "clock" running as we typed characters and had them immediately echoed. Now we will arrange for the system to keep running an even more complicated program and still respond to input but not echo the characters immediately. We will now place the characters in a buffer and only print them in response to the *<Enter>* key. We could also buffer the output but this will serve as an example.

Dr. Hermann Harrison originally wrote the code for this new exception handler. It has been modified to follow the author's conventions. It appears in Appendix C. Assuming we use the "Settings" window to use the file *PGAexceptions.s* as our exception handler, the following is an interesting test program.

```
## PGAXDemo.s
#
#    Driver to test PGAexceptions.s as an extended exception handler.
#    Modification of code originally written by Dr. Herman Harrison.
#    It uses new operations involving the timer and buffered I/O.
#
            .data
title:      .asciiz   "\nDemonstrate Coprocessor _0 Exceptions:\n"
options:  .ascii    "\n\nTest of I/O and Timer Interrupts:"
          .ascii    "\n------------------------------"
          .ascii    "\n1)Type character(s) then <Enter> key"
          .ascii    "\n2)Type \"<Ctrl-T>\" Toggle Timer messages on/off"
          .ascii            " (default=off)"
          .ascii    "\n3)Type \"<Ctrl-V>\" rapidly to View timer Values"
          .ascii            " (default=100)"
          .ascii    "\n4)Type \"<Ctrl-S>\" Make the timer speed slower"
          .ascii    "\n5)Type \"<Ctrl-F>\" Make the timer speed faster"
          .ascii    "\n6)Type \"<Ctrl-X>\" eXit from the program"
          .ascii    "\n7)Type \"<Ctrl-O>\" to see these Options again"
          .asciiz   "\n\n"
CountTick: .asciiz "\n[Count:Tick]="
newvalue:  .asciiz  "\nNew Tick value=0:"
colon:      .asciiz  ":"
confirm:    .asciiz  "\nAre you sure(y/n)?"
bye:        .asciiz  "\nGood bye\n"
tm_display:  .word    0               # initialize to OFF

            .text
            .globl  main
main:
            la      $a0, title
            li      $v0, 4
            syscall
restart:
            la      $a0, options
            li      $v0, 4
            syscall
            lw      $a0, tm_display  # Turn on timer display messages
            jal     .TIMER_display
mainloop:
            jal     .IO_getc        # returns -1 if no char /\
            blez    $v0, mainloop   # wait for some input   \/
            move    $s0, $v0
            beq     $s0, 10, bufferit # <Enter> (actually LF)
            beq     $s0, 13, bufferit # <Enter> (actually CR)
            bge     $s0, 32, bufferit # printable character
            b       what              # not printable character
bufferit:
            move    $a0, $v0          # put character in buffer
            jal     .IO_putc
# Analyse command
```

```
what:   bne     $s0, 20, notT  # <Ctrl-T> Toggle timer display on/off
        lw      $a0, tm_display
        xor     $a0, $a0, 1
        sw      $a0, tm_display
        jal     .TIMER_display
notT:
        bne     $s0, 19, notS  # <Ctrl-S> make slower
        la      $a0, newvalue  # by doubling timer value
        li      $v0, 4
        syscall
        jal     .TIMER_get
        sll     $a0, $v0, 1     # *2
        jal     .TIMER_set
        li      $v0, 1
        syscall
notS:
        bne     $s0, 6, notF   # <Ctrl-F> make faster
        la      $a0, newvalue  # by halfing timer value
        li      $v0, 4
        syscall
        jal     .TIMER_get
        srl     $a0, $v0, 1     # /2
        jal     .TIMER_set
        li      $v0, 1
        syscall
notF:
        bne     $s0, 22, notV  # <Ctrl-V> View timer Value
        la      $a0, CountTick
        li      $v0, 4
        syscall
        jal     .TIMER_getClock  # get current Clock value
        move    $a0, $v0
        li      $v0, 1
        syscall
        la      $a0, colon       # print ":"
        li      $v0, 4
        syscall
        jal     .TIMER_get        # get current Timer tick value
        move    $a0, $v1
        li      $v0, 1
        syscall
notV:
        bne     $s0, 15, notO  # <Ctrl-O> show Options again
        la      $a0, options
        li      $v0, 4
        syscall
notO:
        beq     $s0, 24, eXit  # <Ctrl-X> eXit from program
        bne     $s0, 0x0a, mainloop # <Enter> (actually ^J = LF)
        jal     .IO_flush        # flush kernel I/O output buffer
        b       mainloop
#-------Leave main loop-------------------------------------------
eXit:
        li      $a0, 0           # Turn off Timer display messages
        jal     .TIMER_display
        jal     .IO_flush        # clear out I/O buffer
floop:  jal     .IO_empty        # wait for flush to complete
```

```
        bnez      $v0, floop
        la        $a0, confirm     # Confirmation request
        li        $v0, 4
        syscall
rloop:  jal       .IO_getc         # check for a "y" response
        blez      $v0, rloop
        bne       $v0, 'y', restart # restart and print out options
#-------Exit to kernel-------------------------------------
        la        $a0, bye
        li        $v0, 4
        syscall
        li        $v0, 10
        syscall
```

The comments explain most of this program and the new exception handler. Notice that this program uses a *jal* command to access the new functions such as *.IO_getc* and *.TIMER_get*. These are defined and made available in *PGAexceptions.s*. Since their code is in the operating system's part of memory (above 0x80000000), while user's code starts at 0x400000, they are very far apart and that is why the special linkages are used at the end of the *PGAexceptions.s* code.

The interrupt handler *PGAexceptions.s* works as follows. It first initializes the kernel/exception handlers by jumping to *_init_kernel* that is at (A). There it sets the I/O interface by using a jump to *_IO_init* at (C). Next it sets the TIMER interface by jumping to *_timer_init* at (B). Finally, it sets the Status and Cause registers to enable exceptions. Notice that the standard startup code is performed as usual.

The I/O buffering is based on the "Producer/Consumer" model described in Operating Systems courses. It is a circular buffer but does not have very careful tests for buffer overflow. That will be left to the exercises.

While using both memory mapped I/O and normal *syscall*'s is not recommended, this does work. Notice that we do everything we can to avoid using any other registers and so avoid needing any other memory references. In the previous chapter we discussed why this is so important for efficiency and is particularly important in what ends up being operating system code.

Finally, note that we could extend the services available to us through the few *syscall* functions by writing our own routines and calling on them. Some suggestions will be given in the exercises. It is by reading and modifying complicated code such as these examples that one can learn assembler language programming.

Exercises

1. Insert code into some of your programs to print out the contents of the Status and the Cause registers as it runs.

2. Insert code into the *exceptions.s* to print out the contents of the Status and the Cause registers when it is called and run the programs written in problem 1.

3. Test the error handling capabilities of *exceptions.s* by writing code that assesses illegal locations, divides by zero, and makes other exceptions. Note that there are various "torture tests" supplied by Larus in the SPIM distribution.

4. Insert a *break* statement into a program and write code to check for the values in, say, *$a0* and *$a1* (for example) to see what you might want done.

5. The modified *PGAexceptions.s* described in Section 6 does not check for buffer overflow. That explains how easy it is to write code that allows buffer overflow and hence is a security leak (an opening for a virus). Insert some code that checks for and does not allow such overflow.

6. Write your own asynchronous *.get* and *.put* routines to add to the library of functions available to a user.

7. Write *.push* and *.pop* routines to add your own stack to the library of functions available to a user. Since the size of the stack area you place in the "Additional data area" must be limited, be sure to test for stack overflow (and underflow; i.e., when the stack is empty).

8. Use memory mapped I/O to print out ("flush") the buffer in Section 12.6.

9. Write additional functions using the model of *PGAexceptions.s*. It will be necessary to capture some exception and do your own handling of it. [Hint: While it might be reasonable to try the *syscall* exception (8); if it does not work as expected one might try the trap[3] exception (13) with the command *teq $0,$0*.]

10. Insert the command *mfc3* into your code. Since there is no co-processor 3, what do you expect to happen? Try it. What exception is raised? Where in the *exceptions.s* file should this information be? Can you use this command (or similar commands) to get access to the exception handler?

---

[3] There are comparison instructions called "traps" that, when the condition is satisfied, transfer control to the exception handler. They are not described in Appendix D but are similar in form to the conditional branch instructions.

A. ASCII Standard Character Set

Char	Ctrl	Dec	Hex	Char	Dec	Hex	Char	Dec	Hex	Char	Dec	Hex
NUL	^@	0	00	space	32	20	@	64	40	`	96	60
SOH	^A	1	01	!	33	21	A	65	41	a	97	61
STX	^B	2	02	"	34	22	B	66	42	b	98	62
ETX	^C	3	03	#	35	23	C	67	43	c	99	63
EOT	^D	4	04	$	36	24	D	68	44	d	100	64
ENQ	^E	5	05	%	37	25	E	69	45	e	101	65
ACK	^F	6	06	&	38	26	F	70	46	f	102	66
BEL	^G	7	07	'	39	27	G	71	47	g	103	67
BS	^H	8	08	(	40	28	H	72	48	h	104	68
HT	^I	9	09	)	41	29	I	73	49	i	105	69
LF	^J	10	0A	*	42	2A	J	74	4A	j	106	6A
VT	^K	11	0B	+	43	2B	K	75	4B	k	107	6B
FF	^L	12	0C	,	44	2C	L	76	4C	l	108	6C
CR	^M	13	0D	-	45	2D	M	77	4D	m	109	6D
SO	^N	14	0E	.	46	2E	N	78	4E	n	110	6E
SI	^O	15	0F	/	47	2F	O	79	4F	o	111	6F
DLE	^P	16	10	0	48	30	P	80	50	p	112	70
DC1	^Q	17	11	1	49	31	Q	81	51	q	113	71
DC2	^R	18	12	2	50	32	R	82	52	r	114	72
DC3	^S	19	13	3	51	33	S	83	53	s	115	73
DC4	^T	20	14	4	52	34	T	84	54	t	116	74
NAK	^U	21	15	5	53	35	U	85	55	u	117	75
SYN	^V	22	16	6	54	36	V	86	56	v	118	76
ETB	^W	23	17	7	55	37	W	87	57	w	119	77
CAN	^X	24	18	8	56	38	X	88	58	x	120	78
EM	^Y	25	19	9	57	39	Y	89	59	y	121	79
SUB	^Z	26	1A	:	58	3A	Z	90	5A	z	122	7A
ESC	^[	27	1B	;	59	3B	[	91	5B	{	123	7B
FS	^\	28	1C	<	60	3C	\	92	5C	|	124	7C
GS	^]	29	1D	=	61	3D	]	93	5D	}	125	7D
RS	^^	30	1E	>	62	3E	^	94	5E	~	126	7E
US	^_	31	1F	?	63	3F	_	95	5F	delete	127	7F

Abbreviations for Control Characters

NULl	**BackS**pace	**Data Link Escape**	**CAN**cel
Start Of Heading	**Horizontal Tab**	**Device Control 1**	**End of Medium**
Start of TeXt	**Line Feed**	**Device Control 2**	**SUB**stitute
End of TeXt	**Vertical Tab**	**Device Control 3**	**ESC**ape
End Of Transmission	**Form Feed**	**Device Control 4**	**File Separator**
ENQuiry	**Carriage Return**	**Negative AcK**nowledge	**Group Separator**
ACKnowledge	**Shift Out**	**SYN**chronous idle	**Record Separator**
BELl	**Shift In**	**End Transmission Block**	**Unit Separator**

B. System Calls

Code	Name	Argument and Result Registers
1	print_int	$a0 = integer
2	print_float	$f12 = float
3	print_double	$f12 (and $f13) = double
4	print_string	$a0 → string
5	read_int	;$v0 = integer
6	read_float	;$f0 = float
7	read_double	;$f0 (and $f1) = double
8	read_string	$a0 →buffer, $a1 = length
9	malloc	$a0 = amount; $v0 = address
10	exit	
11	print_char	$a0 = character (low 8 bits)
12	read_char	;$v0 = character (no LF) echoed
13	file_open	$a0 → full path (zero terminated string with no LF), $a1=flags* $a2 = permission (R=0x100,W=0x80); $v0 = file descriptor (-1=error)
14	file_read	$a0 = file descriptor, $a1 → buffer, $a2 = amount; $v0 = result**
15	file_write	$a0 = file descriptor, $a1 → buffer, $a2 = amount; $v0 = result**
16	file_close	$a0 = file descriptor

*flags: Read=0x0, Write=0x1, Read/Write=0x2
OR   Create=0x100, Truncate=0x200, Append=0x8
OR   Text=0x4000, Binary=0x8000

**result: Amount of data in buffer to/from file (-1=error, 0=EOF)

C. PGAexceptions.s

```
### PGAexceptions.s ### A modified version of "exceptions.s"    #
### as distributed with PCSpim Version 7.2 by James Larus.      #
### Developed by Dr. Hermann Harrison of The University of      #
### Texas at Dallas. It may be used for any program but was     #
### designed to demonstrate features in "PGAXDemo.s".           #
###                                                             #
### It defines new user I/O operations named ".IO_getc" and     #
### ".IO_putc" which get or put characters through a buffer     #
### that may be checked to be empty with ".IO_empty", and       #
### emptied with ".IO_flush". These are accessed with jal.      #
###                                                             #
### In addition, a timer is introduced with the new operations  #
### ".TIMER_set", ".TIMER_get", ".TIMER_display", and           #
### ".TIMER_getClock". These are also accessed with jal.        #
#==============================================================#
# SPIM S20 MIPS simulator.
# The default exception handler for spim.
#
# Copyright (C) 1990-2004 James Larus, larus@cs.wisc.edu.
# ALL RIGHTS RESERVED.
#
# SPIM is distributed under the following conditions:
#
# You may make copies of SPIM for your own use and modify
# those copies.
#
# All copies of SPIM must retain my name and copyright notice.
#
# You may not sell SPIM or distributed SPIM in conjunction
# with a commercial product or service without the expressed
# written consent of James Larus.
#
# THIS SOFTWARE IS PROVIDED ``AS IS'' AND WITHOUT ANY EXPRESS
# OR IMPLIED WARRANTIES, INCLUDING, WITHOUT LIMITATION, THE
# IMPLIED WARRANTIES OF MERCHANTABILITY AND FITNESS FOR A
# PARTICULAR PURPOSE.
#
# $Header: $
# Define the exception handling code.  This must go first!
#==============================================================
#
#===KERNEL DATA DEFINITIONS==================================
        .kdata

#--Kernel Data Variables--------------
__m01_: .asciiz  "  Exception "
__m02_: .asciiz  " occurred and ignored\n"
__e00_: .asciiz  "  [Interrupt] "
__e01_: .asciiz  "  [TLB]"
__e02_: .asciiz  "  [TLB]"
```

```
__e03_:   .asciiz   "   [TLB]"
__e04_:   .asciiz   "   [Address error in inst/data fetch] "
__e05_:   .asciiz   "   [Address error in store] "
__e06_:   .asciiz   "   [Bad instruction address] "
__e07_:   .asciiz   "   [Bad data address] "
__e08_:   .asciiz   "   [Error in syscall] "
__e09_:   .asciiz   "   [Breakpoint] "
__e10_:   .asciiz   "   [Reserved instruction] "
__e11_:   .asciiz   "   [Coprocessor error]"
__e12_:   .asciiz   "   [Arithmetic overflow] "
__e13_:   .asciiz   "   [Trap] "
__e14_:   .asciiz   ""
__e15_:   .asciiz   "   [Floating point] "
__e16_:   .asciiz   ""
__e17_:   .asciiz   ""
__e18_:   .asciiz   "   [Coproc 2]"
__e19_:   .asciiz   ""
__e20_:   .asciiz   ""
__e21_:   .asciiz   ""
__e22_:   .asciiz   "   [MDMX]"
__e23_:   .asciiz   "   [Watch]"
__e24_:   .asciiz   "   [Machine check]"
__e25_:   .asciiz   ""
__e26_:   .asciiz   ""
__e27_:   .asciiz   ""
__e28_:   .asciiz   ""
__e29_:   .asciiz   ""
__e30_:   .asciiz   "   [Cache]"
__e31_:   .asciiz   ""

__excp_:  .word __e00_, __e01_, __e02_, __e03_, __e04_, __e05_
          .word __e06_, __e07_, __e08_, __e09_, __e10_, __e11_
          .word __e12_, __e13_, __e14_, __e15_, __e16_, __e17_
          .word __e18_, __e19_, __e20_, __e21_, __e22_, __e23_
          .word __e24_, __e25_, __e26_, __e27_, __e28_, __e29_
          .word __e30_, __e31_

__s01_:   .word 0
__s02_:   .word 0

#--Exceptions in Branch Delay Slot---------------
_bds_msg: .asciiz  "\nException in Branch_Delay_Slot"
#--

#--TIMER Data Variables---------------
_TIMER_MSG:      .asciiz  "\nTIMER_events="
_TIMER_CLOCK:    .word 0
_TIMER_DISPLAY: .word 0

#--I/O Buffers/Data Variables---------
_bufsiz:       .word  128
_bufin:        .space 128
_bufin_end:                            # Must immediately follow "bufin:"
_bufin_put:  .word _bufin     # input buffer "producer" pointer
_bufin_get:  .word _bufin     # input buffer "consumer" pointer
_bufout:       .space 128
_bufout_end:                           # Must immediately follow "bufout:"
```

```
_bufout_put: .word    _bufout    # output buffer "producer" pointer
_bufout_get: .word    _bufout    # output buffer "consumer" pointer


#====KERNEL INTERRUPT SERVICE ROUTINES===========================
# This is the exception handler code that the processor runs when
# an exception occurs. It only prints some information about the
# exception, but can server as a model of how to write a handler.
#
# Because we are running in the kernel, we can use $k0/$k1
# without saving their old values.
#---------------------------------------------------------------
# This is the exception vector address for MIPS32:
        .ktext 0x80000180


#(1)====SAVE THE CPU ENVIRONMENT/STATE===========================

        .set   noat             #                      these avoid
        move   $k1 $at          # Save $AT($1)
        .set   at               #                      warning messages
        sw     $v0, __s01_      # Not re-entrant, can't trust $sp
        sw     $a0, __s02_      # But, we need to use these registers
#****************************************************************
        mfc0   $k0, $13         # C0_CAUSE register($13)
        nop                     ##Delay Slot
        srl    $a0, $k0, 2      # Extract Exc_Code Field
# If External Interrupt, do not print information
        andi   $a0, $a0, 0x1f
        beqz   $a0,_Ext_Interrupts  ####Ext Interrupt Handlers#####
        nop                     # Branch-delay-slot


#(2)===INTERNAL EXCEPTION HANDLERS===============================
# Print information about exception. (Could handle them here)
        li     $v0, 4           # syscall 4 (print_str)
        la     $a0, __m01_
        syscall

        li     $v0, 1           # syscall 1 (print_int)
        srl    $a0, $k0 2       # Extract ExcCode Field
        andi   $a0, $a0 0x1f
        syscall

        li     $v0, 4           # syscall 4 (print_str)
        andi   $a0, $k0 0x7c
        lw     $a0, __excp_($a0)
        nop
        syscall

        andi   $a0, $k0, 0x7c
        bne    $a0, 0x18, _ok_pc # Bad PC exception requires
        nop                     # special case

        mfc0   $a0, $14         # EPC
        nop                     ##Delay Slot
        andi   $a0, $a0, 0x3    # Is EPC word-aligned?
        beq    $a0, 0, _ok_pc
        nop
        li     $v0, 10          # Exit on really bad PC
```

```
        syscall

_ok_pc:
        li      $v0, 4                  # syscall 4 (print_str)
        la      $a0, __m02_
        syscall

        andi    $a0, $k0, 0x7c   # Extract Exc_Code Field
        bne     $a0, $zero, _ret # 0 means exception was interrupt
        nop


#(3)===EXTERNAL INTERRUPT HANDLERS===============================
# External/Interrupt-specific code goes here!
# Don't skip instruction at EPC since it has not executed.

_Ext_Interrupts:

#---------TIMER-------------------------------------------
_timer:
        andi    $a0, $k0, 0x8000 # Bit 15 means timer interrupt
        beqz    $a0, _timer_end
        nop                     # Branch-delay-slot
#       ----------------------
        mtc0    $zero, $9       # Reset C0_Timer_Register
        lw      $a0, _TIMER_CLOCK # Increment the clock tick count
        lw      $v0, _TIMER_DISPLAY # Load delay slot
        addi    $a0, $a0, 1
        sw      $a0, _TIMER_CLOCK
#       ----------------------
        beqz    $v0, _timer_end # Check for display toggle
        nop                     # Branch-delay-slot
        la      $a0, _TIMER_MSG
        li      $v0, 4
        syscall
        lw      $a0, _TIMER_CLOCK
        li      $v0, 1
        syscall
_timer_end:

#---------TERMINAL INPUT ------------------------------------
_IO_in:
        andi    $a0, $k0, 0x0800 # Bit 11 indicates keyboard input
        beqz    $a0, _IO_out
        nop                     # Branch-delay-slot
#       ------------------------
        li      $a0, 0xffff0000  # Read the character from the input device
        lw      $v0, 4($a0)
        lw      $a0, _bufin_put
        nop                     # Load-delay-slot
        sb      $v0, 0($a0)     # Store character in buffer

        addiu   $a0, $a0, 1     # Increment buffer input pointer
        la      $v0, _bufin_end # Check for buffer wrap
        bne     $v0, $a0, _IO_in1
        nop                     # Branch-delay-slot
        la      $a0, _bufin     # (BDS)Wrap to start of buffer
_IO_in1:
```

```
    sw      $a0, _bufin_put
    sb      $zero, 0($a0)     ##### needs to handle buffer overrun
#---------TERMINAL OUTPUT-----------------------------------------
_IO_out:
    andi    $a0, $k0, 0x400   # Bit 10 indicates display output
    beqz    $a0, _IO_out_1
    nop                       # Branch-delay-slot
#    --------------------
    lw      $a0, _bufout_get  # Check for character to output
    nop                       # Load-delay-slot
    lbu     $v0, 0($a0)
    nop                       # Load-delay-slot
    beqz    $v0, _IO_out_1    # buffer empty?
    nop                       # Branch-delay-slot
    sb      $zero, 0($a0)     # Clear current buffer location
    addiu   $a0, $a0, 1       # Increment buffer output pointer
    sw      $a0, _bufout_get  # Update the pointer
    li      $a0, 0xffff0000   # Write the character to output device
    sw      $v0, 12($a0)

    lw      $a0, _bufout_get  # Check for buffer wrap
    la      $v0, _bufout_end
    bne     $v0, $a0, _IO_out_1
    nop                       # Branch-delay-slot
    la      $a0, _bufout      # Wrap to start of buffer
    sw      $a0, _bufout_get  # Update the pointer
_IO_out_1:
#-----------------------------
    b       _ret_1
    nop                       # Branch-delay-slot

#(4)====RESTORE THE CPU ENVIRONMENT/STATE=================
_ret:
# Return from (non-interrupt) exception. Skip offending
# instruction at EPC to avoid infinite loop.
    li      $a0, 0x80000000
    and     $a0, $a0, $k0     # check the BD bit
    beqz    $a0, _ret_2
    nop                       # Branch-delay-slot
#///////////////////////exception in Branch_Delay_Slot
    la      $a0, _bds_msg
    li      $v0, 4
    syscall
    b       _ret_1            #### ASSUMES ONLY "NOP" in BDS
    nop                       # Branch-delay-slot
_ret_2:
    mfc0    $k0, $14          # Bump EPC register
    nop                       ##Delay Slot
    addiu   $k0, $k0, 4       # Skip faulting instruction
    mtc0    $k0, $14

# Restore registers and reset processor state
_ret_1:
    mtc0    $zero, $13        # Clear Cause register
#************************************************
# Return from exception on MIPS32:
    lw      $a0, __s02_       # Restore other registers
```

```
        lw       $v0,  __s01_
        .set     noat
        move     $at, $k1          # Restore $at
        .set     at
# *** NO PSEUDO INSTRUCTION PASSED THIS POINT IN HANDLER ***
        eret               # New instruction in MIPS32; replaces rfe
        nop
#========================================================================

#(A)=========KERNEL INITIALIZATION w/EXCEPTION PROCESSING===========
_init_kernel:
    addiu $sp, $sp, -4      # Push
    sw     $ra, 0($sp)      # Save return address
    mtc0   $zero, $12       # DISABLE ALL interrupts(C0_STATUS=$12)
    mtc0   $zero, $13       # Clear/ACK ALL interrupts(C0_CAUSE=$13)
#---------Reset IO Interface-----------------------------------------
    la     $a0, 0xFFFF0000  # RESET Console I/O to polled(default)
    sw     $zero, 0($a0)    # Disable receiver(0xffff0000)
    sw     $zero, 8($a0)    # Disable transmitter(0xffff0008)
#---
    jal    _IO_init         # Initialization for IO interrupts
    nop                     # Branch-delay-slot
#----------Reset/Enable TIMER Interface----------------------------
    mtc0   $zero, $9        # CLEAR C0_Timer_Register($9)
    mtc0   $zero, $11       # Clear C0_Compare_Register($11)
#---                               (Disable compare)
    li     $a0,   100       # Compare timer value (default=100)
    li     $a1,   0         # Turn off debug mode (default=off)
    jal    _timer_init      # Setup Timer for interrupts
    nop                     # Branch-delay-slot
#----------Initialize COPROCESOR_0 Interface (Status/Cause)
    mtc0   $zero, $13       # CLEAR entire C0_CAUSE register
    mfc0   $a0, $12         ### Configure C0_STATUS Register
    nop                     ##Delay Slot
    ori    $a0, $a0, 0x0011 ### Select User mode and enable
#                               global interrupts
    mtc0,  $a0, $12         # ENABLE selected interrupts in
#                               C0_STATUS(0x8c11)
#----------------------------------------------------------------
    lw     $ra, 0($sp)      # Restore return address
    addiu  $sp, $sp, 4      # Pop
    jr     $ra
    nop                     # Branch-delay-slot

#(B)---------TIMER INITIALIZATION------------------------------
_timer_init:               # $a0 = compare reg, $a1 = debug on/off
    mtc0   $a0,   $11      # SET C0_Compare_Register($11)
    sw     $a1,   _TIMER_DISPLAY # set/reset debug mode
    sw     $zero, _TIMER_CLOCK   # clear Timer clock
    #---------- Select TIMER Interrupt
    mfc0   $a0, $12         ### Configure C0_STATUS Register
    nop                     ##Delay Slot
    ori    $a0, $a0, 0x8000 ### Select/enable TIMER
    mtc0,  $a0, $12         ### Set interrupt mask in C0_STATUS
    jr     $ra
    nop                     # Branch-delay-slot
#----------
```

```
#(B)========USER ACCESSABLE TIMER ROUTINES====================
_setTimer:                    # $a0 = compare register tick count
    mtc0    $zero, $9       # CLEAR CO_Timer_Register($9)
    mtc0    $a0,   $11      # SET CO_Compare_Register($11)
    sw      $zero, _TIMER_CLOCK # clear Timer clock
    jr      $ra
    nop                     # Branch-delay-slot
#-----------
_getTimer:                    # $v0 returns current timer value
    mfc0    $v1, $9         # READ CO_Timer_Register($9)
    mfc0    $v0, $11        # READ CO_Compare_Register($11)
    jr      $ra
    nop                     # Branch-delay-slot
    #-----------
_getTmClock:                  # $v0 returns current timer cycle count
    lw      $v0, _TIMER_CLOCK
    jr      $ra
    nop                     # Branch-delay-slot
#-----------
_displayTimer:                # display print $a0=(on=1, off=0)
    sw      $a0, _TIMER_DISPLAY
    jr      $ra
    nop                     # Branch-delay-slot
#(C)---------TERMINAL INITIALIZATION----------------------------
_IO_init:
#---------Enable I/O INTR here
    la      $v0, 0xFFFF0000    # Setup Console I/O for interrupts
    li      $v1, 2             # Load interrupt enable bits
    sw      $v1, 0($v0)        # SET receiver on
    sw      $v1, 8($v0)        # SET transmitter on
#----------Initialize I/O BUFFERS
    la      $a0, _bufin
    sw      $a0, _bufin_put
    sw      $a0, _bufin_get
    sw      $zero, 0($a0)
    la      $a0, _bufout
    sw      $a0, _bufout_put
    sw      $a0, _bufout_get
    sw      $zero, 0($a0)
#---------- Select I/O Interrupts
    mfc0    $a0, $12              ### Configure C0_STATUS Register
    nop                          ### Delay Slot
    ori     $a0, $a0, 0x0c00     ### Select/enable IO
    mtc0,   $a0, $12             ### Set interrupt mask in C0_STATUS
    jr      $ra
    nop         # Branch-delay-slot
#========USER ACCESSABLE IO I/O ROUTINES=========================
#--------TERMINAL INPUT-----------------------------------------
_IO_getc:
    lw      $a0, _bufin_get  # Read character from kernel buffer
    nop                      # Load-delay-slot
    lbu     $v0, 0($a0)
    nop                      # Load-delay-slot
    beqz    $v0, _tgetc_2    # Check for empty buffer
    nop                      # Branch-delay-slot
    sb      $zero, 0($a0)    # Clear current buffer location
    addiu   $a0, $a0, 1      # Increment buffer output pointer
```

```
        la      $v1, _bufin_end     # Check for buffer wrap
        bne     $v1, $a0, _tgetc_1
        nop                         # Branch-delay-slot
        la      $a0, _bufin         # Wrap to start of buffer
_tgetc_1:
        sw      $a0, _bufin_get
        jr      $ra
        nop                         # Branch-delay-slot
#------------------------------
_tgetc_2:
        li      $v0, -1
        jr      $ra
        nop         # Branch-delay-slot
#---------TERMINAL OUTPUT-------------------------------------------
_IO_putc:
        lw      $v0, _bufout_put    # Check for empty buffer
        nop                         # Load-delay-slot
        lb      $v1, 0($v0)
        nop                         # Load-delay-slot
        bnez    $v1, _tputc_2
        nop                         # Branch-delay-slot
        lw      $v0, _bufout_put    # Check for full buffer
        nop                         # Load-delay-slot
        lb      $v1, 0($v0)
        nop                         # Load-delay-slot
        bnez    $v1, _tputc_2       # buffer ?
        nop                         # Branch-delay-slot
        sb      $a0, 0($v0)         # Write character to kernel buffer

        addiu   $a0, $v0, 1         # Increment buffer output pointer
        la      $v0, _bufout_end    # Check for buffer wrap
        bne     $v0, $a0, _tputc_1
        nop                         # Branch-delay-slot
        la      $a0, _bufout        # wrap to start of buffer
_tputc_1:
        sw      $a0, _bufout_put    # Update the pointer
        li      $v0, 1              # successful
        jr      $ra
        nop                         # Branch-delay-slot
#------------------------------
_tputc_2:
        li      $v0, 0              # failed
        jr      $ra
        nop                         # Branch-delay-slot
#---------TERMINAL FLUSH--------------------------------------------
_IO_flush:
        lw      $a0, _bufout_get    # Check for character to output
        nop                         # Load-delay-slot
        lbu     $v0, 0($a0)
        nop                         # Load-delay-slot
        beqz    $v0, _tflush_3      # buffer empty?
        nop                         # Branch-delay-slot
#-----------
        sb      $zero, 0($a0)       # Clear current buffer location
        addiu   $a0, $a0, 1         # Increment buffer output pointer
        la      $v1, _bufout_end
        bne     $v1, $a0, _tflush_1
```

```
        nop                             # Branch-delay-slot
        la      $a0, _bufout            # Wrap to start of buffer
_tflush_1:
        sw      $a0, _bufout_get        # Update the pointer
_tflush_2:
        li      $a0, 0xffff0000         # Write the character to output device
        lw      $v1, 8($a0)             # Poll to output first character
        nop                             # Load-delay-slot
        andi    $v1, $v1, 1
        beqz    $v1, _tflush_2
        nop                             # Branch-delay-slot
        sw      $v0, 12($a0)            # Write character to output device
_tflush_3:
        jr      $ra
        nop                             # Branch-delay-slot
#---------TERMINAL EMPTY?----------------------------------------
_IO_empty:
        lw      $a0, _bufout_get        # Check for character to output
        nop                             # Load-delay-slot
        lbu     $v0, 0($a0)
        jr      $ra
        nop                             # Branch-delay-slot


#----------------------------------------------------------------
#=======END OF KERNEL RESIDENT CODE==============================

#=======KERNEL INITIALIZATION/USER PROGRAM LINKAGE======================
        .text
        .globl __start
__start:
# Standard startup code.  Invoke the routine "main" with arguments:
#       main(argc, argv, envp)
        lw      $a0, 0($sp)      # argc
        addiu   $a1, $sp, 4      # argv
        addiu   $a2, $a1, 4      # envp
        sll     $v0, $a0, 2
        addu    $a2, $a2, $v0

# ---Initialize kernel/exception handlers-------------------------
# This is far away in the kernel (different 256K block) so a jump
# register is needed. Other handlers could be initialized here.
        la      $ra, _init_kernel
        jalr    $ra
        nop                             # Branch-delay-slot
# ---End of kernel/exception handlers initialization -------------

# Finally jump to the user's program starting at "main":
        jal     main
        nop

        li      $v0, 10                 # syscall 10 (exit)
        syscall


#================================================================
# Special linkage: kernel and user code reside in very far apart 256MB
# blocks so special code is necessary. The following allows user access
# to the IO and TIMER interface routines written above.
```

```
#----------------Memory Mapped I/O Stuff----------------------------------
        .globl  .IO_getc    #   ;$v0 - char(0-255), (-1 = not available)
        .globl  .IO_putc    #   $a0 = char(0-255)
        .globl  .IO_empty   #   ;$v0 = (0==empty)/(!0==!empty)
        .globl  .IO_flush   #   void

.IO_getc:  la   $v1,_IO_getc  ;  jr   $v1 ; nop
.IO_putc:  la   $v1,_IO_putc  ;  jr   $v1 ; nop
.IO_flush: la   $v1,_IO_flush ;  jr   $v1 ; nop
.IO_empty: la   $v1,_IO_empty ;  jr   $v1 ; nop
#----------------Timer/Clock Stuff----------------------------------------
        .globl   .TIMER_set      #   $a0 = compare_reg value
        .globl   .TIMER_get      #   ;$v0 = compare_reg value,
                                 #   ;$v1 = timer_reg value
        .globl   .TIMER_getClock #   ;$v0 = clock value
        .globl   .TIMER_display  #   $a0 = ON=1/OFF=0

.TIMER_set:       la   $v1, _setTimer      ; jr   $v1 ; nop
.TIMER_get:       la   $v1, _getTimer      ; jr   $v1 ; nop
.TIMER_getClock:  la   $v1, _getTmClock    ; jr   $v1 ; nop
.TIMER_display:   la   $v1, _displayTimer  ; jr   $v1 ; nop
#=========================================================================
        .globl __eoth
__eoth:
#=======END OF USER SPACE/PROGRAM LINKAGE/INTERFACE STUB===========
```

SPIM S20: A MIPS R2000 Simulator[*]

$"\frac{1}{25}"^{th}$ the performance at none of the cost"

James R. Larus
larus@cs.wisc.edu
Computer Sciences Department
University of Wisconsin–Madison
1210 West Dayton Street
Madison, WI 53706, USA
608-262-9519

1   SPIM

SPIM S20 is a simulator that runs programs for the MIPS R2000/R3000 RISC computers.[1]
SPIM can read and immediately execute files containing assembly language. SPIM is a self-contained system for running these programs and contains a debugger and interface to a few operating system services.

The architecture of the MIPS computers is simple and regular, which makes it easy to learn and understand. The processor contains 32 general-purpose 32-bit registers and a well-designed instruction set that make it a propitious target for generating code in a compiler.

However, the obvious question is: why use a simulator when many people have workstations that contain a hardware, and hence significantly faster, implementation of this computer? One reason is that these workstations are not generally available. Another reason is that these machine will not persist for many years because of the rapid progress leading to new and faster computers. Unfortunately, the trend is to make computers faster by executing several instructions concurrently, which makes their architecture more difficult to understand and program. The MIPS architecture may be the epitome of a simple, clean RISC machine.

In addition, simulators can provide a better environment for low-level programming than an actual machine because they can detect more errors and provide more features than an actual computer. For example, SPIM has a X-window interface that is better than most debuggers for the actual machines.

---

[*]I grateful to the many students at UW who used SPIM in their courses and happily found bugs in a professor's code. In particular, the students in CS536, Spring 1990, painfully found the last few bugs in an "already-debugged" simulator. I am grateful for their patience and persistence. Alan Yuen-wui Siow wrote the X-window interface.

[1]For a description of the real machines, see Gerry Kane and Joe Heinrich, *MIPS RISC Architecture*, Prentice Hall, 1992.

Finally, simulators are an useful tool for studying computers and the programs that run on them. Because they are implemented in software, not silicon, they can be easily modified to add new instructions, build new systems such as multiprocessors, or simply to collect data.

1.1 Simulation of a Virtual Machine

The MIPS architecture, like that of most RISC computers, is difficult to program directly because of its delayed branches, delayed loads, and restricted address modes. This difficulty is tolerable since these computers were designed to be programmed in high-level languages and so present an interface designed for compilers, not programmers. A good part of the complexity results from delayed instructions. A *delayed branch* takes two cycles to execute. In the second cycle, the instruction immediately following the branch executes. This instruction can perform useful work that normally would have been done before the branch or it can be a **nop** (no operation). Similarly, *delayed loads* take two cycles so the instruction immediately following a load cannot use the value loaded from memory.

MIPS wisely choose to hide this complexity by implementing a *virtual machine* with their assembler. This virtual computer appears to have non-delayed branches and loads and a richer instruction set than the actual hardware. The assembler *reorganizes* (rearranges) instructions to fill the delay slots. It also simulates the additional, *pseudoinstructions* by generating short sequences of actual instructions.

By default, SPIM simulates the richer, virtual machine. It can also simulate the actual hardware. We will describe the virtual machine and only mention in passing features that do not belong to the actual hardware. In doing so, we are following the convention of MIPS assembly language programmers (and compilers), who routinely take advantage of the extended machine. Instructions marked with a dagger (†) are pseudoinstructions.

1.2 SPIM Interface

SPIM provides a simple terminal and a X-window interface. Both provide equivalent functionality, but the X interface is generally easier to use and more informative.

spim, the terminal version, and **xspim**, the X version, have the following command-line options:

-bare
> Simulate a bare MIPS machine without pseudoinstructions or the additional addressing modes provided by the assembler. Implies **-quiet**.

-asm
> Simulate the virtual MIPS machine provided by the assembler. This is the default.

-pseudo
> Accept pseudoinstructions in assembly code.

-nopseudo
> Do not accept pseudoinstructions in assembly code.

-notrap
> Do not load the standard trap handler. This trap handler has two functions that must be assumed by the user's program. First, it handles traps. When a trap occurs, SPIM jumps to location 0x80000080, which should contain code to service the exception. Second,

this file contains startup code that invokes the routine `main`. Without the trap handler, execution begins at the instruction labeled `__start`.

`-trap`

> Load the standard trap handler. This is the default.

`-trap_file`

> Load the trap handler in the file.

`-noquiet`

> Print a message when an exception occurs. This is the default.

`-quiet`

> Do not print a message at an exception.

`-nomapped_io`

> Disable the memory-mapped IO facility (see Section 5).

`-mapped_io`

> Enable the memory-mapped IO facility (see Section 5). Programs that use SPIM syscalls (see Section 1.5) to read from the terminal should not also use memory-mapped IO.

`-file`

> Load and execute the assembly code in the file.

`-s seg size` Sets the initial size of memory segment *seg* to be *size* bytes. The memory segments are named: `text`, `data`, `stack`, `ktext`, and `kdata`. For example, the pair of arguments `-sdata 2000000` starts the user data segment at 2,000,000 bytes.

`-lseg size` Sets the limit on how large memory segment *seg* can grow to be *size* bytes. The memory segments that can grow are: `data`, `stack`, and `kdata`.

1.2.1   Terminal Interface

The terminal interface (`spim`) provides the following commands:

`exit`

> Exit the simulator.

`read "file"`

> Read *file* of assembly language commands into SPIM's memory. If the file has already been read into SPIM, the system should be cleared (see `reinitialize`, below) or global symbols will be multiply defined.

`load "file"`

> Synonym for `read`.

`run <addr>`

> Start running a program. If the optional address *addr* is provided, the program starts at that address. Otherwise, the program starts at the global symbol `__start`, which is defined by the default trap handler to call the routine at the global symbol `main` with the usual MIPS calling convention.

step <N>

Step the program for *N* (default: 1) instructions. Print instructions as they execute

continue

Continue program execution without stepping.

print $N

Print register *N*.

print $fN

Print floating point register *N*.

print addr

Print the contents of memory at address *addr*.

print_sym

Print the contents of the symbol table, i.e., the addresses of the global (but not local) symbols.

reinitialize

Clear the memory and registers.

breakpoint addr

Set a breakpoint at address *addr*. *addr* can be either a memory address or symbolic label.

delete addr

Delete all breakpoints at address *addr*.

list

List all breakpoints.

.

Rest of line is an assembly instruction that is stored in memory.

<nl>

A newline reexecutes previous command.

?

Print a help message.

Most commands can be abbreviated to their unique prefix e.g., **ex**, **re**, **l**, **ru**, **s**, **p**. More dangerous commands, such as **reinitialize**, require a longer prefix.

1.2.2   X-Window Interface

The X version of SPIM, **xspim**, looks different, but should operate in the same manner as **spim**. The X window has five panes (see Figure 1). The top pane displays the contents of the registers. It is continually updated, except while a program is running.

The next pane contains the buttons that control the simulator:

quit

Exit from the simulator.

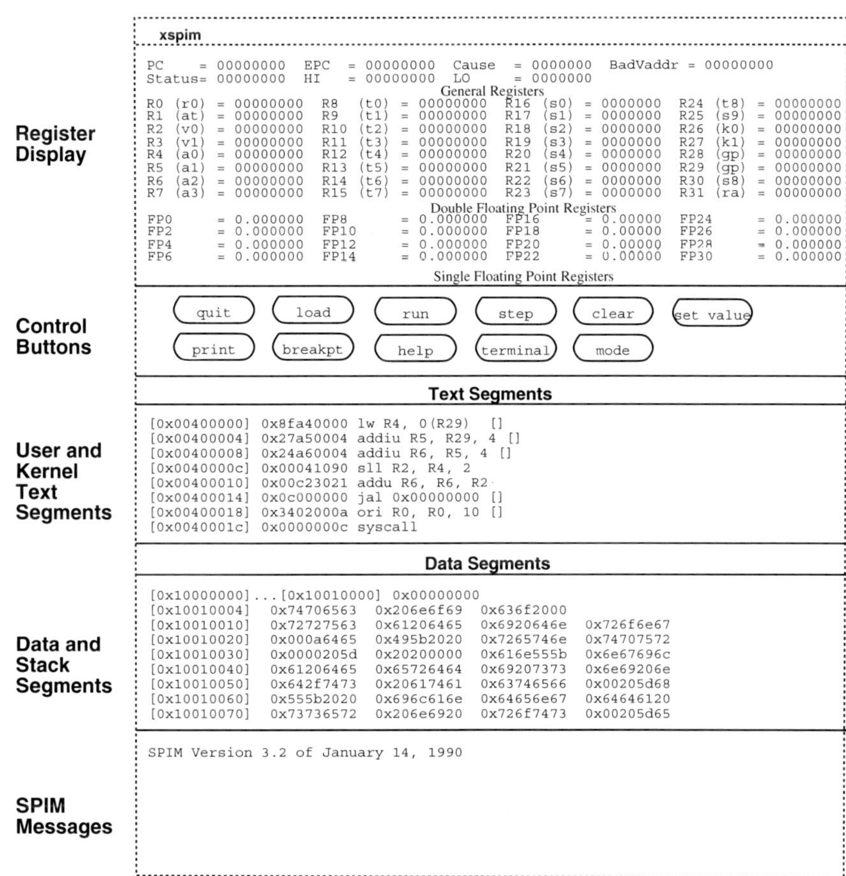

Register Display

Control Buttons

User and Kernel Text Segments

Data and Stack Segments

SPIM Messages

Figure 1: X-window interface to SPIM.

load
Read a source file into memory.

run
Start the program running.

step
Single-step through a program.

clear
Reinitialize registers or memory.

set value
Set the value in a register or memory location.

print
Print the value in a register or memory location.

breakpoint
Set or delete a breakpoint or list all breakpoints.

help
Print a help message.

terminal
Raise or hide the console window.

mode
Set SPIM operating modes.

The next two panes display the memory contents. The top one shows instructions from the user and kernel text segments.[2] The first few instructions in the text segment are startup code (`__start`) that loads `argc` and `argv` into registers and invokes the `main` routine.

The lower of these two panes displays the data and stack segments. Both panes are updated as a program executes.

The bottom pane is used to display messages from the simulator. It does not display output from an executing program. When a program reads or writes, its IO appears in a separate window, called the Console, which pops up when needed.

1.3 Surprising Features

Although SPIM faithfully simulates the MIPS computer, it is a simulator and certain things are not identical to the actual computer. The most obvious differences are that instruction timing and the memory systems are not identical. SPIM does not simulate caches or memory latency, nor does it accurate reflect the delays for floating point operations or multiplies and divides.

Another surprise (which occurs on the real machine as well) is that a pseudoinstruction expands into several machine instructions. When single-stepping or examining memory, the instructions that you see are slightly different from the source program. The correspondence between the two sets of instructions is fairly simple since SPIM does not reorganize the instructions to fill delay slots.

---

[2]These instructions are real—not pseudo—MIPS instructions. SPIM translates assembler pseudoinstructions to 1–3 MIPS instructions before storing the program in memory. Each source instruction appears as a comment on the first instruction to which it is translated.

1.4   Assembler Syntax

Comments in assembler files begin with a sharp-sign (#). Everything from the sharp-sign to the end of the line is ignored.

Identifiers are a sequence of alphanumeric characters, underbars (_), and dots (.) that do not begin with a number. Opcodes for instructions are reserved words that are **not** valid identifiers. Labels are declared by putting them at the beginning of a line followed by a colon, for example:

```
        .data
  item: .word 1
        .text
        .globl main              # Must be global
  main: lw $t0, item
```

Strings are enclosed in double-quotes ("). Special characters in strings follow the C convention:

```
  newline          \n
  tab              \t
  quote            \"
```

SPIM supports a subset of the assembler directives provided by the MIPS assembler:

.align n
> Align the next datum on a 2^n byte boundary. For example, `.align 2` aligns the next value on a word boundary. `.align 0` turns off automatic alignment of `.half`, `.word`, `.float`, and `.double` directives until the next `.data` or `.kdata` directive.

.ascii str
> Store the string in memory, but do not null-terminate it.

.asciiz str
> Store the string in memory and null-terminate it.

.byte b1, ..., bn
> Store the n values in successive bytes of memory.

.data <addr>
> The following data items should be stored in the data segment. If the optional argument *addr* is present, the items are stored beginning at address *addr*.

.double d1, ..., dn
> Store the n floating point double precision numbers in successive memory locations.

.extern sym size
> Declare that the datum stored at `sym` is `size` bytes large and is a global symbol. This directive enables the assembler to store the datum in a portion of the data segment that is efficiently accessed via register `$gp`.

.float f1, ..., fn
> Store the n floating point single precision numbers in successive memory locations.

.globl sym
> Declare that symbol `sym` is global and can be referenced from other files.

Service	System Call Code	Arguments	Result
print_int	1	$a0 = integer	
print_float	2	$f12 = float	
print_double	3	$f12 = double	
print_string	4	$a0 = string	
read_int	5		integer (in $v0)
read_float	6		float (in $f0)
read_double	7		double (in $f0)
read_string	8	$a0 = buffer, $a1 = length	
sbrk	9	$a0 = amount	address (in $v0)
exit	10		

Table 1: System services.

.half h1, ..., hn
Store the n 16-bit quantities in successive memory halfwords.

.kdata <addr>
The following data items should be stored in the kernel data segment. If the optional argument *addr* is present, the items are stored beginning at address *addr*.

.ktext <addr>
The next items are put in the kernel text segment. In SPIM, these items may only be instructions or words (see the `.word` directive below). If the optional argument *addr* is present, the items are stored beginning at address *addr*.

.space n
Allocate n bytes of space in the current segment (which must be the data segment in SPIM).

.text <addr>
The next items are put in the user text segment. In SPIM, these items may only be instructions or words (see the `.word` directive below). If the optional argument *addr* is present, the items are stored beginning at address *addr*.

.word w1, ..., wn
Store the n 32-bit quantities in successive memory words.

SPIM does not distinguish various parts of the data segment (`.data`, `.rdata`, and `.sdata`).

1.5   System Calls

SPIM provides a small set of operating-system-like services through the system call (`syscall`) instruction. To request a service, a program loads the system call code (see Table 1) into register $v0 and the arguments into registers $a0...$a3 (or $f12 for floating point values). System calls that return values put their result in register $v0 (or $f0 for floating point results). For example, to print "`the answer = 5`", use the commands:

```
        .data
str:    .asciiz "the answer = "
        .text
```

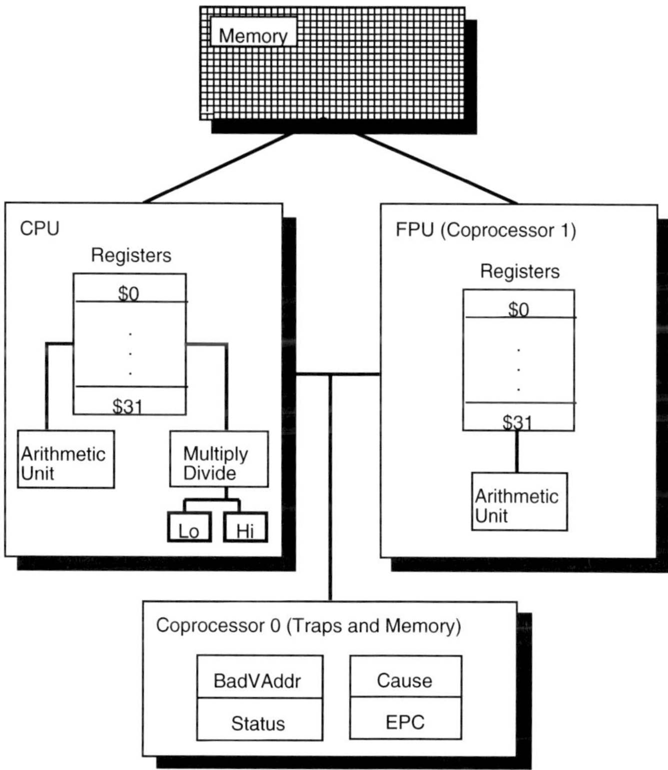

Figure 2: MIPS R2000 CPU and FPU

```
li $v0, 4          # system call code for print_str
la $a0, str        # address of string to print
syscall            # print the string

li $v0, 1          # system call code for print_int
li $a0, 5          # integer to print
syscall            # print it
```

print_int is passed an integer and prints it on the console. **print_float** prints a single floating point number. **print_double** prints a double precision number. **print_string** is passed a pointer to a null-terminated string, which it writes to the console.

read_int, **read_float**, and **read_double** read an entire line of input up to and including the newline. Characters following the number are ignored. **read_string** has the same semantics as the Unix library routine **fgets**. It reads up to $n - 1$ characters into a buffer and terminates the string with a null byte. If there are fewer characters on the current line, it reads through the newline and again null-terminates the string. **Warning:** programs that use these syscalls to read from the terminal should not use memory-mapped IO (see Section 5).

sbrk returns a pointer to a block of memory containing n additional bytes. **exit** stops a program from running.

Register Name	Number	Usage
zero	0	Constant 0
at	1	Reserved for assembler
v0	2	Expression evaluation and
v1	3	results of a function
a0	4	Argument 1
a1	5	Argument 2
a2	6	Argument 3
a3	7	Argument 4
t0	8	Temporary (not preserved across call)
t1	9	Temporary (not preserved across call)
t2	10	Temporary (not preserved across call)
t3	11	Temporary (not preserved across call)
t4	12	Temporary (not preserved across call)
t5	13	Temporary (not preserved across call)
t6	14	Temporary (not preserved across call)
t7	15	Temporary (not preserved across call)
s0	16	Saved temporary (preserved across call)
s1	17	Saved temporary (preserved across call)
s2	18	Saved temporary (preserved across call)
s3	19	Saved temporary (preserved across call)
s4	20	Saved temporary (preserved across call)
s5	21	Saved temporary (preserved across call)
s6	22	Saved temporary (preserved across call)
s7	23	Saved temporary (preserved across call)
t8	24	Temporary (not preserved across call)
t9	25	Temporary (not preserved across call)
k0	26	Reserved for OS kernel
k1	27	Reserved for OS kernel
gp	28	Pointer to global area
sp	29	Stack pointer
fp	30	Frame pointer
ra	31	Return address (used by function call)

Table 2: MIPS registers and the convention governing their use.

2   Description of the MIPS R2000

A MIPS processor consists of an integer processing unit (the CPU) and a collection of coprocessors that perform ancillary tasks or operate on other types of data such as floating point numbers (see Figure 2). SPIM simulates two coprocessors. Coprocessor 0 handles traps, exceptions, and the virtual memory system. SPIM simulates most of the first two and entirely omits details of the memory system. Coprocessor 1 is the floating point unit. SPIM simulates most aspects of this unit.

2.1   CPU Registers

The MIPS (and SPIM) central processing unit contains 32 general purpose 32-bit registers that are numbered 0–31. Register n is designated by \$n. Register \$0 always contains the hardwired value 0. MIPS has established a set of conventions as to how registers should be used. These suggestions are guidelines, which are not enforced by the hardware. However a program that

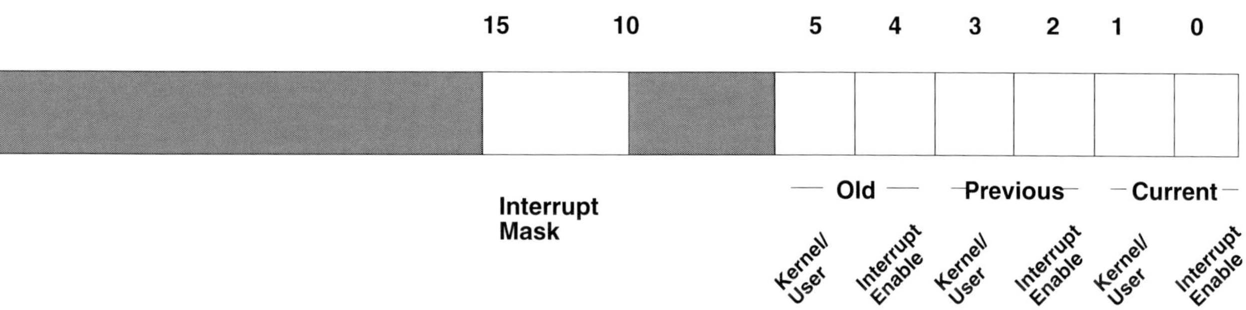

Figure 3: The `Status` register.

violates them will not work properly with other software. Table 2 lists the registers and describes their intended use.

Registers `$at` (1), `$k0` (26), and `$k1` (27) are reserved for use by the assembler and operating system.

Registers `$a0`–`$a3` (4–7) are used to pass the first four arguments to routines (remaining arguments are passed on the stack). Registers `$v0` and `$v1` (2, 3) are used to return values from functions. Registers `$t0`–`$t9` (8–15, 24, 25) are caller-saved registers used for temporary quantities that do not need to be preserved across calls. Registers `$s0`–`$s7` (16–23) are callee-saved registers that hold long-lived values that should be preserved across calls.

Register `$sp` (29) is the stack pointer, which points to the last location in use on the stack.[3] Register `$fp` (30) is the frame pointer.[4] Register `$ra` (31) is written with the return address for a call by the `jal` instruction.

Register `$gp` (28) is a global pointer that points into the middle of a 64K block of memory in the heap that holds constants and global variables. The objects in this heap can be quickly accessed with a single load or store instruction.

In addition, coprocessor 0 contains registers that are useful to handle exceptions. SPIM does not implement all of these registers, since they are not of much use in a simulator or are part of the memory system, which is not implemented. However, it does provide the following:

Register Name	Number	Usage
BadVAddr	8	Memory address at which address exception occurred
Status	12	Interrupt mask and enable bits
Cause	13	Exception type and pending interrupt bits
EPC	14	Address of instruction that caused exception

These registers are part of coprocessor 0's register set and are accessed by the `lwc0`, `mfc0`, `mtc0`, and `swc0` instructions.

Figure 3 describes the bits in the `Status` register that are implemented by SPIM. The **interrupt mask** contains a bit for each of the five interrupt levels. If a bit is one, interrupts at that level are allowed. If the bit is zero, interrupts at that level are disabled. The low six bits of the `Status` register implement a three-level stack for the **kernel/user** and **interrupt enable** bits. The **kernel/user** bit is 0 if the program was running in the kernel when the interrupt occurred and 1 if it was in user mode. If the **interrupt enable** bit is 1, interrupts are allowed.

---

[3]In earlier version of SPIM, `$sp` was documented as pointing at the first free word on the stack (not the last word of the stack frame). Recent MIPS documents have made it clear that this was an error. Both conventions work equally well, but we choose to follow the real system.

[4]The MIPS compiler does not use a frame pointer, so this register is used as callee-saved register `$s8`.

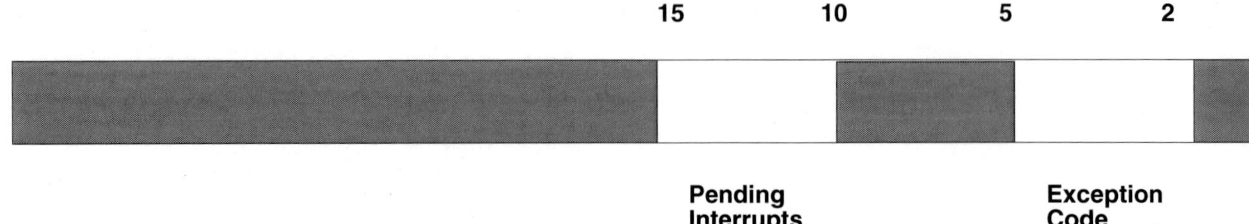

Figure 4: The `Cause` register.

If it is 0, they are disabled. At an interrupt, these six bits are shifted left by two bits, so the current bits become the previous bits and the previous bits become the old bits. The current bits are both set to 0 (i.e., kernel mode with interrupts disabled).

Figure 4 describes the bits in the `Cause` registers. The five **pending interrupt** bits correspond to the five interrupt levels. A bit becomes 1 when an interrupt at its level has occurred but has not been serviced. The **exception code** register contains a code from the following table describing the cause of an exception.

Number	Name	Description
0	INT	External interrupt
4	ADDRL	Address error exception (load or instruction fetch)
5	ADDRS	Address error exception (store)
6	IBUS	Bus error on instruction fetch
7	DBUS	Bus error on data load or store
8	SYSCALL	Syscall exception
9	BKPT	Breakpoint exception
10	RI	Reserved instruction exception
12	OVF	Arithmetic overflow exception

2.2 Byte Order

Processors can number the bytes within a word to make the byte with the lowest number either the leftmost or rightmost one. The convention used by a machine is its *byte order*. MIPS processors can operate with either *big-endian* byte order:

Byte #

0	1	2	3

or *little-endian* byte order:

Byte #

3	2	1	0

SPIM operates with both byte orders. SPIM's byte order is determined by the byte order of the underlying hardware running the simulator. On a DECstation 3100, SPIM is little-endian, while on a HP Bobcat, Sun 4 or PC/RT, SPIM is big-endian.

2.3 Addressing Modes

MIPS is a load/store architecture, which means that only load and store instructions access memory. Computation instructions operate only on values in registers. The bare machine provides only one memory addressing mode: `c(rx)`, which uses the sum of the immediate (integer) `c` and the contents of register `rx` as the address. The virtual machine provides the following addressing modes for load and store instructions:

Format	Address Computation
(register)	contents of register
imm	immediate
imm (register)	immediate + contents of register
symbol	address of symbol
symbol ± imm	address of symbol + or − immediate
symbol ± imm (register)	address of symbol + or − (immediate + contents of register)

Most load and store instructions operate only on aligned data. A quantity is *aligned* if its memory address is a multiple of its size in bytes. Therefore, a halfword object must be stored at even addresses and a full word object must be stored at addresses that are a multiple of 4. However, MIPS provides some instructions for manipulating unaligned data.

2.4   Arithmetic and Logical Instructions

In all instructions below, `Src2` can either be a register or an immediate value (a 16 bit integer). The immediate forms of the instructions are only included for reference. The assembler will translate the more general form of an instruction (e.g., `add`) into the immediate form (e.g., `addi`) if the second argument is constant.

`abs Rdest, Rsrc`   *Absolute Value* [†]
Put the absolute value of the integer from register `Rsrc` in register `Rdest`.

`add Rdest, Rsrc1, Src2`   *Addition (with overflow)*
`addi Rdest, Rsrc1, Imm`   *Addition Immediate (with overflow)*
`addu Rdest, Rsrc1, Src2`   *Addition (without overflow)*
`addiu Rdest, Rsrc1, Imm`   *Addition Immediate (without overflow)*
Put the sum of the integers from register `Rsrc1` and `Src2` (or `Imm`) into register `Rdest`.

`and Rdest, Rsrc1, Src2`   *AND*
`andi Rdest, Rsrc1, Imm`   *AND Immediate*
Put the logical AND of the integers from register `Rsrc1` and `Src2` (or `Imm`) into register `Rdest`.

`div Rsrc1, Rsrc2`   *Divide (signed)*
`divu Rsrc1, Rsrc2`   *Divide (unsigned)*
Divide the contents of the two registers. `divu` treats is operands as unsigned values. Leave the quotient in register `lo` and the remainder in register `hi`. Note that if an operand is negative, the remainder is unspecified by the MIPS architecture and depends on the conventions of the machine on which SPIM is run.

`div Rdest, Rsrc1, Src2`   *Divide (signed, with overflow)* [†]
`divu Rdest, Rsrc1, Src2`   *Divide (unsigned, without overflow)* [†]
Put the quotient of the integers from register `Rsrc1` and `Src2` into register `Rdest`. `divu` treats is operands as unsigned values.

`mul Rdest, Rsrc1, Src2`   *Multiply (without overflow)* [†]
`mulo Rdest, Rsrc1, Src2`   *Multiply (with overflow)* [†]

`mulou Rdest, Rsrc1, Src2`   *Unsigned Multiply (with overflow)* [†]

Put the product of the integers from register `Rsrc1` and `Src2` into register `Rdest`.

`mult Rsrc1, Rsrc2`   *Multiply*
`multu Rsrc1, Rsrc2`   *Unsigned Multiply*

Multiply the contents of the two registers. Leave the low-order word of the product in register `lo` and the high-word in register `hi`.

`neg Rdest, Rsrc`   *Negate Value (with overflow)* [†]
`negu Rdest, Rsrc`   *Negate Value (without overflow)* [†]

Put the negative of the integer from register `Rsrc` into register `Rdest`.

`nor Rdest, Rsrc1, Src2`   *NOR*

Put the logical NOR of the integers from register `Rsrc1` and `Src2` into register `Rdest`.

`not Rdest, Rsrc`   *NOT* [†]

Put the bitwise logical negation of the integer from register `Rsrc` into register `Rdest`.

`or Rdest, Rsrc1, Src2`   *OR*
`ori Rdest, Rsrc1, Imm`   *OR Immediate*

Put the logical OR of the integers from register `Rsrc1` and `Src2` (or `Imm`) into register `Rdest`.

`rem Rdest, Rsrc1, Src2`   *Remainder* [†]
`remu Rdest, Rsrc1, Src2`   *Unsigned Remainder* [†]

Put the remainder from dividing the integer in register `Rsrc1` by the integer in `Src2` into register `Rdest`. Note that if an operand is negative, the remainder is unspecified by the MIPS architecture and depends on the conventions of the machine on which SPIM is run.

`rol Rdest, Rsrc1, Src2`   *Rotate Left* [†]
`ror Rdest, Rsrc1, Src2`   *Rotate Right* [†]

Rotate the contents of register `Rsrc1` left (right) by the distance indicated by `Src2` and put the result in register `Rdest`.

`sll Rdest, Rsrc1, Src2`   *Shift Left Logical*
`sllv Rdest, Rsrc1, Rsrc2`   *Shift Left Logical Variable*
`sra Rdest, Rsrc1, Src2`   *Shift Right Arithmetic*
`srav Rdest, Rsrc1, Rsrc2`   *Shift Right Arithmetic Variable*
`srl Rdest, Rsrc1, Src2`   *Shift Right Logical*
`srlv Rdest, Rsrc1, Rsrc2`   *Shift Right Logical Variable*

Shift the contents of register `Rsrc1` left (right) by the distance indicated by `Src2` (`Rsrc2`) and put the result in register `Rdest`.

`sub Rdest, Rsrc1, Src2`   *Subtract (with overflow)*
`subu Rdest, Rsrc1, Src2`   *Subtract (without overflow)*

Put the difference of the integers from register `Rsrc1` and `Src2` into register `Rdest`.

`xor Rdest, Rsrc1, Src2`   *XOR*
`xori Rdest, Rsrc1, Imm`   *XOR Immediate*

Put the logical XOR of the integers from register `Rsrc1` and `Src2` (or `Imm`) into register `Rdest`.

2.5   Constant-Manipulating Instructions

li Rdest, imm   *Load Immediate* [†]
Move the immediate imm into register Rdest.

lui Rdest, imm   *Load Upper Immediate*
Load the lower halfword of the immediate imm into the upper halfword of register Rdest. The lower bits of the register are set to 0.

2.6   Comparison Instructions

In all instructions below, Src2 can either be a register or an immediate value (a 16 bit integer).

seq Rdest, Rsrc1, Src2   *Set Equal* [†]
Set register Rdest to 1 if register Rsrc1 equals Src2 and to be 0 otherwise.

sge Rdest, Rsrc1, Src2   *Set Greater Than Equal* [†]
sgeu Rdest, Rsrc1, Src2   *Set Greater Than Equal Unsigned* [†]
Set register Rdest to 1 if register Rsrc1 is greater than or equal to Src2 and to 0 otherwise.

sgt Rdest, Rsrc1, Src2   *Set Greater Than* [†]
sgtu Rdest, Rsrc1, Src2   *Set Greater Than Unsigned* [†]
Set register Rdest to 1 if register Rsrc1 is greater than Src2 and to 0 otherwise.

sle Rdest, Rsrc1, Src2   *Set Less Than Equal* [†]
sleu Rdest, Rsrc1, Src2   *Set Less Than Equal Unsigned* [†]
Set register Rdest to 1 if register Rsrc1 is less than or equal to Src2 and to 0 otherwise.

slt Rdest, Rsrc1, Src2   *Set Less Than*
slti Rdest, Rsrc1, Imm   *Set Less Than Immediate*
sltu Rdest, Rsrc1, Src2   *Set Less Than Unsigned*
sltiu Rdest, Rsrc1, Imm   *Set Less Than Unsigned Immediate*
Set register Rdest to 1 if register Rsrc1 is less than Src2 (or Imm) and to 0 otherwise.

sne Rdest, Rsrc1, Src2   *Set Not Equal* [†]
Set register Rdest to 1 if register Rsrc1 is not equal to Src2 and to 0 otherwise.

2.7   Branch and Jump Instructions

In all instructions below, Src2 can either be a register or an immediate value (integer). Branch instructions use a signed 16-bit offset field; hence they can jump $2^{15} - 1$ *instructions* (not bytes) forward or 2^{15} instructions backwards. The *jump* instruction contains a 26 bit address field.

b label   *Branch instruction* [†]
Unconditionally branch to the instruction at the label.

bczt label   *Branch Coprocessor z True*
bczf label   *Branch Coprocessor z False*
Conditionally branch to the instruction at the label if coprocessor z's condition flag is true (false).

beq Rsrc1, Src2, label *Branch on Equal*
Conditionally branch to the instruction at the label if the contents of register Rsrc1 equals Src2.

beqz Rsrc, label *Branch on Equal Zero* [†]
Conditionally branch to the instruction at the label if the contents of Rsrc equals 0.

bge Rsrc1, Src2, label *Branch on Greater Than Equal* [†]
bgeu Rsrc1, Src2, label *Branch on GTE Unsigned* [†]
Conditionally branch to the instruction at the label if the contents of register Rsrc1 are greater than or equal to Src2.

bgez Rsrc, label *Branch on Greater Than Equal Zero*
Conditionally branch to the instruction at the label if the contents of Rsrc are greater than or equal to 0.

bgezal Rsrc, label *Branch on Greater Than Equal Zero And Link*
Conditionally branch to the instruction at the label if the contents of Rsrc are greater than or equal to 0. Save the address of the next instruction in register 31.

bgt Rsrc1, Src2, label *Branch on Greater Than* [†]
bgtu Rsrc1, Src2, label *Branch on Greater Than Unsigned* [†]
Conditionally branch to the instruction at the label if the contents of register Rsrc1 are greater than Src2.

bgtz Rsrc, label *Branch on Greater Than Zero*
Conditionally branch to the instruction at the label if the contents of Rsrc are greater than 0.

ble Rsrc1, Src2, label *Branch on Less Than Equal* [†]
bleu Rsrc1, Src2, label *Branch on LTE Unsigned* [†]
Conditionally branch to the instruction at the label if the contents of register Rsrc1 are less than or equal to Src2.

blez Rsrc, label *Branch on Less Than Equal Zero*
Conditionally branch to the instruction at the label if the contents of Rsrc are less than or equal to 0.

bgezal Rsrc, label *Branch on Greater Than Equal Zero And Link*
bltzal Rsrc, label *Branch on Less Than And Link*
Conditionally branch to the instruction at the label if the contents of Rsrc are greater or equal to 0 or less than 0, respectively. Save the address of the next instruction in register 31.

blt Rsrc1, Src2, label *Branch on Less Than* [†]
bltu Rsrc1, Src2, label *Branch on Less Than Unsigned* [†]
Conditionally branch to the instruction at the label if the contents of register Rsrc1 are less than Src2.

bltz Rsrc, label *Branch on Less Than Zero*
Conditionally branch to the instruction at the label if the contents of Rsrc are less than 0.

```
bne Rsrc1, Src2, label
```
Branch on Not Equal

Conditionally branch to the instruction at the label if the contents of register `Rsrc1` are not equal to `Src2`.

```
bnez Rsrc, label
```
Branch on Not Equal Zero [†]

Conditionally branch to the instruction at the label if the contents of `Rsrc` are not equal to 0.

```
j label
```
Jump

Unconditionally jump to the instruction at the label.

```
jal label
jalr Rsrc
```
Jump and Link
Jump and Link Register

Unconditionally jump to the instruction at the label or whose address is in register `Rsrc`. Save the address of the next instruction in register 31.

```
jr Rsrc
```
Jump Register

Unconditionally jump to the instruction whose address is in register `Rsrc`.

2.8   Load Instructions

```
la Rdest, address
```
Load Address [†]

Load computed *address*, not the contents of the location, into register `Rdest`.

```
lb Rdest, address
lbu Rdest, address
```
Load Byte
Load Unsigned Byte

Load the byte at *address* into register `Rdest`. The byte is sign-extended by the `lb`, but not the `lbu`, instruction.

```
ld Rdest, address
```
Load Double-Word [†]

Load the 64-bit quantity at *address* into registers `Rdest` and `Rdest + 1`.

```
lh Rdest, address
lhu Rdest, address
```
Load Halfword
Load Unsigned Halfword

Load the 16-bit quantity (halfword) at *address* into register `Rdest`. The halfword is sign-extended by the `lh`, but not the **lhu**, instruction .

```
lw Rdest, address
```
Load Word

Load the 32-bit quantity (word) at *address* into register `Rdest`.

```
lwcz Rdest, address
```
Load Word Coprocessor

Load the word at *address* into register `Rdest` of coprocessor z (0–3).

```
lwl Rdest, address
lwr Rdest, address
```
Load Word Left
Load Word Right

Load the left (right) bytes from the word at the possibly-unaligned *address* into register `Rdest`.

```
ulh Rdest, address
ulhu Rdest, address
```
Unaligned Load Halfword [†]
Unaligned Load Halfword Unsigned [†]

Load the 16-bit quantity (halfword) at the possibly-unaligned *address* into register `Rdest`. The halfword is sign-extended by the `ulh`, but not the `ulhu`, instruction

`ulw Rdest, address`   *Unaligned Load Word* [†]
Load the 32-bit quantity (word) at the possibly-unaligned *address* into register `Rdest`.

2.9   Store Instructions

`sb Rsrc, address`   *Store Byte*
Store the low byte from register `Rsrc` at *address*.

`sd Rsrc, address`   *Store Double-Word* [†]
Store the 64-bit quantity in registers `Rsrc` and `Rsrc + 1` at *address*.

`sh Rsrc, address`   *Store Halfword*
Store the low halfword from register `Rsrc` at *address*.

`sw Rsrc, address`   *Store Word*
Store the word from register `Rsrc` at *address*.

`swcz Rsrc, address`   *Store Word Coprocessor*
Store the word from register `Rsrc` of coprocessor z at *address*.

`swl Rsrc, address`   *Store Word Left*
`swr Rsrc, address`   *Store Word Right*
Store the left (right) bytes from register `Rsrc` at the possibly-unaligned *address*.

`ush Rsrc, address`   *Unaligned Store Halfword* [†]
Store the low halfword from register `Rsrc` at the possibly-unaligned *address*.

`usw Rsrc, address`   *Unaligned Store Word* [†]
Store the word from register `Rsrc` at the possibly-unaligned *address*.

2.10   Data Movement Instructions

`move Rdest, Rsrc`   *Move* [†]
Move the contents of `Rsrc` to `Rdest`.

The multiply and divide unit produces its result in two additional registers, hi and lo. These instructions move values to and from these registers. The multiply, divide, and remainder instructions described above are pseudoinstructions that make it appear as if this unit operates on the general registers and detect error conditions such as divide by zero or overflow.

`mfhi Rdest`   *Move From hi*
`mflo Rdest`   *Move From lo*
Move the contents of the hi (lo) register to register `Rdest`.

```
mthi Rdest                                                              Move To hi
mtlo Rdest                                                              Move To lo
```
Move the contents register `Rdest` to the hi (lo) register.

Coprocessors have their own register sets. These instructions move values between these registers and the CPU's registers.

```
mfcz Rdest, CPsrc                                             Move From Coprocessor z
```
Move the contents of coprocessor z's register `CPsrc` to CPU register `Rdest`.

```
mfc1.d Rdest, FRsrc1                                    Move Double From Coprocessor 1 †
```
Move the contents of floating point registers `FRsrc1` and `FRsrc1 + 1` to CPU registers `Rdest` and `Rdest + 1`.

```
mtcz Rsrc, CPdest                                              Move To Coprocessor z
```
Move the contents of CPU register `Rsrc` to coprocessor z's register `CPdest`.

2.11 Floating Point Instructions

The MIPS has a floating point coprocessor (numbered 1) that operates on single precision (32-bit) and double precision (64-bit) floating point numbers. This coprocessor has its own registers, which are numbered `$f0`–`$f31`. Because these registers are only 32-bits wide, two of them are required to hold doubles. To simplify matters, floating point operations only use even-numbered registers—including instructions that operate on single floats.

Values are moved in or out of these registers a word (32-bits) at a time by `lwc1`, `swc1`, `mtc1`, and `mfc1` instructions described above or by the `l.s`, `l.d`, `s.s`, and `s.d` pseudoinstructions described below. The flag set by floating point comparison operations is read by the CPU with its `bc1t` and `bc1f` instructions.

In all instructions below, `FRdest`, `FRsrc1`, `FRsrc2`, and `FRsrc` are floating point registers (e.g., `$f2`).

```
abs.d FRdest, FRsrc                              Floating Point Absolute Value Double
abs.s FRdest, FRsrc                              Floating Point Absolute Value Single
```
Compute the absolute value of the floating float double (single) in register `FRsrc` and put it in register `FRdest`.

```
add.d FRdest, FRsrc1, FRsrc2                          Floating Point Addition Double
add.s FRdest, FRsrc1, FRsrc2                          Floating Point Addition Single
```
Compute the sum of the floating float doubles (singles) in registers `FRsrc1` and `FRsrc2` and put it in register `FRdest`.

```
c.eq.d FRsrc1, FRsrc2                                          Compare Equal Double
c.eq.s FRsrc1, FRsrc2                                          Compare Equal Single
```
Compare the floating point double in register `FRsrc1` against the one in `FRsrc2` and set the floating point condition flag true if they are equal.

```
c.le.d FRsrc1, FRsrc2                              Compare Less Than Equal Double
c.le.s FRsrc1, FRsrc2                              Compare Less Than Equal Single
```
Compare the floating point double in register `FRsrc1` against the one in `FRsrc2` and set the floating point condition flag true if the first is less than or equal to the second.

```
c.lt.d FRsrc1, FRsrc2
c.lt.s FRsrc1, FRsrc2
```
Compare Less Than Double
Compare Less Than Single

Compare the floating point double in register `FRsrc1` against the one in `FRsrc2` and set the condition flag true if the first is less than the second.

```
cvt.d.s FRdest, FRsrc
cvt.d.w FRdest, FRsrc
```
Convert Single to Double
Convert Integer to Double

Convert the single precision floating point number or integer in register `FRsrc` to a double precision number and put it in register `FRdest`.

```
cvt.s.d FRdest, FRsrc
cvt.s.w FRdest, FRsrc
```
Convert Double to Single
Convert Integer to Single

Convert the double precision floating point number or integer in register `FRsrc` to a single precision number and put it in register `FRdest`.

```
cvt.w.d FRdest, FRsrc
cvt.w.s FRdest, FRsrc
```
Convert Double to Integer
Convert Single to Integer

Convert the double or single precision floating point number in register `FRsrc` to an integer and put it in register `FRdest`.

```
div.d FRdest, FRsrc1, FRsrc2
div.s FRdest, FRsrc1, FRsrc2
```
Floating Point Divide Double
Floating Point Divide Single

Compute the quotient of the floating float doubles (singles) in registers `FRsrc1` and `FRsrc2` and put it in register `FRdest`.

```
l.d FRdest, address
l.s FRdest, address
```
Load Floating Point Double [†]
Load Floating Point Single [†]

Load the floating float double (single) at `address` into register `FRdest`.

```
mov.d FRdest, FRsrc
mov.s FRdest, FRsrc
```
Move Floating Point Double
Move Floating Point Single

Move the floating float double (single) from register `FRsrc` to register `FRdest`.

```
mul.d FRdest, FRsrc1, FRsrc2
mul.s FRdest, FRsrc1, FRsrc2
```
Floating Point Multiply Double
Floating Point Multiply Single

Compute the product of the floating float doubles (singles) in registers `FRsrc1` and `FRsrc2` and put it in register `FRdest`.

```
neg.d FRdest, FRsrc
neg.s FRdest, FRsrc
```
Negate Double
Negate Single

Negate the floating point double (single) in register `FRsrc` and put it in register `FRdest`.

```
s.d FRdest, address
s.s FRdest, address
```
Store Floating Point Double [†]
Store Floating Point Single [†]

Store the floating float double (single) in register `FRdest` at `address`.

```
sub.d FRdest, FRsrc1, FRsrc2
sub.s FRdest, FRsrc1, FRsrc2
```
Floating Point Subtract Double
Floating Point Subtract Single

Compute the difference of the floating float doubles (singles) in registers `FRsrc1` and `FRsrc2` and put it in register `FRdest`.

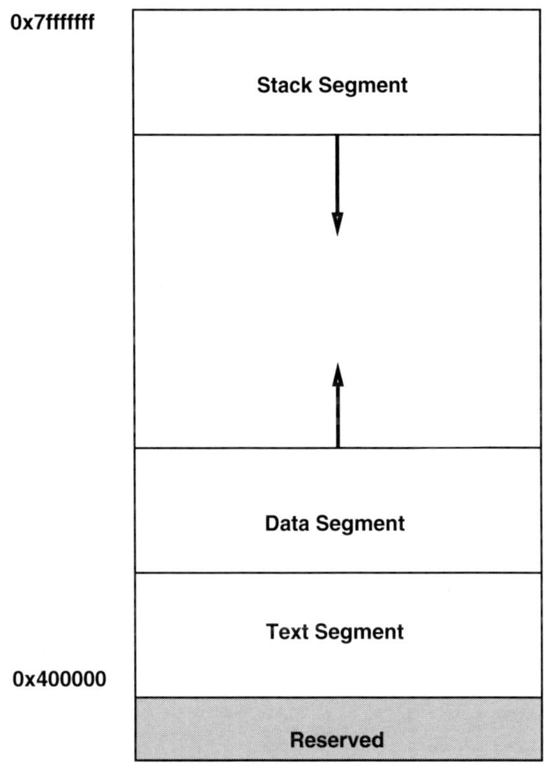

Figure 5: Layout of memory.

2.12   Exception and Trap Instructions

`rfe`   *Return From Exception*
Restore the Status register.

`syscall`   *System Call*
Register $v0 contains the number of the system call (see Table 1) provided by SPIM.

`break n`   *Break*
Cause exception n. Exception 1 is reserved for the debugger.

`nop`   *No operation*
Do nothing.

3   Memory Usage

The organization of memory in MIPS systems is conventional. A program's address space is composed of three parts (see Figure 5).

At the bottom of the user address space (0x400000) is the text segment, which holds the instructions for a program.

Above the text segment is the data segment (starting at 0x10000000), which is divided into two parts. The static data portion contains objects whose size and address are known to the

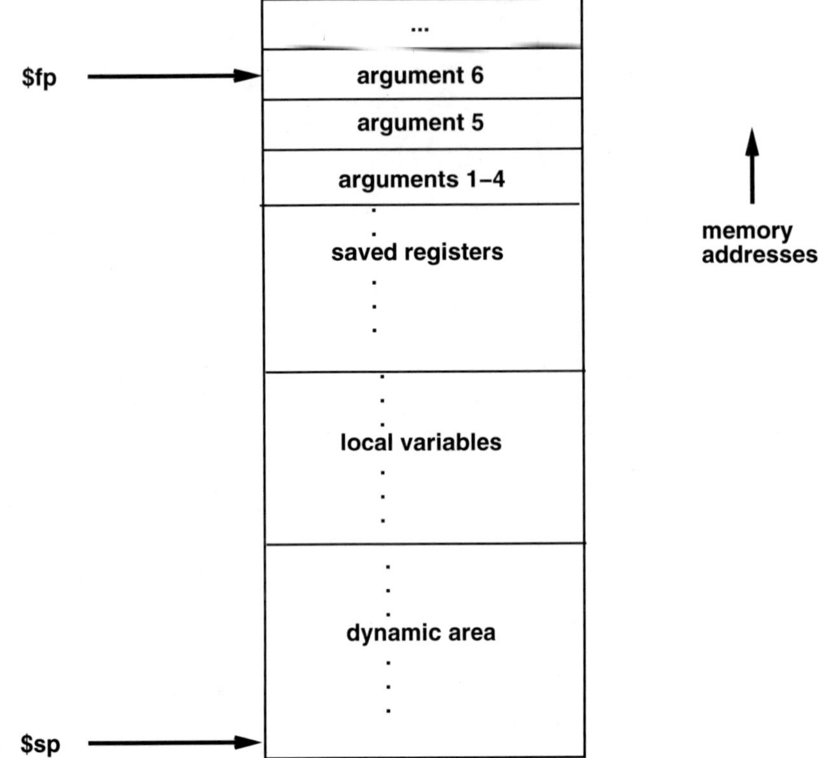

Figure 6: Layout of a stack frame. The frame pointer points just below the last argument passed on the stack. The stack pointer points to the last word in the frame.

compiler and linker. Immediately above these objects is dynamic data. As a program allocates space dynamically (i.e., by `malloc`), the `sbrk` system call moves the top of the data segment up.

The program stack resides at the top of the address space (0x7fffffff). It grows down, towards the data segment.

4   Calling Convention

The calling convention described in this section is the one used by *gcc*, not the native MIPS compiler, which uses a more complex convention that is slightly faster.

Figure 6 shows a diagram of a stack frame. A frame consists of the memory between the frame pointer (`$fp`), which points to the word immediately after the last argument passed on the stack, and the stack pointer (`$sp`), which points to the last word in the frame. As typical of Unix systems, the stack grows down from higher memory addresses, so the frame pointer is above stack pointer.

The following steps are necessary to effect a call:

1. Pass the arguments. By convention, the first four arguments are passed in registers `$a0`–`$a3` (though simpler compilers may choose to ignore this convention and pass all arguments via the stack). The remaining arguments are pushed on the stack.

2. Save the caller-saved registers. This includes registers `$t0`–`$t9`, if they contain live values at the call site.

3. Execute a `jal` instruction.

 Within the called routine, the following steps are necessary:

1. Establish the stack frame by subtracting the frame size from the stack pointer.

2. Save the callee-saved registers in the frame. Register `$fp` is always saved. Register `$ra` needs to be saved if the routine itself makes calls. Any of the registers `$s0`–`$s7` that are used by the callee need to be saved.

3. Establish the frame pointer by adding the stack frame size - 4 to the address in `$sp`.

 Finally, to return from a call, a function places the returned value into `$v0` and executes the following steps:

1. Restore any callee-saved registers that were saved upon entry (including the frame pointer `$fp`).

2. Pop the stack frame by adding the frame size to `$sp`.

3. Return by jumping to the address in register `$ra`.

5   Input and Output

In addition to simulating the basic operation of the CPU and operating system, SPIM also simulates a memory-mapped terminal connected to the machine. When a program is "running," SPIM connects its own terminal (or a separate console window in `xspim`) to the processor. The program can read characters that you type while the processor is running. Similarly, if SPIM executes instructions to write characters to the terminal, the characters will appear on SPIM's terminal or console window. One exception to this rule is control-C: it is not passed to the processor, but instead causes SPIM to stop simulating and return to command mode. When the processor stops executing (for example, because you typed control-C or because the machine hit a breakpoint), the terminal is reconnected to SPIM so you can type SPIM commands. To use memory-mapped IO, `spim` or `xspim` must be started with the `-mapped_io` flag.

 The terminal device consists of two independent units: a *receiver* and a *transmitter*. The receiver unit reads characters from the keyboard as they are typed. The transmitter unit writes characters to the terminal's display. The two units are completely independent. This means, for example, that characters typed at the keyboard are not automatically "echoed" on the display. Instead, the processor must get an input character from the receiver and re-transmit it to echo it.

 The processor accesses the terminal using four memory-mapped device registers, as shown in Figure 7. "Memory-mapped" means that each register appears as a special memory location. The Receiver Control Register is at location 0xffff0000; only two of its bits are actually used. Bit 0 is called "ready": if it is one it means that a character has arrived from the keyboard but has not yet been read from the receiver data register. The ready bit is read-only: attempts to write it are ignored. The ready bit changes automatically from zero to one when a character is typed at the keyboard, and it changes automatically from one to zero when the character is read from the receiver data register.

 Bit one of the Receiver Control Register is "interrupt enable". This bit may be both read and written by the processor. The interrupt enable is initially zero. If it is set to one by the

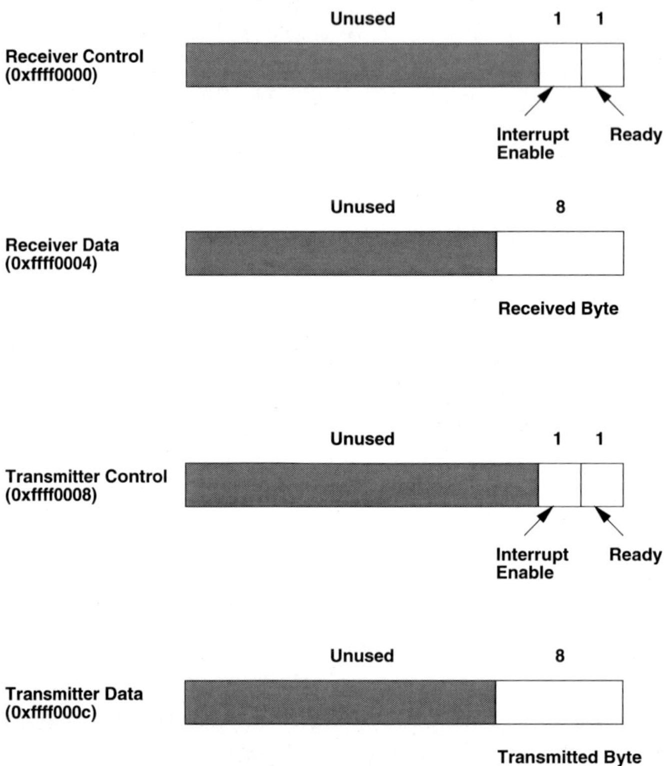

Figure 7: The terminal is controlled by four device registers, each of which appears as a special memory location at the given address. Only a few bits of the registers are actually used: the others always read as zeroes and are ignored on writes.

processor, an interrupt is requested by the terminal on level zero whenever the ready bit is one. For the interrupt actually to be received by the processor, interrupts must be enabled in the status register of the system coprocessor (see Section 2).

Other bits of the Receiver Control Register are unused: they always read as zeroes and are ignored in writes.

The second terminal device register is the Receiver Data Register (at address 0xffff0004). The low-order eight bits of this register contain the last character typed on the keyboard, and all the other bits contain zeroes. This register is read-only and only changes value when a new character is typed on the keyboard. Reading the Receiver Data Register causes the ready bit in the Receiver Control Register to be reset to zero.

The third terminal device register is the Transmitter Control Register (at address 0xffff0008). Only the low-order two bits of this register are used, and they behave much like the corresponding bits of the Receiver Control Register. Bit 0 is called "ready" and is read-only. If it is one it means the transmitter is ready to accept a new character for output. If it is zero it means the transmitter is still busy outputting the previous character given to it. Bit one is "interrupt enable"; it is readable and writable. If it is set to one, then an interrupt will be requested on level one whenever the ready bit is one.

The final device register is the Transmitter Data Register (at address 0xffff000c). When it is written, the low-order eight bits are taken as an ASCII character to output to the display. When the Transmitter Data Register is written, the ready bit in the Transmitter Control Register will be reset to zero. The bit will stay zero until enough time has elapsed to transmit the character to the terminal; then the ready bit will be set back to one again. The Transmitter Data Register should only be written when the ready bit of the Transmitter Control Register is one; if the transmitter isn't ready then writes to the Transmitter Data Register are ignored (the write appears to succeed but the character will not be output).

In real computers it takes time to send characters over the serial lines that connect terminals to computers. These time lags are simulated by SPIM. For example, after the transmitter starts transmitting a character, the transmitter's ready bit will become zero for a while. SPIM measures this time in instructions executed, not in real clock time. This means that the transmitter will not become ready again until the processor has executed a certain number of instructions. If you stop the machine and look at the ready bit using SPIM, it will not change. However, if you let the machine run then the bit will eventually change back to one.

INDEX